IFIP Advances in Information and Communication Technology 614

Editor-in-Chief

Kai Rannenberg, Goethe University Frankfurt, Germany

Editorial Board Members

IFIP – The International Federation for Information Processing

IFIP was founded in 1960 under the auspices of UNESCO, following the first World Computer Congress held in Paris the previous year. A federation for societies working in information processing, IFIP's aim is two-fold: to support information processing in the countries of its members and to encourage technology transfer to developing nations. As its mission statement clearly states:

IFIP is the global non-profit federation of societies of ICT professionals that aims at achieving a worldwide professional and socially responsible development and application of information and communication technologies.

IFIP is a non-profit-making organization, run almost solely by 2500 volunteers. It operates through a number of technical committees and working groups, which organize events and publications. IFIP's events range from large international open conferences to working conferences and local seminars.

The flagship event is the IFIP World Computer Congress, at which both invited and contributed papers are presented. Contributed papers are rigorously refereed and the rejection rate is high.

As with the Congress, participation in the open conferences is open to all and papers may be invited or submitted. Again, submitted papers are stringently refereed.

The working conferences are structured differently. They are usually run by a working group and attendance is generally smaller and occasionally by invitation only. Their purpose is to create an atmosphere conducive to innovation and development. Refereeing is also rigorous and papers are subjected to extensive group discussion.

Publications arising from IFIP events vary. The papers presented at the IFIP World Computer Congress and at open conferences are published as conference proceedings, while the results of the working conferences are often published as collections of selected and edited papers.

IFIP distinguishes three types of institutional membership: Country Representative Members, Members at Large, and Associate Members. The type of organization that can apply for membership is a wide variety and includes national or international societies of individual computer scientists/ICT professionals, associations or federations of such societies, government institutions/government related organizations, national or international research institutes or consortia, universities, academies of sciences, companies, national or international associations or federations of companies.

More information about this series at http://www.springer.com/series/6102

Eunika Mercier-Laurent · M. Özgür Kayalica ·
Mieczyslaw Lech Owoc (Eds.)

Artificial Intelligence
for Knowledge Management

8th IFIP WG 12.6 International Workshop, AI4KM 2021
Held at IJCAI 2020
Yokohama, Japan, January 7–8, 2021
Revised Selected Papers

 Springer

Editors
Eunika Mercier-Laurent ⓘ
University of Reims Champagne-Ardenne
Reims, France

M. Özgür Kayalica ⓘ
Istanbul Technical University
Istanbul, Turkey

Mieczyslaw Lech Owoc ⓘ
Wroclaw University of Economics
and Business
Wroclaw, Poland

ISSN 1868-4238　　　　　　　ISSN 1868-422X　(electronic)
IFIP Advances in Information and Communication Technology
ISBN 978-3-030-80849-5　　　　ISBN 978-3-030-80847-1　(eBook)
https://doi.org/10.1007/978-3-030-80847-1

This Springer imprint is published by the registered company Springer Nature Switzerland AG
The registered company address is: Gewerbestrasse 11, 6330 Cham, Switzerland

Preface

Welcome to the proceedings of the 8th IFIP WG 12.6 International Workshop on Artificial Intelligence for Knowledge Management (AI4KM 2021), which was held in conjunction with the 29th International Joint Conference on Artificial Intelligence and the 17th Pacific Rim International Conference on Artificial Intelligence (IJCAI-PRICAI 2020). IJCAI-PRICAI 2020 was planned to take place in Yokohama, Japan, during August 2020, but the COVID-19 pandemic changed the initial plan and the conference went online in January 2021. The virtual conference was as amazing as the previous in-person editions of IJCAI, with both engaging discussions and social events.

The technical program of IJCAI-PRICAI 2020 was very rich with new topics such as Artificial Intelligence (AI) ethics, and the main conference touched on components of knowledge management (KM) such as knowledge representation, dynamics of knowledge, knowledge base, knowledge transfer, shared knowledge, knowledge engineering, visual knowledge, and combining knowledge with deep convolutional neural networks.

Knowledge management is a large multidisciplinary field having its roots in both management and AI. Knowledge is one of the intangible capitals that influence the performance of organizations and their capacity to innovate. Since the beginning of the KM movement in the early 1990s, companies and nonprofit organizations have experimented with various approaches. AI has brought additional knowledge modeling, knowledge processing, and problem-solving techniques. The AI4KM workshop aims to bridge the gap between AI and knowledge management to advance new methods for organizing, accessing, and exploiting multidisciplinary knowledge.

Understanding the benefits of knowledge management for research, organizations, and business and applying it is still a challenge for many. The overall process involving people, big data, and all kinds of computers and applications has the potential to accelerate discovery and innovation by organizing and optimizing the flow of knowledge. This collection of selected, extended, and updated papers from AI4KM 2021 aims to raise awareness among AI researchers and practitioners about KM challenges so that we can better explore all fields of AI and integrate real-world feedback from experience of AI in KM applications.

The first AI4KM workshop was organized by the International Federation for Information Processing (IFIP) Working Group 12.6 (Knowledge Management) in partnership with the European Conference on Artificial Intelligence (ECAI) in 2012, and the second workshop was held two years later during the Federated Conference on Computer Science and Information Systems (FedCSIS) in conjunction with the 20th Conference on Knowledge Acquisition and Management conference (KAM 2014). The third edition of the workshop saw the beginning of the partnership with the International Joint Conference on Artificial Intelligence (IJCAI) in 2015. The fourth AI4KM workshop was held as part of IJCAI 2016 in New York, USA, and the fifth workshop took place in Melbourne, Australia, co-located with IJCAI 2017, followed by the sixth edition at IJCAI-ECAI 2018 in Stockholm, Sweden, and the seventh edition at IJCAI 2019 in Macao, China.

The objectives of AI4KM 2021 were to continue to promote the interest of AI researchers and practitioners in knowledge management challenges, to discuss methodological, technical and organizational aspects of AI used for knowledge management, and to share feedback on KM applications in various fields using AI.

The topic of this year's workshop was "AI for Sustainable Future".

AI4KM 2021 took place virtually during January 7–8, 2021. The workshop opened with our invited talk given by Anthony Wong, Vice President of IFIP, who addressed a timely and controversial topic: **"Ethics and Regulation of Artificial Intelligence"**. Paradoxically AI helps humans and is an object of controversy, fear, and imaginary threats. As with many inventions, AI can be used for peaceful as well as military applications. Manipulation of data to obtain the desired results leads to the infamous problem of bias. Our invited talk discussed the main threats and the ways to avoid some of them.

The first session devoted to AI for Society and Education began with a presentation on **"Ontologies Cooperation to Model the Needs of Disabled Persons"**. In France, various forms of assistance are available for people with disabilities and it is not easy to know what type of aid a given person may be entitled to. Proposed distributed ontology groups information from heterogeneous sources. A workflow guides the impaired person in finding adequate help.

The second paper proposed a **"Conceptual Framework of Intelligent Management Control System for Higher Education"**. The university management control system should consider the processing of management information for management purposes, allowing for the relationships between different groups of stakeholders. The specificity of the university operation assumes that long-term scientific research and educational programs are conducted.

The next presentation entitled **"Curriculum Vitae (CVs) Evaluation Using Machine Learning Approach"** concerned the continuation of PhD research on knowledge management powered by AI for the evaluation of international students' profiles, which was first presented during AI4KM 2018. Based on his own experience in recruitment of students, the author explains why machine learning is the most appropriate method for CV text mining. Some experiments were presented, and the results were discussed.

"University Students' Research on Artificial Intelligence and Knowledge Management. A Review and Report of Multi-case Studies" presented and discussed the analysis of students' thesis topics defended in the last 10 years in business informatics and computer science at two selected universities in Poland. This study relied on a detailed review and analysis of qualitative data.

The second session on AI for Business and Sustainable Cities began with a paper on **"Customer Churn Prediction in FMCG Sector Using Machine Learning Applications"**. The authors experimented with the contribution of various machine learning algorithms applied on a real data set obtained in the Turkish market to predict the churn behavior of the most valuable part of the existing customer base of some FMCG brands.

The next three presentations were devoted to various aspects of Smart Cities.

The first, entitled **"Crowdsourcing as a Tool Supporting Intra-city Communication"** discussed various aspects of the development of Smart City, such as civic budget and the interaction between local administration, residents, and stakeholders. The author described the concept of crowdsourcing applied to knowledge aquisition by city leaders and its impact on the decisions in a Smart City.

The following speaker addressed the **"Importance of the Internet of Things for Smart Cities"**. After defining the scope of a smart city, she presented an overview of IoT technologies and discussed their potential usefulness for the city.

Metropolitan cities are all concerned by climate change. While many conferences express wishes, the authors of the paper entitled **"Developing a Knowledge Base for Climate Change for Metropolitan Cities"** presented an incremental approach for building collaboratively a knowledge base of best practices in recycling products, beginning with the recycling of electronic devices.

The session that took place on January 8, 2021, devoted to AI for Industry and Sustainability began with the question **"Can Artificial Intelligence Effectively Support Sustainable Development?"** Sustainable development is currently among the most important challenges, and 'sustainability' and 'development' may, on the face of it, appear to be opposing objectives. However, AI can help in protecting our planet by allowing decision makers to evaluate the likely impacts of various applications and technologies, and thus apply the "right technique for the right problem".

"Holistic Approach to Smart Factory" provided an overall view of the techniques deployed in a smart factory. The author explained how to apply AI to digital twins and how it can be integrated with the other components of a smart factory.

The next article **"Development of Big Data Analytics in a Multi-site Enterprise on the Example of Supply Chain Management"** discussed the importance of an analytical platform for multi-source data and proposed the development of analytical processing for SCM in a multi-site industrial enterprise.

"Analysing Natural Gas Prices for Turkey in the Light of a Possible Hub" provided an outlook of the global natural gas market and Turkey's position in this business. Turkey depends on importing gas from Russia, Iran, and Azerbaijan through pipelines and LNG suppliers. The natural gas market in Turkey can become more independent by defining an international gas hub in the global gas trade system. In this respect, the pricing of large trading volumes will be an issue for the near future. This article aims to underline the importance of hub pricing through structuring a virtual hub in Turkey.

The authors of **"Predicting Power Deviation in the Turkish Power Market Based on Adaptive Factor Impacts"** presented a study of the short-term prediction of trends in the power market by selecting the influencing factors and choosing those with the highest impacts. The proposed hybrid method reduces the prediction errors.

The last article entitled **"Machine Learning Methods in the Inclinometers Readings Anomaly Detection Issue on the Example of Tailings Storage Facility"** presented methods of finding anomalies in the inclinometer readings at a tailings storage facility (TSF) using machine learning techniques, which significantly simplifies the process of identifying attention-requiring areas. The effectiveness of the algorithms was tested on data samples from various measurement points. The best method involves building learning-based supervised classifiers in the decision-making process regarding TSF stability.

We would like to thank the members of the Program Committee, who reviewed the papers and helped put together an interesting program for AI4KM 2021. We would also like to thank all the authors and our invited speaker, Anthony Wong. Finally, our thanks go to the local Organizing Committee and all the supporting institutions and organizations.

We hope that you enjoy reading these papers.

May 2021   Eunika Mercier-Laurent
                                                            M. Özgür Kayalica
                                                         Mieczyslaw L. Owoc

Organization

Volume Editors

Eunika Mercier-Laurent	University of Reims Champagne Ardenne, France
M. Özgür Kayalica	Istanbul Technical University, Turkey
Mieczyslaw L. Owoc	Wroclaw University of Economics and Business, Poland

Program Committee

Danielle Boulanger	Jean Moulin University Lyon 3, France
Anne Dourgnon	EDF Research Center, France
Otthein Hertzog	Jacobs University, Germany
Knut Hinkelmann	University of Applied Sciences and Arts, Switzerland
Gülgün Kayakutlu	Istanbul Technical University, Turkey
Antoni Ligeza	AGH University of Science and Technology, Poland
Nada Matta	Troyes Technical University, France
Eunika Mercier-Laurent	University of Reims Champagne-Ardenne, France
Mieczyslaw Lech Owoc	Wroclaw University of Economics and Business, Poland
Vincent Ribiere	IKI, Thailand
Michael Stankosky	George Washington University, USA
Abdul Sattar	Griffith University, Australia
Frederique Segond	Inria, France
Guillermo Simari	Universidad Nacional del Sur, Argentina
Hiroshi Takeda	Osaka University, Japan
Mario Tokoro	Sony-CSL, Tokyo, Japan
Eric Tsui	Hong Kong Polytechnic University, Hong Kong
Janusz Wojtusiak	George Mason University, USA

Local Organizing Committee

Eunika Mercier-Laurent	University of Reims Champagne-Ardenne, France
Felip Manya	IIIA-CSIC, Spain

Contents

Ethics and Regulation of Artificial Intelligence

Anthony Wong[1,2,3](✉)

[1] AGW Legal & Advisory, Sydney, Australia
anthonywong@agwconsult.com
[2] IFIP, Laxenburg, Austria
[3] Australian Computer Society (ACS), Sydney, Australia

Abstract. Over the last few years, the world has deliberated and developed numerous ethical principles and frameworks. It is the general opinion that the time has arrived to move from principles and to operationalize on the ethical practice of AI. It is now recognized that principles and standards can play a universal harmonizing role for the development of AI-related legal norms across the globe. However, how do we translate and embrace these articulated values, principles and actions to guide Nation States around the world to formulate their regulatory systems, policies or other legal instruments regarding AI? Our regulatory systems have attempted to keep abreast of new technologies by recalibrating and adapting our regulatory frameworks to provide for new opportunities and risks, to confer rights and duties, safety and liability frameworks, and to ensure legal certainty for businesses. These past adaptations have been reactive and sometimes piecemeal, often with artificial delineation on rights and responsibilities and with unintended flow-on consequences. Previously, technologies have been deployed more like tools, but as autonomy and self-learning capabilities increase, robots and intelligent AI systems will feel less and less like machines and tools. There is now a significant difference, because machine learning AI systems have the ability 'to learn', adapt their performances and 'make decisions' from data and 'life experiences'. This paper presented at the International Joint Conference on Artificial Intelligence - Pacific Rim International Conference on Artificial Intelligence in 2021 provides brief insights on some selected topical developments in ethical principles and frameworks, our regulatory systems and the current debates on some of the risks and challenges from the use and actions of AI, autonomous and intelligent systems [1].

Keywords: AI · Robots · Automation · Regulation · Ethics · Law · Liability · Transparency · Explainability · Data protection · Privacy · Legal personhood · Job transition · Employment

1 Introduction

AI and algorithmic decision-making will over time bring significant benefits to many areas of human endeavour. The proliferation of AI systems imbued with increasingly complex mathematical and data modelling, and machine learning algorithms, are being

© IFIP International Federation for Information Processing 2021
Published by Springer Nature Switzerland AG 2021
E. Mercier-Laurent et al. (Eds.): AI4KM 2021, IFIP AICT 614, pp. 1–18, 2021.
https://doi.org/10.1007/978-3-030-80847-1_1

integrated in virtually every sector of the economy and society, to support and in many cases undertake more autonomous decisions and actions.

Previously, technologies have often been deployed more like tools, as a pen or paintbrush, but as autonomy and self-learning capabilities increase, robots and intelligent AI systems feel less and less like machines or tools. AI will equip robots and systems with the ability to learn using machine-learning and deep-learning algorithms. They will have the ability to interact and work alongside us or to augment our work. They will increasingly be able to take over functions and roles and, perhaps more significantly, the ability 'to make decisions'.

How much autonomy should AI and robots have to make decisions on our behalf and about us in our life, work and play? How do we ensure they can be trusted, and that they are transparent, reliable, accountable and well designed?

While technological advances hold tremendous promise for mankind, they also pose and raise difficult questions in disparate areas including ethics and morality, bias and discrimination, human rights and dignity, privacy and data protection, data ownership, intellectual property, safety, liability, consumer protection, accountability and transparency, competition law, employment and the future of work and, legal personhood. In a world, that is increasingly connected and where machine-based algorithms use available data to make decisions that affect our lives, how do we ensure these automated decisions are not opaque, appropriate and transparent? And what recourse do we have when these decisions intrude on our rights, freedoms, safety and legitimate interests?

The base tenets of our regulatory systems were created long before the advances and confluence of emergent technologies including AI (artificial intelligence), IoT (Internet of Things), blockchain, cloud, quantum computing, to name a few. With the rise of these technologies we have taken many initiatives to address their consequences by recalibrating and adapting our regulatory frameworks to provide for new opportunities and risks, to confer rights and duties, safety and liability frameworks, and ensure legal certainty for business.

Sector-specific regulation has also been adopted and adapted to address market failures and risks in critical and regulated domains. These changes have often been reactive and piecemeal, with artificial delineation of rights and responsibilities. There have been many unintended consequences. More recently we have begun to learn from past mishaps, and these regulatory adaptations are now more likely to be drafted in technologically neutral way avoiding strict technical definition, especially when the field is still evolving rapidly.

Emerging technologies are rapidly transforming the regulatory landscape. They are providing timely opportunities for fresh approaches in the redesign of our regulatory systems to keep pace with technological changes, now and into the future. AI is currently advancing more rapidly than the process of regulatory recalibration. Unlike the past, there is now a significant difference—we must now take into consideration, machine learning AI systems that have the ability to learn, adapt their performances and 'make decisions' from data and 'life experiences'.

The UN Secretary-General in his June 2020 report, commented that, "The world is at a critical inflection point for technology governance, made more urgent by the ongoing pandemic" [2]. He further emphasized the need to redouble our efforts to better harness digital technologies while mitigating the harm that they may cause.

This paper presented at AI4KM 2020 at the International Joint Conference on Artificial Intelligence - Pacific Rim International Conference on Artificial Intelligence (IJCAI-PRICAI 2020), Yokohama, Japan 7th January 2021, provides brief insights on some selected topical developments in our ethical and regulatory systems and, the current debates to address some of the challenges and risks from the use and actions of AI, autonomous and intelligent systems [1]. The paper is partly based on the keynotes, presentations and engagements in Australia [3], Malaysia [4], Zimbabwe [5], Cambodia [6], Sri Lanka [7], Switzerland [8] and Brazil [9]. It extends on the paper published as "The Laws and Regulation of AI and Autonomous Systems" [10].

The paper is organized as follows. Section 2 Briefly reviews the state of ethical principles and frameworks. Section 3 Looks at the responsibility and liability challenges for damages caused by AI. Section 4 discuss transparency and explainability of AI and Sect. 5 on the debates on legal personhoods for AI. Section 6 Briefly looks at AI and Implications of Employment. Section 7 concludes this paper.

2   Ethical Issues Arising from AI

It is perhaps apt at this juncture, that I pause to reflect on the journey that has brought me to the cross-roads of ethics and regulation of AI. In 2016, I initiated a series of articles on AI for The Australian. The columns commenced with a piece on "Ethics must travel as AI's associate" [11], which was followed by a series of closely related topics including: "How far should AI replace human sense?" [12], "We need plans for when robots are in driver's seat" [13], "Complex algorithms can use a little of that human touch" [14], "AI: Are Musk and Hawking right, or is our future in our hands?" [15], "Do robots and artificial intelligence think about copyright?" [16], "Data frameworks critical for AI success" [17] and, "Who is liable when robots and AI get it wrong?" [18].

These columns led to a series of interviews, panels, and presentations looking at the possible risks that AI poses and the notion of building ethics into machine intelligence. These included an ABC TV News interview on "Neurotechnologies and AI, privacy, agency and identity, and bias", panels to explore the social and ethical concerns of AI and, submission to the consultation on Artificial Intelligence, Australia's Ethics Framework [3].

The many topics canvassed included:

- What happens when AI and algorithmic decision-making leads to someone being disadvantaged or discriminated against? There have been numerous instances where this has happened [19], not necessarily due to the algorithm itself, but because the underlying data reflects an inherent bias, statistical distortion or pattern that becomes obvious when the algorithm is applied to it.
- How do you think traditional business models will be disrupted in the future by AI?
- How will AI disruption of traditional business models impact society?
- What options does the government have to constrain or enable artificial intelligence and what should be its focus?

- What ethical considerations must be taken into account when developing artificial intelligence and what are the priorities?

The conclusions derived from algorithms are probabilistic in nature and may carry inherent biases, which may be replicated, amplified and reinforced. Algorithms are not infallible. As algorithmic complexity and autonomy increase, it becomes imperative to build in checks and balance to protect the legitimate interests of Stakeholders [11].

If ethical parameters are programmed into AI, whose ethical and social values are these? This question was Foremost in my mind, When I presented on the "Ethical dimensions of AI & Autonomous Systems" to an audience studying buddhist ethics [20]. Each society, tradition, cultural group, religion, system and country view ethics and morality through the contextual lenses of their underlying philosophical beliefs. The variations in ethical and social values that underpin our global landscape are challenging and, changes with the passage of time.

In response to the challenges articulated above, a range of stakeholders have produced AI ethical principles and frameworks. When I reviewed AI ethical principles and frameworks produced by public, private, and non-governmental organizations in 2019, there were more than 70 in existence. The number continues to grow. In 2019, jurisdictions including Australia [21] and the EU [22] published their frameworks, adding to the lists of contributors including the OECD Principles on Artificial Intelligence [23], the World Economic Forum AI Governance: A Holistic Approach To Implement Ethics Into AI [24] and the Singapore Model AI Governance Framework [25], to name a few.

An analysis of 84 principles and guidelines by Jobin et al. [26] reveals a convergence emerging around five ethical principles (transparency, justice and fairness, non-maleficence, responsibility and privacy).

By 2020, a study by Fjeld et al. [27] of 36 principles and guidelines, revealed an extended list around eight key themes: (1) Privacy, (in 97% of documents), (2) Accountability (in 97% of documents), (3) Safety and Security (in 81% of documents), (4) Transparency and Explainability (in 94% of documents), (5) Fairness and Non-discrimination (in 100% of documents), (6) Human Control of Technology (in 69% of documents), (7) Professional Responsibility (in 78% of documents), (8) Promotion of Human Values (in 69% of documents).

The UN Secretary-General in his 2020 report commented that "there are currently over 160 organizational, national and international sets of artificial intelligence ethics and governance principles worldwide" [28] and calls for a common platform to bring these separate initiatives together.

UNESCO was given the mandate by its Member States to develop an international standard-setting instrument on the ethics of artificial intelligence, which is to be submitted to the General Conference in the later part of 2021.The first draft of UNESCO's Recommendation on the Ethics of Artificial Intelligence was released to Member States in late 2020 [29]. The Recommendation has largely been considered as an inter-disciplinary and multi-stakeholder initiative in light of the proliferation of ethical principles and frameworks.

The Recommendation includes many common or shared ethical concepts and values with an extended list around ten key themes: (1) proportionality and do no harm, (2) safety and security, (3) fairness and non-discrimination, (4) sustainability, (5) privacy, (6) human oversight and determination, (7) transparency and explainability, (8) responsibility and accountability, (9) awareness and literacy and (10) multi-stakeholder and adaptive governance and collaboration.

The debates have matured significantly since 2017, beyond the 'what' of ethical principles to more of the 'how', with detailed guidelines on how such principles can be operationalised in the design and implementation to minimise risks and negative outcomes. But the challenge has always been putting principles into practice and creating accountability mechanisms.

There is a growing consensus that the time has arrived to move from principles and to operationalize on the ethical practice on AI [30]. Many of the proponents for regulatory intervention have argued that abstract high-level AI principles lack the specificity to be used in practice and require legal enforcement mechanisms that are more robust to provide redress when things go wrong. With the growing lists of AI related incidents, there is a general distrust that AI developers could self-regulate effectively.

There is also a growing awareness that principles can play a useful base from which to develop professional ethics, standards, and AI regulatory systems across the globe. But how do we translate and embrace these articulated values, principles and actions to guide Nation States in the formulation of their regulatory systems, policies or other legal instruments regarding AI?

As stated by Fjeld et al., the impact of a set of principles is "likely to depend on how it is embedded in a larger governance ecosystem, including for instance relevant policies (e.g. AI national plans), laws, regulations, but also professional practices and everyday routines" [31]. That view also resonated with those of UNESCO. UNESCO has advocated for Member States to put in place policy actions and oversight mechanisms to operationalize the values and principles in the Recommendation.

Due to the challenges in enforcing ethical principles or frameworks, we are seeing greater regulatory impetus and focus to complement the gaps to improve the public's trust. We are seeing growing awareness that our existing regulatory frameworks are not evolving fast enough to keep pace with the rapid progress in AI. Recently, UNESCO and the EU Parliament have set the regulatory train in motion.

One of the objectives of the UNESCO Recommendation is to provide a universal framework of values, principles and actions to guide Member States in the formulation of their legislation, policies or other instruments regarding AI: "Member States should develop, review and adapt, as appropriate, regulatory and legal frameworks to achieve accountability and responsibility for the content and outcomes of AI systems at the different phases of their life cycle. Member States should introduce liability frameworks or clarify the interpretation of existing frameworks to ensure the attribution of accountability for the outcomes and behaviour of AI systems" [32].

UNESCO has strongly advocated that AI cannot be a no law zone: "There are some legislative vacuums around the industry which needs to be filled fast. The first step is to agree on exactly which values need to be enshrined, and which rules need to be enforced. Many frameworks and guidelines exist, but they are implemented unevenly, and none are truly global. AI is global, which is why we need a global instrument to regulate it" [34].

In October 2020, the European Parliament adopts 3 resolutions to regulate AI, setting the pace as a global leader in AI regulation. The resolutions cover the ethical and legal obligations surrounding AI, civil liability setting fines of up to 2 million euros for damage caused by AI; and intellectual property rights [33]. In response, the European Commission has indicated that it will publish draft legislation in 2021 addressing AI by obliging high-risk AI systems to meet mandatory requirements related to their trustworthiness.

2021 will prove to be an interesting year for AI regulatory developments. However, what will unfold, time will tell. Some of these ethical principles or frameworks may well be adopted alongside or incorporated in legislation.

3   Responsibility and Liability for Damages Caused by AI

How should regulators manage the complexity and challenges arising from the design, development and deployment of robots and autonomous systems? What legal and social responsibilities should we give to algorithms shielded behind statistically data-derived 'impartiality'? Who is liable when robots and AI get it wrong?

There is much debate as to who amongst the various players and actors across the design, development and deployment lifecycle of AI and autonomous systems should be responsible and liable to account for any damages that might be caused. Would autonomy and self-learning capabilities alter the chain of responsibility of the producer or developer as the "AI-driven or otherwise automated machine which, after consideration of certain data, has taken an autonomous decision and caused harm to a human's life, health or property" [35]?

Or has "inserting a layer of inscrutable, unintuitive, and statistically-derived code in between a human decisionmaker and the consequences of that decision, AI disrupts our typical understanding of responsibility for choices gone wrong"? [36] Or should the producer or programmer foresee the potential loss or damage even when it may be difficult to anticipate—particularly in unusual circumstances, the actions of an autonomous system? These questions will become more critical as more and more autonomous decisions are made by AI systems.

One of the more advanced regulatory developments in AI is in the trialling of autonomous vehicles [37] and in the regulatory frameworks for drones [38].

The rapid adoption of AI and autonomous systems into more diverse areas of our lives—from business, education, healthcare and communication through to infrastructure, logistics, defence, entertainment and agriculture—means that any laws involving liability will need to consider a broad range of contexts and possibilities.

We are moving rapidly towards a world where autonomous and intelligent AI systems are connected, embedded and integrated in complex environments, and with "the plurality of actors involved, it can be difficult to assess where a potential damage originates and which person is liable for it. Due to the complexity of these technologies, it can be very difficult for victims to identify the liable person and prove all necessary conditions for a successful claim, as required under national law" [39]. That view is also reflected in the more recent European Parliament resolution with recommendations to the Commission on a civil liability regime for artificial intelligence [40]. The burden of proof in a tort fault-based liability system in some countries could significantly increase the costs of litigation.

We will need to establish specific protections for potential victims of AI-related incidents to give consumers confidence that they will have legal recourse if something goes wrong.

One of the proposals being debated is for the creation of a mandatory insurance scheme to ensure that victims of incidents involving robots and intelligent AI systems have access to adequate compensation. This might be similar to the mandatory comprehensive insurance that owners need to purchase before being able to register a motor vehicle [41]. The EU Parliament has recently also proposed for deployers of high-risk AI to have mandatory liability insurance (€10m in the event of death and physical harm and €2m for damage to property) [40].

Another approach is for the creation of strict liability rules to compensate victims for potential harm caused by AI and autonomous systems along the lines of current product liability laws in the EU and Australia. Strict liability rules would ensure that the victim is compensated regardless of fault. The EU Parliament has proposed that deployers of AI designated as "high-risk" would be strictly liable for any damage caused by it. But who amongst the various players and actors should be strictly liable?

Whether the existing mixture of fault-based and strict liability regimes are appropriate is also subject to much debate.

Introducing a robust regulatory framework with relevant input from industry, policymakers and government would create greater incentive for AI developers and manufacturers to reduce their exposure by building in additional safeguards to minimise the potential risks to humanity.

4 Transparency and Explainability of AI

Algorithms are increasingly being used to analyse information and define or predict outcomes with the aid of AI. These AI systems may be embedded in devices and systems and deployed across many industries and increasingly in critical domains, often without the knowledge and consent of the user. Should humans be informed that they are interacting with AI, on the purposes of the AI, and on the data used for the training and evaluation?

To ensure that AI based systems perform as intended, the quality, accuracy and relevance of data are essential. Any data bias, error or statistical distortion will be learned and amplified. In situations involving machine learning—where algorithms and decision rules are trained using data to recognize patterns and to learn to make future decisions based on these observations, regulators and consumers may not easily discern the properties of these algorithms. These algorithms are able to train systems to perform certain tasks at levels that may exceed human ability and raise many challenging questions including calls for greater algorithmic transparency to minimise the risk of bias, discrimination, unfairness, error and to protect consumer interests.

Over the last few years legislators have started to respond to the challenge. In the EU, Article 22 of the General Data Protection Regulation (GDPR) [42] gives individuals the right not to be subject to a decision based solely on automated decision-making (no human involvement in the decision process), except in certain situations including explicit consent and necessity for the performance of or entering into a contract. The GDPR applies only to automated decision-making involving personal data.

In the public sector, AI systems are increasingly being adopted by governments to improve and reform public service processes. In many situations, stakeholders and users of AI will expect reasons to be given for transparency and accountability of government decisions which are important elements for the proper functioning of public administration. It is currently unclear how our regulatory frameworks would adjust to providing a meaningful review by our courts of decisions undertaken by autonomous AI systems, or in what circumstances a sub-delegation by a nominated decision-maker to an autonomous AI systems would be lawful. We may need to develop new principles and standards and "to identify directions for thinking about how administrative law should respond … that makes sense from both a legal and a technical point of view. [43].

As machine learning evolves, AI models [44] often become even more complex, to the point where it may be difficult to articulate and understand their inner workings— even to people who created them. This raises many questions: what types of explanation are suitable and useful to the audience? [45] How and why does the model perform the way it does? How comprehensive does the explanation need to be—is an understanding on how the algorithmic decision was reached required, or should the explanation be adapted in a manner which is useful to a non-technical audience?

In the EU, the GDPR explicitly provides a data subject with the following rights:

a) rights to be provided and to access information about the automated decision-making; [46]
b) rights to obtain human intervention and to contest the decision made solely by automated decision-making algorithm; [47] and
c) places explicit onus on the algorithmic provider to provide "meaningful information about the logic involved" in algorithmic decision, the "significance" and the "envisaged consequences" of the algorithmic processing [48].

But how would these rights operate and be enforced in practice? With recent and more complex non-linear black-box AI models, it can be difficult to provide meaningful explanations, largely due to the statistical and probabilistic character of machine learning and the current limitations of some AI models—raising concerns including accountability, explainability, interpretability, transparency, and human control.

What expertise and competencies would be required from a data subject to take advantage of the rights or for the algorithmic provider to provide the above rights?

"In addition, access to the algorithm and the data could be impossible without the cooperation of the potentially liable party. In practice, victims may thus not be able to make a liability claim. In addition, it would be unclear, how to demonstrate the fault of an AI acting autonomously, or what would be considered the fault of a person relying on the use of AI" [49].

This opacity will also make it difficult to verify whether decisions made with the involvement of AI are fair and unbiased, whether there are possible breaches of laws, and whether they will hamper the effective access to the traditional evidence necessary to establish a successful liability action and to claim compensation.

Should organisations consider and ensure that specific types of explanation be provided for their proposed AI system to meet the requisite needs of the audience before starting the design process? Should the design and development methodologies adopted have the flexibility to embrace new tools and explanation frameworks, ensuring ongoing improvements in transparency and explainability in parallel with advancement in the state of the art of the technology throughout the lifecycle of the AI system?

While rapid development methodologies may have been adopted by the IT Industry, embedding transparency and explainability into AI system design requires more extensive planning and oversight, and requiring input and knowledge from a wider mix of multi-disciplinary skills and expertise.

New tools and better explanation frameworks need to be developed to instill the desired human values and to reconcile the current tensions and trade-off between accuracy, cost and explainability of AI models. Developing such tools and frameworks is far from trivial, warranting further research and funding.

5   Legal Personhoods for AI

Historically, our regulatory systems have granted rights and legal personhood to slaves, women, children, corporations and more recently to landscape and nature. Two of India's rivers, the Ganga and the Yamuna, have been granted legal status. In New Zealand legislation was enacted to grant legal personhoods to the Whanganui river, Mount Taranaki and the Te Urewera protected area. Previously, corporations were the only non-human entities recognised by the law as legal persons.

"To be a legal person is to be the subject of rights and duties" [50]. Granting legal personality [51] to AI and robots will entail complex legal considerations and is not a simple case of equating them to corporations.

Who foots the bill when a robot or an intelligent AI system makes a mistake, causes an accident or damage, or becomes corrupted? The manufacturer, the developer, the person controlling it, or the robot itself? Or is it a matter of allocating and apportioning risk and liability?

As autonomic and self-learning capabilities increase, robots and intelligent AI systems will feel less and less like machines and tools. Self-learning capabilities for AI have added complexity to the equation. Will granting 'electronic rights' to robots assist with some of these questions? Will human actors use robots to shield themselves from liability or shift any potential liabilities from the developers to the robots? Or will the spectrum, allocation and apportionment of responsibility keep step with the evolution of self-learning robots and intelligent AI systems? Regulators around the world are wrestling with these questions.

The EU is leading the way on these issues. In 2017 the European Parliament, in an unprecedented show of support, adopted a resolution on Civil Law Rules on Robotics [52] by 396 votes to 123. One of its key recommendations was to call on the European Commission to explore, analyse and consider "a specific legal status for robots ... so that at least the most sophisticated autonomous robots could be established as having the status of electronic persons responsible for making good any damage they may cause, and possibly applying electronic personality to cases where robots make autonomous decisions" [53].

The EU resolution generated considerable debate and controversy, because it calls for sophisticated autonomous robots to be given specific legal status as electronic persons. The arguments from both sides are complex and require fundamental shifts in legal theory and reasoning.

In an open letter, experts in robotics and artificial intelligence have cautioned the European Commission that plans to grant robots legal status are inappropriate and "non-pragmatic" [54].

The European Group on Ethics in Science and New Technologies, in its Statement on Artificial Intelligence, Robotics and Autonomous Systems, advocated that the concept of legal personhood is the ability and willingness to take and attribute moral responsibility. "Moral responsibility is here construed in the broad sense in which it may refer to several aspects of human agency, e.g. causality, accountability (obligation to provide an account), liability (obligation to compensate damages), reactive attitudes such as praise and blame (appropriateness of a range of moral emotions), and duties associated with social roles. Moral responsibility, in whatever sense, cannot be allocated or shifted to 'autonomous' technology" [55].

In 2020, the EU Commission presented its "White Paper on Artificial Intelligence—A European approach to excellence and trust for regulation of artificial intelligence (AI)" [56] and a number of other documents including a "Report on the safety and liability implications of Artificial Intelligence, the Internet of Things and robotics" [57] for comments. The White Paper is non-committal on the question of endowing robots with specific legal status as electronic persons. It proposes a risk-based approach to create an 'ecosystem of trust' as one of the key elements of a future regulatory framework for AI in Europe, so that the regulatory burden is not excessively prescriptive or disproportionate.

I concur with the conclusions reached by Bryson et al. [58] that the case for electronic personhood is weak. With the current capabilities and state-of-the-art of AI systems, it is essential that human stays 'in the loop'. The negatives outweigh the benefits in the current debate on shifting legal and moral responsibility to AI systems—at least for the foreseeable future. That view is consistent with those reached by UNESCO: "when developing regulatory frameworks, Member States should, in particular, take into account that ultimate responsibility and accountability must always lie with natural or legal persons and that AI systems should not be given legal personality themselves" [32].

In October 2020, the EU Parliament reversed its earlier resolution and makes it clear that it would not be appropriate to grant legal personhood to AI [59].

As evidenced by the historical debates on the status of slaves, women, corporations and, more recently landscape and nature, the question of granting legal personality to autonomous robots will not be resolved any time soon. There is no simple answer to the question of legal personhood, and one size will not fit all.

Should legal personhood for robots or autonomous systems eventuate in the future, any right invoked on behalf of robots, or obligation enforced against them, will require new approaches and significant recalibration of our regulatory systems. Legal person-hood could potentially allow autonomous robots to own their creations, as well as being open to liability for problems or negative outcomes associated with their actions.

6 AI and Implications of Employment

Over the past few years we have been inundated with predictions that robots and automation will devastate the workplace, replacing many job functions within the next 10 to 15 years. We have already seen huge shifts in manufacturing, mining, agriculture, administration and logistics, where a wide range of manual and repetitive tasks have been automated. More recently, cognitive tasks and data analyses are increasingly being performed by AI and machines.

Historically, new technologies have always affected the structure of the labour market, leading to a significant impact on employment, especially lower skilled and manual jobs. But now the pace and spread of autonomous and intelligent technologies are outperforming humans in many tasks and radically challenging the base tenets of our labour markets and laws. These developments have raised many questions.

Where are the policies, strategies and regulatory frameworks to transition workers in the jobs that will be the most transformed, or those that will disappear altogether due to automation, robotics and AI?

Our current labour and employment laws, such as sick leave, hours of work, tax, minimum wage and overtime pay requirements, were not designed for robots. What is the legal relationship of robots to human employees in the workplace? In relation to workplace safety— what liabilities should apply if a robot harms a human co-worker? Would the 'employer' of the robot be vicariously liable? What is the performance management and control plan for work previously undertaken by human employees working under a collective bargaining agreement, now performed or co-performed with AI or robots? How would data protection and privacy regulations apply to personal information collected and consumed by robots? Who would be responsible for cyber security and the criminal use of robots or AI? [60].

Are there statutory protection and job security for humans displaced by automation and robots? Should we tax robot owners to pay for training for workers who are displaced by automation, or should there be a universal minimum basic income for people displaced? Should we have social plans, such as exist in Germany and France, if restructuring through automation disadvantages employees?

There are many divergent views on all these questions. All are being hotly debated. Governments, policy makers, institutions and employers all have important roles to play in the development of digital skills, in the monitoring of long-term job trends, and in the creation of policies to assist workers and organisations adapt to an automated future. If these issues are not addressed early and proactively, they may worsen the digital divide and increase inequalities between countries and people.

ICT professionals are also being impacted as smart algorithms and other autonomous technologies supplement software programming, data analysis and technical support roles. With AI and machine learning developing at an exponential rate, what does the future look like?

6.1 Case Study - Line Between Human and Robo Advisers in Financial Services

FinTech (financial technology) start-ups are emerging to challenge the roles of banks and traditional financial institutions. FinTechs are rapidly transforming and disrupting the marketplace by providing 'robo-advice' using highly sophisticated algorithms operating on mobile and web-based environments. The technology is called robotic process automation (RPA) and is becoming widespread in business, and particularly in financial institutions. Robo-advice or automated advice is the provision of automated financial product advice using algorithms and technology and without the direct involvement of a human adviser [61].

Robo-advice and AI capabilities have the potential to increase competition and lower prices for consumers in the financial advice and financial services industries by radically reshaping the customer experience. They are designed, modelled and programmed by human actors. Often they operate behind the scenes 24/7 assisting the people who interact with consumers. There are considerable tasks and risks involved in writing algorithms to accurately portray the full offerings and complexity of financial products.

In 2017 Australia, after a number of scandals, introduced professional standards legislation for human financial advisers [62]. These regulations set higher competence and ethical standards, including requirements for relevant first or higher degrees, continuing professional development requirements and compliance with a code of ethics. The initiatives were introduced into a profession already under pressure from the robo environment.

Because robo-advice is designed, modelled and programmed by human actors, should these requirements also apply to robo-advice? Should regulators also hold ICT developers and providers of robots and autonomous systems to the same standards demanded from human financial advisers? What should be the background, skills and competencies of these designers and ICT developers?

Depending on the size and governance framework of an organisation, various players and actors could be involved in a collaborative venture in the development, deployment and lifecycle of AI systems. These might include the developer, the product manager, senior management, the service provider, the distributor and the person who uses the AI or autonomous system. Their domain expertise could be in computer science, or mathematics or statistics, or they might be an interdisciplinary group composed of financial advisers, economists, social scientists or lawyers.

In 2016 the Australian regulator laid down sectoral guidelines [63] for monitoring and testing algorithms deployed in robo-advice. The regulatory guidance requires businesses offering robo-advice to have people within the business who understand the "rationale, risk and rules" used by the algorithms and have the skills to review the resulting robo-advice. What should be the competencies and skills of the humans undertaking the role?

The EU General Data Protection Regulation (GDPR) [64] went further, by placing an explicit onus on the algorithmic provider to provide "meaningful information about the logic involved" [65]. In addition, GDPR provides an individual with explicit rights including the rights to obtain human intervention, to express their point of view and to contest the decision made solely by automated systems [66] that has legal or similarly significant impact. GDPR applies only when AI uses personal data within the scope of the legislation.

Revealing the logic behind an algorithm may potentially risk and disclose commercially sensitive information and trade secrets used by the AI model and on how the system works.

The deployment of robo-advice raises many new, interesting and challenging questions for regulators accustomed only to assessing and regulating human players and actors.

7   Conclusion

This paper raises some of the major topical issues and debates relating to ethics of AI, AI liability, transparency and meaningful AI explanation, aspects of data protection and privacy, legal personhood, job transition and employment law.

In the wake of the 2020 "black lives matter" protests, a number of technology companies have announced limitations on plans to sell facial recognition technology. There have also been renewed calls for a moratorium on certain uses of facial recognition technology that has legal or significant effects on individuals until appropriate legal framework has been established [67].

The need to address AI and autonomous system challenges has increased in urgency as the adverse potential impact could be significant in specific critical domains. If not appropriately addressed, human trust will suffer, impacting on adoption and oversight and in some cases posing significant risks to humanity and societal values.

From this brief exploration, it is clear that the values and issues outlined in the paper will benefit from much broader debate, research and consultation. There are no definitive answers to some of the questions raised—as for many, it is a matter of perspective. I trust that this paper will embark you on your own journey as to what our future regulatory systems should encapsulate. Different AI applications create and pose different benefits, risks and issues. The solutions that might be adopted in the days ahead, will potentially challenge our traditional beliefs and systems for years to come. We are facing a major disruptive shift which is capable of dislodging some of our legal assumptions and may require significant rethink of some of our long-established legal principles—as we must now take into consideration, machine learning AI systems that have the ability to learn, adapt and 'make decisions' from data and 'life experiences'.

Technologists and AI developers understand better than most in relation to the trends and trajectories of emergent technologies and their potential impact on the economic, safety and social constructs of the workplace and society. Is it incumbent on them to raise these issues and ensure they are widely debated, so that appropriate and intelligent decisions can be made for the changes, risks and challenges ahead? Technologists and AI developers are well placed to address some of the risks and challenges during the design and lifecycle of AI-enabled systems. It would be beneficial to society for ICT professionals to assist government, legislators, regulators and policy formulators with their unique understanding of the strengths and limitations of the technology and its effects.

Historically, our regulatory adaptations have been conservative and patchworked in their ability to keep pace with technological changes. Perhaps the drastic disruptions that COVID-19 has caused in our work, life and play beyond the normal will provide sufficient impetus and tenacity to consider and re-think on how our laws and regulatory systems should recalibrate with AI and autonomous systems, now and into the future.

References

1. This paper is for general reference purposes only. It does not constitute legal or professional advice. It is general comment only. Before making any decision or taking any action you should consult your legal or professional advisers to ascertain how the regulatory system applies to your particular circumstances in your jurisdiction
2. United Nation, Report of the Secretary-General, Road map for digital cooperation: implementation of the recommendations of the High-level Panel on Digital Cooperation June 2020, p 3, www.un.org/en/content/digital-cooperation-roadmap/, www.un.org/en/content/digital-cooperation-roadmap/. Accessed Jan 2021
3. Neurotechnologies and AI, privacy, agency and identity, and bias, ABC TV News 24 November 2017; Re-engineering industries with Artificial Intelligence & the social contract - The intended outcome, 26th International Joint Conference on Artificial Intelligence, Melbourne August 2017. https://www.acs.org.au/insightsandpublications/media-releases/00000121.html; Automation and The Nature of Work, ACS Canberra Conference, August 2017; Robo-advice & FinTech: More Transparent, Honest & Reliable than Human Actors? Chair and Panel, Sydney University Business School, November 2018; Future AI Forum submission to the consultation, Artificial Intelligence, Australia's Ethics Framework, May 2019, https://consult.industry.gov.au/strategic-policy/artificial-intelligence-ethics-framework/consultation/view_respondent?_b_index=60&uuId=309030657; Ethical Dimensions of AI & Autonomous Systems, Nan Tien Institute, Wollongong, Australia, 24 August 2019
4. International ICT Infrastructure & Digital Economy Conference Sarawak (IDECS) 2017 – Kuching, Sarawak, Malaysia, April 2017; Presentation to Global Conference on Computing Ethics, Kuala Lumpur, Malaysia, August 2012
5. Artificial Intelligence, the Good, and the Ugly, Victoria Falls, Zimbabwe, November 2017
6. AI and Employment Law Implications, LAWASIA 2018, Siem Reap, Cambodia, November 2018
7. The Ethics & Regulation of Artificial Intelligence, Keynote to NITC 2019 "Embrace Digital" Colombo, Sri Lanka, 9 October 2019
8. Duty of Care and Ethics on Digital Technologies, Internet Governance Forum (IGF), Geneva, December 2017; How do we maximise the benefits of Innovative 4.0 technologies, without unnecessary risks and consequences?, World Summit on the Information Society (WSIS), Geneva, May 2019; AI: Complementing Codes of Ethics with Law and Regulation, Session 131 "Living the standard – how can the Information and Knowledge Society live to an ethical and FAIR Standard", World Summit on the Information Society (WSIS), Geneva, July 2020
9. Ethics & Regulation of Artificial Intelligence, SECOMU 2020 - "Artificially Human or Humanly Artificial? Challenges for Society 5.0", Brazil, 18 November 2020
10. A Wong 2020 The laws and regulation of AI and autonomous systems L Strous R Johnson DA Grier D Swade Eds Unimagined Futures – ICT Opportunities and Challenges IFIP Advances in Information and Communication Technology IAICT 555 Springer Cham 38 54 https://doi.org/10.1007/978-3-030-64246-4_4
11. "Ethics must travel as AI's associate", The Australian, 13 September 2016
12. "How far should AI replace human sense?", The Australian, 27 September 2016
13. "We need plans for when robots are in driver's seat", The Australian, 22 November 2016
14. "Complex algorithms can use a little of that human touch", The Australian, 24 January 2017

15. "AI: Are Musk and Hawking right, or is our future in our hands?", The Australian, 23 August 2017
16. "Do robots and artificial intelligence think about copyright?", The Australian, 5 September 2017
17. "Data frameworks critical for AI success", The Australian, 4 October 2017
18. "Who is liable when robots and AI get it wrong?", The Australian, 19 September 2017
19. Refer to examples in the AI Incident database. https://incidentdatabase.ai/summaries/incidents
20. Ethical Dimensions of AI & Autonomous Systems, Nan Tien Institute, Wollongong, Australia, 24 August 2019
21. Australian AI Ethics Framework (2019). https://www.industry.gov.au/data-and-publications/building-australias-artificial-intelligence-capability/ai-ethics-framework. Accessed 6 June 2020
22. European Commission: Ethics guidelines for trustworthy AI (2019). https://ec.europa.eu/digital-single-market/en/news/ethics-guidelines-trustworthy-ai. Accessed 6 June 2020
23. OECD, OECD Principles on Artificial Intelligence (22 May 2019), https://www.oecd.org/going-digital/ai/principles/. Accessed 20 June 2020
24. World Economic Forum: AI Governance: A Holistic Approach to Implement Ethics into AI. https://www.weforum.org/whitepapers/ai-governance-a-holistic-approach-to-implement-ethics-into-ai. Accessed 20 June 2020
25. Singapore Model AI Governance Framework. https://www.pdpc.gov.sg/-/media/files/pdpc/pdf-files/resource-for-organisation/ai/sgmodelaigovframework2.pdf. Accessed 20 June 2020
26. Jobin, A., Ienca, M., Vayena, E.: The global landscape of AI ethics guidelines. Nat. Mach. Intell. 1, 389–399 (2019). https://doi.org/10.1038/s42256-019-0088-2
27. Fjeld, J., Achten, N., Hilligoss, H., Nagy, A., Srikumar, M.: Principled Artificial Intelligence: Mapping Consensus in Ethical and Rights-Based Approaches to Principles for AI (January 15, 2020). Berkman Klein Center Research Publication No. 2020-1. https://ssrn.com/abstract=3518482 or https://doi.org/10.2139/ssrn.3518482
28. United Nation, Report of the Secretary-General, Road map for digital cooperation: implementation of the recommendations of the High-level Panel on Digital Cooperation. www.un.org/en/content/digital-cooperation-roadmap/, June 2020 p 18, www.un.org/en/content/digital-cooperation-roadmap/. Accessed January 2021
29. The first draft of the recommendation submitted to Member States proposes options for action to Member States and other stakeholders and is accompanied by concrete implementation guidelines. The first draft of the AI Ethics Recommendation. https://unesdoc.unesco.org/ark:/48223/pf0000373434
30. See also the opinion of the High Level Panel Follow-up Roundtable 3C Artificial Intelligence - 1st Session. www.un.org/en/pdfs/HLP%20Followup%20Roundtable%203C%20Artificial%20Intelligence%20-%201st%20Session%20Summary.pdf
31. Fjeld, J., Achten, N., Hilligoss, H., Nagy, A., Srikumar, M.: Principled Artificial Intelligence: Mapping Consensus in Ethical and Rights-Based Approaches to Principles for AI (January 15, 2020). Berkman Klein Center Research Publication No. 2020–1, p. 5. https://ssrn.com/abstract=3518482or http://dx.doi.org/https://doi.org/10.2139/ssrn.3518482
32. UNESCO first draft of the AI Ethics Recommendation, Resolution 68. https://unesdoc.unesco.org/ark:/48223/pf0000373434
33. European Parliament three Resolutions on the ethical and legal aspects of Artificial Intelligence software systems ("AI"): Resolution 2020/2012(INL) on a Framework of Ethical Aspects of Artificial Intelligence, Robotics and related Technologies (the "AI Ethical Aspects Resolution"), Resolution 2020/2014(INL) on a Civil Liability Regime for Artificial Intelligence (the "Civil Liability Resolution"), and Resolution 2020/2015(INI) on Intellectual

Property Rights for the development of Artificial Intelligence Technologies (the "IPR for AI Resolution")

34. Elaboration of a Recommendation on ethics of artificial intelligence (unesco.org). https://en.unesco.org/artificial-intelligence/ethics

35. The World Economic Forum; White Paper on AI Governance A Holistic Approach to Implement Ethics into AI, p. 6. Geneva, Switzerland (2019). https://www.weforum.org/whitepapers/ai-governance-a-holistic-approach-to-implement-ethics-into-ai. Accessed 9 June 2020

36. Selbst, Andrew D.: Negligence and AI's Human Users. In: Public Law & Legal Theory Research Paper No. 20-01, p 1. UCLA School of Law (2018)

37. For a brief rundown of the regulatory frameworks and developments in selected countries refer to the Australian National Transport Commission 2020, Review of 'Guidelines for trials of automated vehicles in Australia': Discussion paper, NTC, Melbourne, pp. 16–18. https://www.ntc.gov.au/sites/default/files/assets/files/NTC%20Discussion%20Paper%20-%20Review%20of%20guidelines%20for%20trials%20of%20automated%20vehicles%20in%20Australia.pdf. Accessed 6 June 2020. For examples of Australian legislation refer to: Motor Vehicles (Trials of Automotive Technologies) Amendment Act 2016 (SA), Transport Legislation Amendment (Automated Vehicle Trials and Innovation) Act 2017 (NSW), Road Safety Amendment (Automated Vehicles) Act 2018 (Vic)

38. For the new European Union drone rules refer to. https://www.easa.europa.eu/domains/civil-drones-rpas/drones-regulatory-framework-background. For the Australia drone rules refer to. https://www.casa.gov.au/knowyourdrone/drone-rules and the Civil Aviation Safety Amendment (Remotely Piloted Aircraft and Model Aircraft—Registration and Accreditation) Regulations 2019

39. European Commission: Report on the safety and liability implications of Artificial Intelligence, the Internet of Things and robotics, COM (2020) 64 (Feb. 19, 2020), p 14. https://ec.europa.eu/info/files/commission-report-safety-and-liability-implications-ai-internet-thingsand-robotics_en. Accessed June 2020

40. European Parliament resolution of 20 October 2020 with recommendations to the Commission on a civil liability regime for artificial intelligence. www.europarl.europa.eu/doceo/document/TA-9-2020-0276_EN.pdf

41. Australian National Transport Commission 2020, Review of 'Guidelines for trials of automated vehicles in Australia': Discussion paper, NTC, Melbourne, pp. 26–27. https://www.ntc.gov.au/sites/default/files/assets/files/NTC%20Discussion%20Paper%20-%20Review%20of%20guidelines%20for%20trials%20of%20automated%20vehicles%20in%20Australia.pdf. Accessed 6 June 2020

42. General Data Protection Regulation (GDPR) art.22; Recital 71; see also Article 29 Data Protection Working Party, 2018a, Guidelines on Automated individual decision-making and Profiling for the purposes of Regulation 2016/679, 17/EN WP251rev.01, p.19. http://ec.europa.eu/newsroom/article29/item-detail.cfm?item_id=612053. Accessed 4 June 2020

43. Cobbe, Jennifer.: Administrative Law and the Machines of Government: Judicial Review of Automated Public-Sector Decision-Making. Legal Studies, p. 3 (2019)

44. For the interpretability characteristics of various AI models, refer to ICO and Alan Turing Institute: Guidance on explaining decisions made with AI (2020), annexe 2. https://ico.org.uk/media/for-organisations/guide-to-data-protection/key-data-protection-themes/explaining-decisions-made-with-artificial-intelligence-1-0.pdf. Accessed June 2020

45. For the types of explanation that an organisation may provide, refer to ICO and Alan Turing Institute: Guidance on explaining decisions made with AI (2020), p. 20. https://ico.org.uk/media/for-organisations/guide-to-data-protection/key-data-protection-themes/explaining-decisions-made-with-artificial-intelligence-1-0.pdf. Accessed June 2020

46. General Data Protection Regulation (GDPR) art.15
47. General Data Protection Regulation (GDPR) art.22
48. General Data Protection Regulation (GDPR) arts.13–14
49. European Commission: Report on the safety and liability implications of Artificial Intelligence, the Internet of Things and robotics, COM (2020) 64 (Feb. 19, 2020), p 15, https://ec.europa.eu/info/files/commission-report-safety-and-liability-implications-ai-int ernet-thingsand-robotics_en. Accessed 9 June 2020
50. Smith, B.: Legal personality. Yale Law J. 37(3), 283–299, 283 (1928)
51. For a discussion on the concept and expression "legal personality" refer to Bryson, J. J., Diamantis, M. E., Grant, T.D.: Of, for, and by the people: the legal lacuna of synthetic persons. Artificial Intelligence and Law. 25(3) (2017), p. 277
52. European Parliament: European Parliament resolution of 16 February 2017 with recommendations to the Commission on Civil Law Rules on Robotics (2015/2103(INL)). https://eur-lex. europa.eu/legal-content/EN/TXT/?uri=CELEX%3A52017IP0051. Accessed 9 June 2020
53. Ibid paragraph 59(f)
54. Refer http://www.robotics-openletter.eu/, last accessed 2020/6/9
55. European Group on Ethics in Science and New Technologies: Statement on Artificial Intelligence, Robotics and 'Autonomous' Systems, p 10. European Commission, Brussels (2018), http://ec.europa.eu/research/ege/pdf/ege_ai_statement_2018.pdf. Accessed 9 June 2020
56. European Commission: White Paper on Artificial Intelligence - A European approach to excellence and trust, COM(2020) 65, 19 February 2020. https://ec.europa.eu/info/sites/info/ files/commissionwhite-paper-artificial-intelligence-feb2020_en.pdf. Accessed 9 June 2020
57. European Commission: Report on the safety and liability implications of Artificial Intelligence, the Internet of Things and robotics, COM (2020) 64, 19 February 2020. https://ec.europa.eu/info/files/commission-report-safety-and-liability-implications-ai-internet-thingsand-robotics_en. Accessed 9 June 2020
58. JJ Bryson ME Diamantis TD Grant 2017 Of, for, and by the people: the legal lacuna of synthetic persons Artif. Intell. Law 25 3 273 291 https://doi.org/10.1007/s10506-017-9214-9
59. Resolution 2020/2014(INL) on a Civil Liability Regime for Artificial Intelligence (the "Civil Liability Resolution"), "any required changes in the existing legal framework should start with the clarification that AI-systems have neither legal personality nor human conscience, and that their sole task is to serve humanity" (Civil Liability Resolution, Annex, (6)); European Parliament resolution of 20 October 2020 on intellectual property rights for the development of artificial intelligence technologies (2020/2015(INI)), "that it would not be appropriate to seek to impart legal personality to AI technologies and points out the negative impact of such a possibility on incentives for human creators", para 13
60. This section on employment implications is based on the presentation to LAWASIA 2018 at Siem Reap, Cambodia - 4 November 2018: Artificial Intelligence & Employment Law Implications
61. Definition from the Australian Securities & Investments Commission: Regulatory Guide 255 - Providing digital financial product advice to retail client, https://asic.gov.au/regulatory-res ources/find-a-document/regulatory-guides/rg-255-providing-digital-financial-product-adv ice-to-retail-clients/. Accessed 6 June 2020
62. Corporations Amendment (Professional Standards of Financial Advisers) Act 2017
63. Australian Securities & Investments Commission: Regulatory Guide 255 - Providing digital financial product advice to retail client. https://asic.gov.au/regulatory-resources/find-a-document/regulatory-guides/rg-255-providing-digital-financial-product-advice-to-retail-cli ents/. Accessed 6 June 2020
64. Regulation (EU) 2016/679 of the European Parliament and of the Council of 27 April 2016 on the protection of natural persons with regard to the processing of personal data and on

the free movement of such data, and repealing Directive 95/46/EC (General Data Protection Regulation), 2016 O.J. (L 119/1) [GDPR].

65. Ibid art. 15(1)(h)
66. Ibid art. 22(3)
67. Australian Human Rights Commission: Discussion Paper on Human Rights and Technology (2019), p. 104. https://humanrights.gov.au/our-work/rights-and-freedoms/publications/human-rights-and-technology-discussion-paper-2019. Accessed 20 June 2020; For a US perspective, refer to Flicker, Kirsten: The Prison of Convenience, The Need for National Regulation of Biometric Technology in Sports Venues. In: 30 Fordham Intell. Prop. Media & Ent. L. J. 985 (2020), p. 1015. https://ir.lawnet.fordham.edu/iplj/vol30/iss3/7/. Accessed 20 June 2020

Ontologies Cooperation to Model the Needs of Disabled Persons

Guilaine Talens[(✉)] and Caroline Wintergerst[(✉)]

University of Lyon, UJML3, iaelyon School of Management, Magellan, Lyon, France
{guilaine.talens,caroline.wintergerst}@univ-lyon3.fr

Abstract. In French society, many aids are proposed for each kind of population. In the particular case of disabled persons, it is quite difficult to deal with
all the different information coming from heterogeneous contexts. Such different knowledge cannot be directly integrated, so we propose to build ontologies
for each aspect. Then, we manage the cooperation of these distributed ontologies
through a relational structure. Finally, to ensure the representation of the guidance interactive process, we model a workflow to follow through the successive
steps of an individual file. This file will go with the disabled person, first with its
own information, then with some administrative information and lastly with service propositions. The process is recursive allowing a better long-term assistance
monitoring.

Keywords: Distributed ontology · Process ontology · Knowledge organization ·
Domain ontology · Workflow

1 Introduction

We live in a growing environment of data, but the important problem is knowledge. In
order to represent knowledge issued from different sources, the ontology concept can be
used. The ontologies allow to identify the concepts contained in the different sources;
these concepts can be linked with synonymy, homonymy … relations between sources.

The definition of Studer [1] based on [2] is: "An *ontology is a formal, explicit
specification of a shared conceptualization*". A 'conceptualization' refers to an abstract
model of some phenomenon in the world by identifying the relevant concepts of that
phenomenon. 'Explicit' means that the type of concepts used and the constraints on
their use are explicitly defined. 'Formal' refers to the fact that the ontology should be
machine understandable and thus excludes natural language. 'Shared' reflects the notion,
an ontology captures consensual knowledge, that is, it is not private to some individual,
but accepted by a group.

Distributed ontology is a relevant framework for the articulation between ontology
domain, knowledge management and activity. We propose first application of this
principle in the domain of disability. In this framework, we develop the foundations of
an infrastructure that connects libraries, processes and services. These document structures are associated to processes but have an internal specific logic. Our first objective is

E. Mercier-Laurent et al. (Eds.): AI4KM 2021, IFIP AICT 614, pp. 19–34, 2021.
https://doi.org/10.1007/978-3-030-80847-1_2

the characterization of each ontology with the objective of its articulation to the others. In France, disabled persons can be helped in many different ways, for example adapting one's home or private teacher assisted learning. Philosophically, [3] points out the necessity for human society to have a good aid for the weak or different disabled people. Every case is individual however there can be similar proposals. For the people and their family concerned, it may be baffling to know one's rights. In fact, they have to summon up a lot of heterogeneous knowledge and build a personal file to obtain help and services. At the end, we hope to propose a tool for managing these individual files. In this paper we propose to follow the construction of the file through different steps using dedicated ontologies. After a brief description of the context and some related works, we present our generic model, then the relational structure before the workflow in our system and a conclusion.

2   Context

First of all, we must have a look on the complexity for a person with a disability or his carers to find and summon up the huge amount of knowledge available. In France, many propositions are held by state-controlled structures but you have also dedicated associations linked with a particular problem like being blind or spastic.

Six public actors are listed when you simply begin with a "Wikipedia search" [4] and, reading further, more public actors appear on regional and local levels.

L'Assurance Maladie, french public health insurance, on its website recommends to apply to six different organizations public or not and point out that there can be other solutions… rather tricky for people already in a difficult situation.

[5] describes the problem with amyotrophic lateral sclerosis (ALS). To help correctly the patient, different assistances have to be proposed:

- Human assistance for the daily life, eating, washing, dressing…
- Technical assistance like identification of the best wheelchair regarding the person abilities
- Social assistance to ask for the right aids
- And medical assistance.

To our knowledge and like Cardoso and al. [5], we didn't find any ontology including simultaneously those multiple points of view. It is not only the management of multiple points of view but also the use of multiple heterogeneous knowledge sources.

How can we associate and use together scientific resources, individual information and rehabilitation service documentation in the framework of an activity? We propose a distributed model that articulates different types of resources in the framework of an activity.

This activity is founded on personal files and its objective is the proposition of services to a person. Of course, this person can receive one service: in this case the activity evaluates the relevance of this service and if it is in keeping with their needs. This process is then recursive.

Our purpose is anchored on a specific activity: guidance of persons with a disability to relevant services. We focus on the conceptual model that allows the organization of the different information sources: bibliographic resources, personal files and service description. These sources are very distinctive both in their structure, description and organization.

We propose a distributed model that represents independently each component. Each component is structured in a way to be used by the activity.

We describe by ontology the three dimensions of this process: the knowledge organization, the service and the activity of decision and regulation. These three dimensions are about persons or individuals. But each considers the individual distinctively: for the knowledge organization, this is an instance. For the activity and the process, the individual is the object of the activity, but distinctively: for the activity, the object is the instance and for the process this is the type.

The individual is the central notion that allows the distribution of the ontology. The need is the central concept that organizes the structure of each distributed conceptual structure. The need is the issue of the deductions in the disability ontology. The activity is founded on the expression and evaluation of the needs. Lastly, the process begins with a need and is ended with its satisfaction.

The disability domain is distinctive to medical and health because it is a dynamic construction that begins with the identification of a disease or disorder and that ends with the individual rehabilitation. This process requires a succession of scientific investigations, comprising sociology, on the individual.

The organization of the scientific knowledge is only a part of the model. The process ontology represents how the individual expresses his need in the social context of an aid and the attribution of a rehabilitation service. The last ontology represents this service in relation to the need and the individual rehabilitation. It represents schematically an activity.

These three ontologies to manage heterogeneous types, instances and references are partly inspired by [6] in their methodology for coordinated evolution of scientific ontologies.

Each module has a distinctive function:

- Workflow for document elaboration and sharing.
- Knowledge organization to articulate libraries to practice, especially for individual description.
- Knowledge organization for service description in relation to individual needs.

In a more general way and including the individual, we distinguish three generic objects for the ontology:

- The characterization of a course of the action.
- An individual character, expressed by its classification.
- An action strategy, manifested by the actor's behaviors and actions.

3 Related Works

We have chosen not to use an existing model, like HI-ONTO [7] for example, because these models are not founded on the association of heterogeneous entities and they postulate the unity of the domain. In our case the domain is itself distributed and oriented to an individual satisfaction of a need. The disability is described by an international classification [8]. This has been criticized because logical conceptual construction is not consistent. The second knowledge organization is the French thesaurus [9]. These tools organize the domain following a modular principle. In this way they are organized by "micro-thesaurus" or sub-domains [10]. Some efforts are engaged to build ontology on the basis of the classification [11]. We propose the elaboration of a specific ontology level that maps classes and thesaurus concepts to ontology. Our ontology integrates active and dynamic dimensions defined by a social characterization of disability. In this framework, a handicap or disability is considered as phenomena that aggregates different points of views, from medicine to social. We follow this principle, considering that these different approaches are dependent. The ordering of these dependencies allows the consistency of the ontology and the use of the BFO vocabulary [12].

As in Basic Formal Ontology (BFO) [13], the three top-level categories of independent continuant, dependent continuant and occurrent are used in our framework.

We do not create an ontology centered on the notion of service availability [14] but a part of our ontology allows to follow the evolution of a document through different activities. Therefore, some attributes characterize specific activities and agent roles.

Our ontologies do not have an upper level as DOLCE [15], but a lightweight that focus on the needs of a specific domain: disability domain.

Disability can be considered in the framework of non-formal ontology by G. Edwards et al. [16]. They propose a social and embodied ontology that "provides a theoretical framework for situating disability in the "ground of being," as an encapsulation of the limitations that are essential to the body-environment ensemble. Hence embodied ontol-ogy moves beyond both the medical and social models of disability, both these models seek to reject limitation in different ways. Within the medical model, physical limita-tions are considered to be surmountable, while the social model rejects environmental limitations. From an embodied perspective, both physical and environmental limitations are essential to our humanity".

IAO-Intel contains ontologies applied to the explication of data models and other terminology resources. The terms in these ontologies are linked together. Each ontology uses terms which are defined in terms of other ontologies [17]. In our framework, the ontologies are also linked and we have also different levels as IAO-Intel.

We have chosen to consider the individual as the foundation of the relations between the different structures. The unity is first characterized at the instance level. At the type level, the concept of the individual is a guarantee of generality. The second foundational concept is the need which can be defined at the two levels too. This realistic foundation for ontology is articulated to a dynamic representation of a domain. These positions have been defined by B. Smith [6] but have never been applied on complex domains like disability. This domain is intrinsically built by the articulation between a scientific knowledge, processes and services. These considerations are evidence for the actors but they have not been applied: knowledge organization always stays static without any connection to the other dimensions of the domain: the proposition of services and the process have never been represented. Especially, the relation between these three dimensions has never been conceptualized. This fact can be explained by the distinction between library, knowledge management and service representation.

Studying recent works on ontology management, we can also relate our proposition to modular ontologies. For Pathak et al. [18], "an ontology module is a reusable component of a larger or more complex ontology, which is self-contained but bears a definite association to other ontology modules, including the original ontology." Although the techniques proposed in this field may be relevant to build the cooperation between our different ontologies, we are not yet in this perspective. However, even if the disability ontology seems to be a module extracted from a more general medical ontology, we argued before for its specificity.

4 Generic Model

We propose a generic model to articulate three sorts of information sources:

- Scientific publications on disability. The disability ontology is essentially relational.
- (Personalized) service. This ontology characterizes the matching of a personalized service.
- Process of attribution of a service for a person. This ontology characterizes a workflow of documents implying different actors and a decision.

As opposed to a monolithic domain ontology, we have proposed a distributed ontology to capture the different dimensions of a domain. This domain is built on an activity: the rehabilitation of persons with disabilities. This activity requires different actors and firstly the person called individual and one objective: the rehabilitation of this person.

The academic knowledge organization is unsatisfying to represent a pluri-disciplinary knowledge structure that integrates both scientific knowledge, individual expression and the availability of rehabilitation services in a specific location and time. We can wonder: How can we associate and use together scientific resources, individual information and rehabilitation service documentation in the framework of an activity? We propose a distributed model that articulates different types of resources in the framework of an activity.

The distribution is foundational because an activity associates systematically embedded situations and abstract framework. The articulation of these different dimensions is founded on the individual that is the object of the activity. This individual has needs and the satisfaction of these needs is the goal of the activity.

The process is the actors and documents structure that allows the individual expression of the need and the representation of its evolution in time. We have centered this representation on the workflow: it will be extended to the document level.

The process representation is intrinsically dynamic and requires for the examination of the individual situation a similarly logically knowledge representation. We have postulated that the construction of the knowledge domain follows the progressive path from a health perspective to a particular social, individual or contextual disability. This progressive path is fundamental for the characterization of a need and identification of the tools or services that allow the satisfaction of this need.

Different users interact in our model. A disabled person creates its individual file. The information is stored in the "workflow ontology". To create and select the different information, he is guided to choose the impairments and the needs in the "disability ontology" and the services in the "service ontology". After, case workers and the medical staff will complete the individual file in coordination with the concerned person. At the end, the CDAPH assigns services linked with the needs of the disabled person and the potential places offered by the local services. The CDAPH is the committee in charge of the rights and the autonomy of disabled people in France (see Fig. 1).

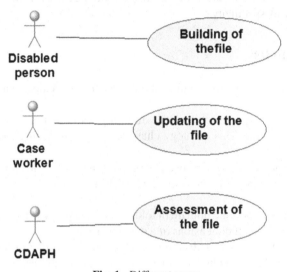

Fig. 1. Different users

We focus on the conceptual model that allows the organization of the different information sources: bibliographic resources, personal files and service description. These sources are very distinctive both in their structure, description and organization.

4.1 Methodology

Our aim and challenge are to manage two different levels of abstraction. On the one hand, we try to deal with a large amount of knowledge stored in heterogeneous documents. On the other hand, we cope with individual information about the person's impairments and life. We then propose, to connect these individual data with documented and referenced information. The PROV-Ontology is shortly described by the following: "It provides a set of classes, properties, and restrictions that can be used to represent and interchange provenance information generated in different systems and under different contexts." [19]. So, we have chosen to work with the PROV-Ontology to manage our dual issues described above.

4.2 Foundational Model

Our three sorts of information sources are heterogeneous but they are in solidarity.

At a high level of generality, we clearly distinguish three sorts of entities:

– Individuals
– Tools or services
– Artifacts.

These structuring entities are always situated in context. Individual is a singular entity which participates to the different ontologies, as shown in Fig. 2:

– As a categorized entity, an individual is a person with disability.
– As a person with needs, he participates to the personalized services.
– As a person that produces files and expresses his needs for the social services, he participates to the workflow.

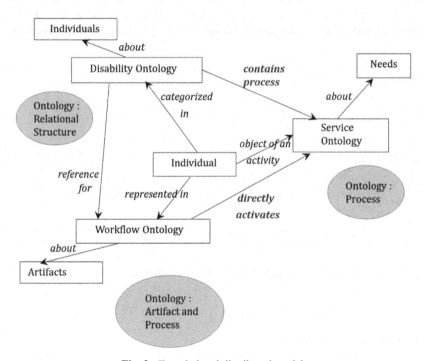

Fig. 2. Foundational distributed model.

4.3 Process

The committee of the rights and the autonomy of disabled people called CDAPH in France allocates services. But, it is in the "regional office of the disabled people" (MDPH in France) that an individual can find all the information and the help to fill in the file.

The impairments and the needs expressed in the file are chosen respectively among these drawn up by the thesaurus handicap [9] and SERAFIN-PH nomenclature [20]. The individual entity contains many attributes such as the birth date, profession etc. and refers to the different caregivers who can help him in the social context. It is the role of each of them which is displayed in Fig. 3. The OBO Relations Ontology [21] has been used to represent the relations between the concepts. We have chosen OBO Relations as they are meant for biological ontologies and each relation is well defined.

When he creates his file, the individual must describe his situation (medical and social). With this information, the system proposes needs according to impairments. The Disability ontology contains the description of the disabilities but also the social context in order to better choose the needs. With these needs, the service ontology selects the different services and proposes them. The individual chooses services. After the social worker studies the individual file and helps to complete it and select potential services in relation to local services. At the end, the CDAPH's assessment determines personalized services. Each year, the file must be updated by the individual and the process starts again. The workflow ontology manages the process and its regular iterations to adapt the proposed services with the personal evolution of the concerned person and his circle.

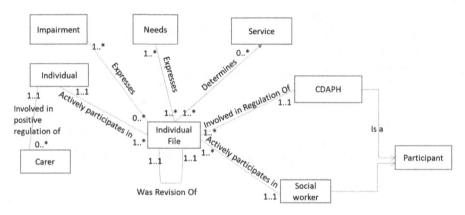

Fig. 3. General file distribution.

5   Relational Structure

The individual is central in the three modules but is described by categorization in the disability ontology. Artifacts are about this individual but represent only some relevant categories for the decision. Lastly, the process associates a tool considered as a service devoted to this individual considering some of its specificities.

These three ontologies are dependent. We do not have a mapping between different ontologies but a knowledge distribution in accordance with the action relatively to persons with disability.

Disability is a complex domain that cannot be reduced to disease aspects or social action. In a way to represent the consistency of the domain, we propose phases to characterize the trajectory from a disease to a social action.

The ontology is a cognitive representation characterized by a two-level structure:

- At the high level, the characterization of the person with the potential disability. This is the global consistency of the handicap domain.
- At the low level, the context of the person where the disability is segmented into a succession of situations where the internal disease is evolved into successive frames. In this level, the accommodation and the identifiable helpers around the disabled person are described.

This representation (see Fig. 4) is about individuals (or the level of reality). The publicly accessible concretizations are recorded in thesauri and classifications.

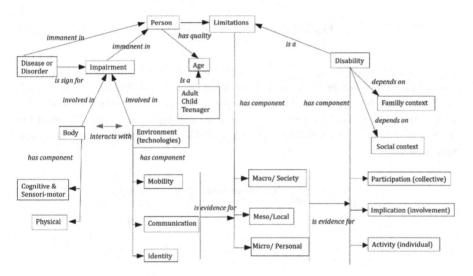

Fig. 4. Resource disability ontology.

We now present, in the Fig. 5, the ontology of the rehabilitation process. This process allows the characterization of the satisfaction of the need. It integrates some characteristics of the service ontology such as the distinction between a service prescription and a service description. This distinction allows the articulation between the generic SERAFIN-PH [20] nomenclature and the local organizations presentation of services.

After the description of individual context, a need is identified (service prescription) and after a solution for this individual need is proposed.

We insist on the individual participation by the concept of "rehabilitation content" that describes the benefit of the service.

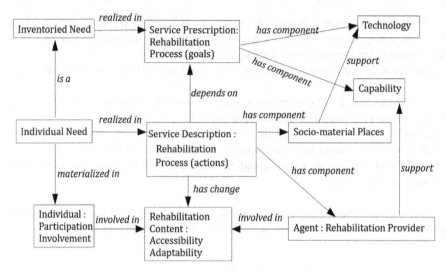

Fig. 5. Rehabilitation process ontology.

We describe a need as a relation between an identified disability, an individual expression and a rehabilitation process (see Fig. 6). Need has a dual definition: at a type level, it is the relation between a disability, an expression and a rehabilitation service. By this information flow, we characterize how the three ontologies are connected under the question of the needs. A need is then defined both by the disability and the individual expression.

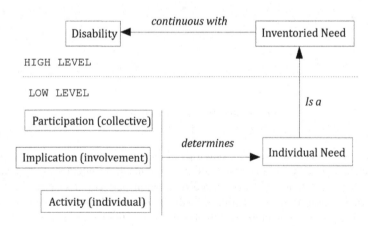

Fig. 6. Need characterization.

6 Workflow

The workflow ontology is based on the individual needs. The individual file describes the person, this one is an entity but also an actor who participates in the building of his file. The person must also list his caregivers. The individual, with the help of the case worker, expresses his impairments and his needs. Finally, services are determined. Therefore, the case worker is also an entity and an actor. The CDAPH determines the possible services linked with the request and real life (places available in special institutes, home helpers…). It is a recursive process. Each year, the individual updates his request and it is re-evaluated by the CDAPH.

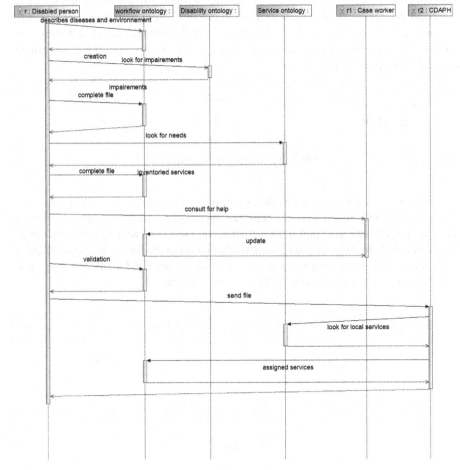

Fig. 7. Awarding of services

Therefore, there are 3 actors interacting to build the file and the response to each need depending on the context.

The disabled person describes his diseases and his environment. He chooses the impairments and his needs thanks to the disability ontology. In fact, many propositions are made to him from his situation. After, the request is evaluated by the social worker and the medical staff and is updated in agreement with the concerned person. For example, many services are automatically selected in the service ontology by the system and are proposed. The staff helps the user to choose the right ones. Finally, the CDAPH studies the request and offers services in connection with the demand and with the local possibilities. The sequence diagram [22] depicted in the Fig. 7 explains the interaction between the different actors and the ontologies in order to assign services to a disabled person.

The PROV Ontology [19] has been used to describe the "individual file" creation and evolution. At the end, services are or are not attributed to the individual who has expressed the needs. PROV-Ontology contains three classes: prov:Agent, prov:Entity and prov:Activity (see Fig. 8). The agents take act on the entities through activities. The activities can generate entities but also modify and use, the entities. The entity can be physical, conceptual or other.

Fig. 8. Classes of PROV ontology

The scenario allows to describe the provenance of individual files. The entities are the file, the selected impairments, the needs among all the existing ones and the attributed services. Three agents take part in the activities: an individual who describes his needs corresponding to his impairments, a case worker modifies the file by adding or deleting needs relatively to the impairments and the individual situation. Finally, the concerned CDAPH studies the file and decides the services to allocate.

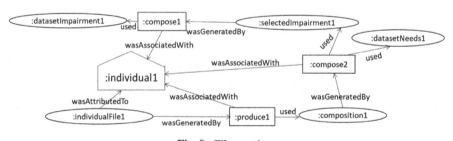

Fig. 9. File creation.

As you can see in Fig. 9, an individual creates his "individual file" which contains, at the beginning, a descriptive analysis of his impairments and a first needs list. The composition activity (:compose1) uses the selected impairments by the individual1. The composed data are generated by this activity. After which, another composition activity generates the selected needs. Finally, the:individualFile1 is produced by individual1. He is an agent, a person described by attributes: age, name, profession and the caregivers that can help him.

In a second step (see Fig. 10), a case worker completes the:IndividualFile1.: caseWorker1 is an agent, a person, who works in an organization which is itself an agent. The selected needs by individual1 are corrected and a new composition is created. A new individual file with better expression of needs is produced; it is a revision of the previous. Note that, in the figure, grey ellipsis are coming from the preceding step.

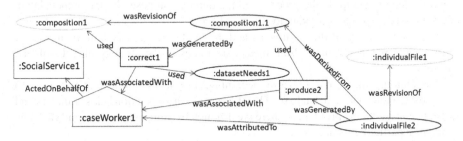

Fig. 10. File revision.

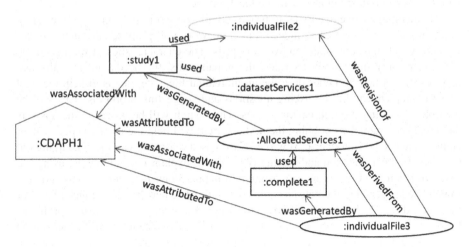

Fig. 11. File update.

Then, an instance of the CDAPH studies the individualFile2 with the data set of existing services (see Fig. 11). With all this information, the allocated services are decided. A new "individual file" is created, it is a revision of ":individualFile2", allocated services are added to it by the ":CDAPH1". This ":individualFile3" is not a final one. The individual can go to appeal and, then create an ":individualFile4" to argue for a new analysis of his case and rights. Furthermore, from time to time, at least each year, a case worker will inspect the individual and may revise his individual file. This

":individualFileN" will, then, be studied again by the CDAPH. The process is gradual and iterative.

7   Conclusion

We have presented a first conceptual structure that allows the organization of a domain characterized by a process. The further step of the project will concern the connection to the thesaurus that indexes the scientific documents, the characterization of the information artifacts that compose the process and the duality composed by the nomenclature and the available services in time, location and actors.

The heterogeneity of the documents and the modalities to accede to their content (information extraction, indexation, metadata) argues to the strategy of a distributed ontology.

The building of the ontologies is beginning. The service collection is very hard because there is no national database of local services. An association helps us understand and collect data but the problem is: there are different existing associations and each one concerns a particular disability.

Our goal is to create a computer aided system which can be used by anyone, that is to say by a specialist of a particular disability but also by a final user which has a disability. We aim for this one to find all the propositions of potential services linked with his social context but also with the local services.

Another perspective to enrich our proposal will be to propose to an user the existing cases similar to his own case. Indeed, our framework will propose allocated services to a file which has a similar context and needs. The characteristics of the person do not appear, only the caregiver's roles, the impairments, the needs and the allocated services. It is a help to better describe an individual file. The idea is to help the final user to complete the file by asking questions and suggesting proposals. This will be possible by tracing through existing cases. This search will be based on the answers and therefore gradually enriching them, the system will help the users to specify their context and needs. Kolodner [23] wrote "Case-based reasoning can mean adapting old solutions to meet new demands; using old cases to explain new situations; using old cases to critique new solutions; or reasoning from precedents to interpret a new situation (much like lawyers do) or create an equitable solution to a new problem (much like labor mediators do)". The basic idea of CBR (Case-Based Reasoning) is to solve new problems by comparing them to problems already solved [24]. The idea to associate case-based reasoning and ontology is not a new idea [25] showed a strong relationship between both approaches with respect to technological but also to methodological issues. Therefore, adding the concept of CBR to our approach seems very interesting to aid the final user to complete his file and find the most appropriate services for his needs.

References

1. Studer, R., Benjamins, D., Fensel, D.: Knowledge engineering: principles and methods. IEEE Trans. Data Knowl. Eng. **25**(1–2), 161–197 (1998)

2. Gruber, T.R.: A translation approach to portable ontologies. Knowl. Acquis. **5**(2), 199–220 (1993)
3. Doat, D.: Vers une ontologie humaine intégratrice du handicap et de la fragilité en contexte évolutionniste. René-Michel Roberge **69**(3), 549–583 (2013)
4. Prise en charge du handicap en France. https://fr.wikipedia.org/wiki/Prise_en_charge_du_handicap_en_France. Accessed 24 Feb 2021
5. Cardoso, S., Aime, X., Meininger, V., Grabli, D., Cohen, K., et al.: De l'intérêt des ontologies modulaires. Application à la modélisation de la prise en charge de la SLA. 29es Journées Francophones d'Ingénierie des Connaissances, IC 2018, AFIA, Nancy, France, pp. 121–128. hal-01839571 (2018)
6. Smith, B., Ceusters, W.: Ontological realism: a methodology for coordinated evolution of scientific ontologies. J. App. Ontol. **5**(3–4), 139–188 (2010)
7. El-Diraby, T.E., Kashif, K.F.: Distributed ontology architecture for knowledge management in highway construction. J. Constr. Eng. Manag. **131**(5), 591–603 (2005)
8. ICF: International Classification of Functioning, Disability and Health. World Health Organization Geneva (2001). http://apps.who.int/iris/bitstream/10665/42407/7/9241545429_tha%2Beng.pdf
9. French Thesaurus (2012). http://mssh.ehesp.fr/wp-content/uploads/2012/10/THESAURUS-HANDICAP_FINAL_V_3.pdf
10. Ruggieri, A.P., Elkin, P.L., Solbrig, H., Chute, C.G.: Expression of a domain ontology model in unified modeling language for the World Health Organization International classification of impairment, disability, and handicap, version 2. In: Proceedings of the AMIA Symposium. American Medical Informatics Association (2001)
11. Cuenot, M.: Améliorer les cadres de référence pour le suivi de l'application de la Convention des Nations Unies relative aux droits des personnes handicapées: une illustration à travers le processus de mise à jour de l'International Classification of Functioning, Disability and Health (ICF). ALTER-Eur. J. Disability Res./Revue Européenne de Recherche sur le Handicap **9**(1), 64–74 (2015)
12. Arp, R., Smith, B., Spear, A.D.: Building Ontologies with Basic Formal Ontology. MIT Press, Cambridge (2015)
13. Grenon, P., Smith, B.: SNAP and SPAN: towards dynamic spatial ontology. Spat. Cogn. Comput. **4**(1), 69–103 (2004)
14. Ferrario, R., Guarino, N.: Towards an ontological foundation for services science. In: Domingue, J., Fensel, D., Traverso, P. (eds.) FIS 2008. LNCS, vol. 5468, pp. 152–169. Springer, Heidelberg (2009). https://doi.org/10.1007/978-3-642-00985-3_13
15. Gangemi, A., Guarino, N., Masolo, C., Oltramari, A., Schneider, L.: Sweetening ontologies with DOLCE. In: Gómez-Pérez, A., Benjamins, V.R. (eds.) EKAW 2002. LNCS (LNAI), vol. 2473, pp. 166–181. Springer, Heidelberg (2002). https://doi.org/10.1007/3-540-45810-7_18
16. Edwards, G., et al.: Disability, rehabilitation research and post-Cartesian embodied ontologies–has the research paradigm changed? In: Environmental Contexts and Disability, pp. 73–102. Emerald Group Publishing Limited (2014)
17. Smith, B., et al.: IAO-Intel: an ontology of information artifacts in the intelligence domain. In: Laskey, K.B., Costa, P.C.G. (eds.) Proceedings of the Eighth International Conference on Semantic Technologies for Intelligence, Defense, and Security, Fairfax, VA, (STIDS 2013), vol. 1097, pp. 33–40. CEUR (2013)
18. Pathak, J., Solbrig, H.R., Johnson, T.M., Buntrock, J.D., Chute, C.G.: Survey of modular ontology techniques and their applications in the biomedical domain. Integr. Comput.-Aided Eng. **16**(3), 225–242 (2009)
19. PROV 2013. https://www.w3.org/TR/prov-o/. Accessed 24 Feb 2021

20. SERAFIN-PH 2016 NOMENCLATURES BESOINS ET PRESTATIONS DETAILLEES Services et établissements: réforme pour une adéquation des financements aux parcours des personnes handicapées. http://solidarites-sante.gouv.fr/IMG/pdf/nomenclatures_serafin phdetaillees_mars_16.pdf

21. Oborel. https://raw.githubusercontent.com/oborel/obo-relations/master/ro.obo. Accessed 02 Feb 2017

22. Booch, G., Rumbaugh, J., Jacobson, I.: The Unified Modeling Language Reference Manual, 550 p. Prentice Hall (2000)

23. Kolodner, J.L.: An introduction to case-based reasoning. Artif. Intell. Rev. **6**(1), 3–34 (1992)

24. Aamodt, A., Plaza, E.: Case-based reasoning: foundational issues, methodological variations, and system approaches. AICOM **7**(1), 39–59 (1994)

25. Bergmann, R., Schaaf, M.: Structural case-based reasoning and ontology-based knowledge management: a perfect match? J. UCS **9**(7), 608–626 (2003)

A Conceptual Framework of Intelligent Management Control System for Higher Education

Helena Dudycz[1], Marcin Hernes[1(✉)], Zdzislaw Kes[1], Eunika Mercier-Laurent[2], Bartłomiej Nita[1], Krzysztof Nowosielski[1], Piotr Oleksyk[1], Mieczysław L. Owoc[1], Rafał Palak[3], Maciej Pondel[1], and Krystian Wojtkiewicz[3]

[1] Wrocław University of Economics and Bussiness, Komandorska 118/120, 53-345 Wrocław, Poland
{helena.dudycz,marcin.hernes,aw.kes,omiej.nita,
krzysztof.nowosielski,piotr.oleksyk,aw.owoc,
maciej.pondel}@ue.wroc.pl
[2] University of Reims Champagne Ardennes, Reims, France
eunika@innovation3d.fr
[3] Wroclaw University of Science and Technology, Wrocław, Poland
{rafal.palak,krystian.wojtkiewicz}@pwr.edu.pl

Abstract. The utilization of management control systems in university management poses a considerable challenge because university's strategic goals are not identical to those applied in profit-oriented management. A university's management control system should take into account the processing of management information for management purposes, allowing for the relationships between different groups of stakeholders. The specificity of the university operation assumes conducting long-term scientific research and educational programmes. Therefore, the controlling approach to university management should considerat long-term performance measurement as well as management in key areas such as research, provision of education to students, and interaction with the tertiary institution's socio-economic environment. This paper aims to develop a conceptual framework of the Intelligent Management Control System for Higher Education (IMC-SHE) based on cognitive agents. The main findings are related to developing the assumption, model, and technological basis including the artificial intelligence method.

Keywords: Management control system · Intelligent systems · Artificial intelligence · Higher education · Cognitive technologies

1 Introduction

The use of management control systems (MCS) in university management is a significant challenge because the universities' strategic objectives are not the same as those of profit-oriented businesses. Moreover, unlike enterprises, which mainly attach importance to

E. Mercier-Laurent et al. (Eds.): AI4KM 2021, IFIP AICT 614, pp. 35–47, 2021.
https://doi.org/10.1007/978-3-030-80847-1_3

increasing value for the owners, the competitive advantage - and thus the position - of a university among institutions which focus on scientific and educational activity stems from other sources and is oriented towards meeting the needs of a wide range of stakeholders. It is crucial to translate a university's strategy into its operation, which is intended to serve the purpose of enabling all members of the academic community to understand the strategy while streamlining the process of its implementation in the course of the tertiary institution's day-to-day activity. A university's controlling system structure is closely related to its strategic goals and assumed directions of development. The triple helix concept, promoted by H. Etzkowitz and L. Leydesdorff [1] can be used as a basis for defining the mission and strategy of a university. According to them, the triple helix is a model of relations occurring in the process of the creation of knowledge between three types of entities: scientific centres (academia), the industrial environment (industry), and public administration (state). The knowledge-based economy requires creative cooperation of modern universities with public administration and the economic environment. The so-called quadruple helix and even quintuple helix concepts are being postulated today [2]. The triple helix model is enriched by the media, civil society, and the natural environment.

The MCS of a university should allow for the processing of management information for the executive bodies' needs, taking into account the relations between different stakeholder groups. The specificity of a university's operation assumes conducting long-term research and offering long-term educational programmes. Therefore, university management's controlling approach should allow for long-term performance measurement and management in critical areas, such as conducting research, educating students, and cooperating with the socio-economic environment.

The design of MCS to support university management should include internal and external information. Processing internal information is complicated due to the multi-dimensionality of information aggregation objects and the wide range of stakeholders. Access to prospective information allowing to assess the expected changes in operating conditions and determine future directions of action is limited because scientific research may produce uncertain results (i.e. there are no such methods). A useful tool for any university is to create scenarios for future decisions that can be generated to ensure the adopted development strategy's implementation. Moreover, as far as the decision-making process is concerned, it is necessary to process external information concerning factors including the following:

- the demographic situation,
- changes in legal regulations,
- the demand for graduates with new qualifications,
- competitive entities' activity,
- changes in the methods of education.

Managing a university is a process of making decisions whose accuracy determines the effectiveness and efficiency of its educational and research activities. Therefore, analyses carried out under the MCS should enable the following, among other things:

- evaluation of the university's ability to meet the requirements of the regulations governing higher education,
- identification of the financial needs sources of research and sources of its funding,
- symptoms of threat and the risk of a change in the competitive position,
- directions of changes in the side areas of operation.

A carefully developed and detail-oriented internal information system, constituting a response to signals coming from the environment, plays a vital role in supporting university management. It is necessary to apply a detailed assessment of all aspects of the university's operation. The most common method of managing performance in private and public sectors, including universities, is the Balanced Scorecard. The first generation of the Balanced Scorecard [3] was treated exclusively as a method of measuring performance, while nowadays, it is a much more advanced concept, one that is continuously being developed. Today, R.S. Kaplan and D. P. Norton argue that their proposal can provide a framework for performance management geared towards implementing a strategy using intelligent control systems.

The functioning of the MCS involves the processing of both structured and unstructured knowledge. The artificial intelligence methods and tools can be used in this purpose.

This paper aims to develop a conceptual framework of an Intelligent Management Control System for Higher Education (IMCSHE) based on cognitive agents.

The main contribution is related to the following:

- The application of cognitive agents in a Management Control System for Higher Education,
- A proposal for extending the Learning Intelligent Distribution Agent Architecture with a machine learning module.

2 Related Works

During the theoretical foundations' analysis, attention was paid to the issues raised in studies dedicated to Management Control Systems (MCS) solutions implemented at universities, emphasizing the applications being within this study's scope. The overwhelming majority of the studies concerns the characteristics and evaluation of MSC systems used. Baid [4] researched types of control in schools. Its findings show a positive relationship between teacher control, student control and the institution's performance. Al.-Tarawneh [5] conducted a study involving university professors and students in the context of MSC use. In his view, professors who have less experience in higher education tend to use MSC more than those with many years of experience [5]. Beuren and Teixeira [6] researched the structure and functions of MSC in assessing performance at private universities. Based on the results of the questionnaires sent to managers responsible for the strategy of educational institutions, it was found that the overall evaluation result for MCS reached an average of 3.62 on a 5-degree scale. According to Tanveer and Karim [7], universities must implement performance management (PM) procedures to improve their performance and align their individual goals with the university's strategy. The evaluation must consider the achievements of the researchers and the administration to an equal extent.

A much smaller number of articles included information on the IT solutions being applied. The authors Cantele, Martini, and Campedelli [8] showed in their research an insignificant relationship between the degree of development of MCS and some specific features of state-run universities, such as size, complexity, degree of expenditure rigidity, and availability of human resources assigned to administrative activities. Besides, they found that the planning and control tools used at universities include modules that enable the following:

- economic and financial simulations, including planning under different scenarios;
- processing information on the university's strategy, mission, and objectives;
- building long-term business plans that define strategies, goals, programmes, initiatives, and projects, as well as their implementation schedules, project managers, allocated financial and human resources, and objectives to be achieved;
- using management dashboards which provide performance indicators that can be used for both internal management and external communication;
- cost calculation in sections such as master's studies, research projects, activities and processes, responsibility centres;
- budgeting and operational planning;
- deviation analysis.

Labas and Bacs [9] present an MCS concept that includes a software structure. The MCS should be at the junction of field-specific systems (e.g. fixed assets management, financial management, financial accounting, or human resources management) and the management information system (MIS). Based on preliminary research carried out, it can be concluded that there is a cognitive gap in IT support for MCS in organizations involved in academic teaching.

Z Alach [10] proposes a model for assessing the maturity of performance management systems in higher education controlling, which includes seven elements. This model was built based on normative research conducted by many authors. Z Alach integrated these recommendations and empirically verified them, grouping all criteria into three sets. The first group concerns the use of information on performance in university management and on whether the obtained results stem from the use of this information. The second group is focused on designing a performance management system and its internal coherence. The last group refers to the elements that determine the system's usefulness. McCormack et al. [11] propose using 17 measures for the evaluation and design of a university's controlling system. All the measures are divided into four categories: operational activity, monitoring, targeting of measures, and motivation systems.

3   Research Methodology

In our research, we use the Design Science Research Process (DSRP) methodology [12]. This methodology involves the realization of research works as process-dependent steps responsible for implementing basic tasks and delivering primary work artefacts.

This methodology is based on five necessary steps. The first, "Awareness of problem", focuses on preparing a preliminary proposal for a new research topic. It results from the analysis of already available achievements and results in related scientific disciplines and industry (in our paper this phase is realized in the introduction. The second, development of the proposal ("Suggestion"), follows the initial proposal and is a creative step to define new models, methods, and functionalities based on new configurations of existing or new elements. This phase is realized in the related works section. The third, constituting further development of the proposal ("Development"), is where the initial research is developed and extended. The development is performed in the Framework of the system section. The fourth, "Evaluation", is when the prepared artefacts are evaluated according to the adopted criteria. The fifth, "Conclusion", can be the end of a given research cycle or end the entire research undertaking. The evaluation and conclusion are related in the Conclusions section. As outlined, each stage ends with a specific result, which then forms the basis for and enables the next step in the process. Besides, this methodology assumes that it is possible to return to the previous steps under the observed restrictions. We use the literature of subject analysis, as a research method in the Awareness of the problem and the Suggestion stages. In the development stage, we use such research methods, as modelling, design and implementation and observation of phenomena's. The Evaluation we use research experiment method. Conclusion phase we based on synthesis, analysis, induction and deduction research methods.

4   The Framework of the System

The Intelligent Management Control System for Higher Education (IMCSHE) aims to provide information for the UEW's Balanced Scorecard (BSC). The scorecard includes four perspectives focusing on the following information:

The financial perspective (F):

- financial plans including a material and financial plan, the central budget of the university, partial budgets (budgets of subunits, tasks, or projects);
- control aspects in terms of income and expenses (in cross-section of subunits, tasks and projects) and financial and economic indicators.

The customer perspective (C):

- student segmentation;
- change dynamics in student segments (degrees, types of studies, fields of study);
- quality of education from the perspective of students and graduates (tracking the path of graduates' professional development) broken down into fields of study, specialties, modules, and subjects;
- education quality indicators.

The internal processes perspective (P):

- human resources potential, including the structure and dynamics of employment broken down into degrees and academic titles, positions held, and functions performed;

- scientific potential, including the number and quality of publications (IF and quality of publications), citation indicators, experience in research projects, the number of promoted doctoral students, the level of scientific research commercialization, the impact of scientific activity on the functioning of the society and economy, research infrastructure, as well as the organization of conferences and scientific seminars;
- educational potential, including flexibility in adopting the educational offer to market needs, employee evaluation from the perspective of both, the student and the graduate, the number of promoted students, supervision of scientific associations, initiatives in the field of cooperation with students and their organizations, as well as teaching facilities;
- organizational potential, including the ability to develop pro-efficiency and pro-quality intra-organisational projects, work for the university environment, and the organization of the internal units' operation.

The development perspective (D):

- acquiring and conducting development projects, fully informed at HR development, as well as management structures and infrastructure;
- development level and evolution of IT systems supporting the implementation of all university processes;
- level of organizational maturity.

The diversity of perspectives enables the development of multidimensional reports for managerial purposes. It also determines the architecture of the data aspect of the IMCSHE. The class diagram in Fig. 1 represents the simplified hierarchical structure of a university. Also, it shows how reports are generated. At this point, there were four types of reports distinguished concerning the identified perspectives, namely:

- Financial report,
- Customer report,
- Internal process report,
- Development report.

However, a new type of report could be defined if needed, since the generalization set is not complete.

The composition used between all levels of university management indicates that reports generated for each level of the university are used to calculate reports for higher university structures, e.g. in the case of a financial report, the sum of all expenses for projects in a given division will give the expense value in the financial report for this division. One of the project approach's main assumptions is that business as usual (BAU) is also treated as a separate project. At first, we distinguished two types of organization unit: Faculty and Administration. The lower level is a division, which serves as a universal type of second-level descendant in the structure. The division report is created as a result of the aggregation of projects, i.e. the lowest level of university structure decomposition. Reports are complex structures built from various fields, for each of which a separate aggregation function needs to be defined. At the top of the hierarchy is the university, which has reports derived from lower structure levels. The aggregation function allows us to derive the final report based on a chosen organizational structure level due to such a hierarchical structure. In particular, we do not need to include all levels in defining aggregation, instead only focusing on the minimum needed set of projects. However, each report is based on an arbitrary set of report types, i.e., Financial report, Customer report, Internal process report, and Development report. All of them inherit from a report, which means that they share some properties, but at the same time, they focus on different perspectives. Final Report should reflect all the mentioned perspectives and creates summarised (including different measurable results) view on the university state.

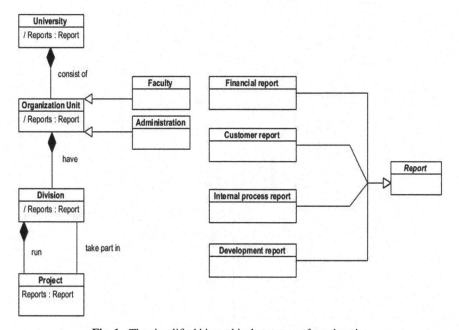

Fig. 1. The simplified hierarchical structure of a university

The component diagram (Fig. 2) shows the system's concept with a strong emphasis on data sources, i.e., the university's core IT systems. The integrated system communicates with each source component through a dedicated API and obtains the data from each of them. At first, the data feeds the data warehouse, where it is processed, and then the aggregated data is sent via a dedicated interface to the target iSIC component. Thus, the data warehouse is a crucial part of the system. The quality and structure of data delivered to the warehouse is undoubtedly the key indicator of system performance. In our concept, we focused on the following data sources:

– Employee evaluation system – provides data about employee results;
– USOS – provides data related to teaching, such as student surveys or data on financial settlements with students;

- Lecture planning system – a system for sharing data on the allocation of items and teachers to rooms;
- Publication repository – provides data on employees' publications;
- ERP – a system focusing on data such us: HR and payroll, organizational structure, and cost centres;
- Budget Planning System (SIC) – a system used to define unit budgets (tasks and project budgets);
- Expenses Control – a system focusing on tracking expenses;
- Project repository - shares information on scientific, R&D, and organizational projects;
- Infrastructure Management – provides information regarding the infrastructure.

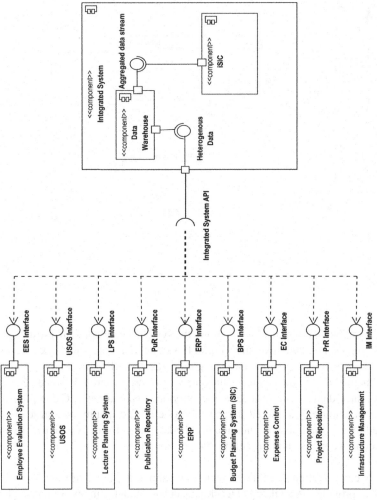

Fig. 2. A concept of the management control system for higher education.

Such diverse data sources allow generating distinguished types of reports by the iSIC component. The iSIC component consists of the artificial intelligence module. We use the Learning Intelligent Distribution Agent Architecture (LIDA), developed by Cognitive Computing Research Group (CCRG) [13, 14]. CCRG also developed the software framework of LIDA (in Java and Python). The reason for choosing this architecture is our many years' scientific experience in applying this architecture in management information systems [15, 16]. LIDA is a cognitive architecture, performing tasks within a cognitive cycle. The knowledge is represented by a "slipnet" - a semantic network with nodes' and links' activation level. The learning process is permanently performed. LIDA consists of the following modules:

- sensory memory,
- perceptual memory,
- episodic memory,
- declarative memory,
- workspace,
- attentional codelets,
- global workspace,
- action selection,
- sensory-motor memory.

The communication between modules is handled by codelets - mobile software programs processing information. LIDA's functioning was described in detail in [Franklin et al. 2016, McCall et al. 2020]. LIDA's advantage is related to the ability to process both symbolic and numerical knowledge (a slipnet allows the representation of such kinds of knowledge). This form of knowledge representation is beneficial in the areas of management and economics [17]. However, the disadvantage of LIDA is its complexity when processing large amounts of knowledge. Moreover, it entails high resource consumption. Therefore, we propose extending the LIDA architecture with a machine learning module, making it possible to process faster numerical knowledge (which cannot be represented as a slipnet, e.g. knowledge related to the prediction of costs, or the number of students). The extension is presented in Fig. 3.

The machine learning module is connected to episodic memory (this memory stores data related to past events) and workspace memory. Input data for the machine learning module is required from the historical data and workspace memory. Machine learning module consists of 2 units:

- Experimental platform,
- Operational platform.

The experimental platform is the first unit, where ideas for Machine learning analyses are examined. Models are created, tested, validated and if necessary, tuned to archive better results. After a technical perspective of a model is verified, the business attractiveness of results is also evaluated. Positively verified models are documented, virtualized and deployed to the operational platform, where then return on a regular basis and generate results. The operational platform is also monitored, and it is checked if results accuracy does not drop below defined thresholds. If such a situation happens, the experimental platform is employed, and the model is again verified, tuned and in a corrected version again deployed to the operational platform.

The results are sent to the workspace memory. The results (e.g. predictions) are taken into consideration in forming a current situational model in the global workspace, which influences action selection and action forming.

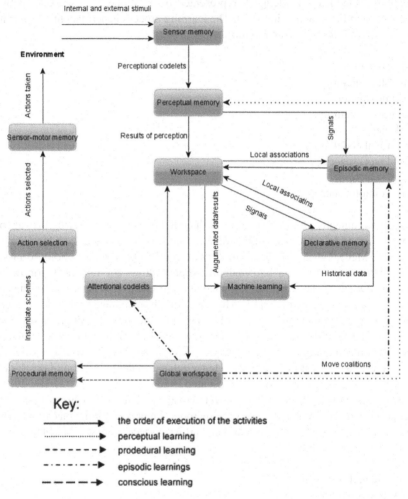

Fig. 3. The extended architecture of LIDA.

Next, the set of alternative decisions is presented to the user. Each of decision has the level of confidence. Also consensus of the set of decisions is calculated [15].

5 Conclusions

Universities try to develop following the strategies they adopted, which will enable long-term activities plans. The university management must constantly analyze the information coming from available databases pertaining to many areas and its surrounding environment. This article presents a concept of an intelligent management control system for higher education. The essence of this solution is a combination of an MCS's ideas, the balanced scorecard, and machine learning. The premise of this system is a controlling-oriented approach to supporting university management. The executed operational tasks must serve to implement the adopted strategy. The proposed system is expected to involve long-term measurement and management in key areas, i.e. to conduct research, providing education to students, and cooperating with the socio-economic environment.

Furthermore, it should support the university's management staff in carrying out various types of financial analyses so that the tertiary institution's activity does not bring financial losses. The university's MCS is based on the Balanced Scorecard, which comprises four perspectives: The Financial Perspective, the Customer Perspective, the Internal Process Perspective, and Development Perspective. The Balanced Scorecard is one of the methods used to support knowledge management, which is important because the university's employees' knowledge constitutes its essential capital. As far as universities are concerned, adaptation to the technological change, effective knowledge sharing and communication, operational efficiency, time saved due to knowledge sharing, and the growth and enhancement in the collaboration culture are becoming essential elements of knowledge management. Especially knowledge sharing allows generating new ideas, improving organizational performance, and helping employees to stay motivated. The Balanced Scorecard makes it possible to generate various reports for the university management with a focus on four perspectives.

The proposed concept of an intelligent control system requires an appropriate IT system architecture. A basis is a typical approach applied in Business Intelligence class IT systems, i.e. the transformation of data in various heterogeneous databases into information and knowledge for the management staff. There are many databases within the university (mentioned in the previous section) from which the necessary data will be obtained and loaded into a data warehouse after using ETL tools (initial concepts addressed to educational/customer area was proposed in [18]). Aggregate data located in a data warehouse is the primary resource for an Intelligent Management Control System for Higher Education. The use of the Learning Intelligent Distribution Agent Architecture and the machine learning module application are important elements of the proposed system. The use of these elements makes our proposal different from a typical Business Intelligence class system.

The proposed Intelligent Management Control System for Higher Education, applying four perspectives following the Balanced Scorecard and machine learning, allows the development of scenarios for future decisions that can be generated to ensure the adopted development strategy's execution. Scenarios may concern the processing of information from databases existing at the university. They may also include data and information from the university's environment, i.e. the demographic situation, changes in legal regulations, the demand for graduates with new qualifications, and competitive entities' activity.

Acknowledgement. The project is financed by the Ministry of Science and Higher Education in Poland under the programme "Regional Initiative of Excellence" 2019 - 2022 project number 015/RID/2018/19 total funding amount 10 721 040,00 PLN.

References

1. Etzkowitz, E., Leydesdorff, L.: The dynamics of innovation: from national systems and "mode 2" to a triple helix of university–industry-government relations. Res. Policy **29**, 109–123 (2000)
2. Carayannis, E.G., Campbell, D.F.: Open innovation diplomacy and a 21st century fractal research, education and innovation (FREIE) ecosystem: building on the quadruple and quintuple helix innovation concepts and the "mode 3" knowledge production system. J. Knowl. Econ. **2**(3), 327–372 (2011)
3. Baid, D.: A study of management control systems (MCS) and school performance. Metamorphosis: J. Manag. Res. **16**(2), 92–106 (2017). https://journals.sagepub.com/doi/full/10.1177/0972622517731407. Accessed 28 Apr 2020
4. Kaplan, R.S., Norton, D.P.: The balanced scorecard – measures that drive performance. Harvard Bus. Rev. **70**(1), 71–79 (1992)
5. Al-Tarawneh, H.A.: Design and use of management accounting and control systems in the Jordanian Universities. Int. J. Account. Financ. Report. **1**(1), 242–254 (2011)
6. Beuren, I.M., Teixeira, S.A.: Evaluation of management control systems in a higher education institution with the performance management and control. J. Inf. Syst. Technol. Manag. **11**(1), 169–192 (2014)
7. Tanveer, M., Karim, A.M.: Higher education institutions and the performance. Library Philos. Pract. (2183) (2018). ISSN 1522-0222
8. Cantele, S., Martini, M., Campedelli, B.: The implementation of management control systems in Italian universities: moving towards New University Management? In: CMS7 – 7th Critical Management Studies Conference (2011)
9. Lábas, I., Bács, Z.: Management control system in the University of Debrecen. Process Econ. Finance **32**, 408–415 (2015)
10. Alach, Z.: Performance measurement maturity in a national set of universities. Int. J. Prod. Perform. Manag. **66**(2) (2017)
11. McCormack, J., Propper, C., Smith, S.: Herding cats? Management and university performance. Econ. J. **124**(578), F534–F564 (2014)
12. Vaishnavi, V., Kuechler, W., Petter, S. (eds.): Design Science Research in Information Systems, 20 January 2004 (created in 2004 and updated until 2015 by Vaishnavi, V. and Kuechler, W.); last updated (by Vaishnavi, V. and Petter, S.), 30 June 2019. http://www.desrist.org/design-research-in-information-systems/
13. Franklin, S., et al.: A LIDA cognitive model tutorial. Biol. Inspired Cogn. Archit. 105–130 (2016). https://doi.org/10.1016/j.bica.2016.04.003
14. McCall, R., Franklin, S., Faghihi, U., Snaider, J., Kugele, S.: Artificial motivation for cognitive software agents. J. Artif. General Intell. **11**(1), 38–69 (2020). https://doi.org/10.2478/jagi-2020-0002
15. Hernes, M.: Consensus theory for cognitive agents' unstructured knowledge conflicts resolving in management information systems. In: Nguyen, N.T., Kowalczyk, R., Hernes, M. (eds.) Transactions on Computational Collective Intelligence XXXII. LNCS, vol. 11370, pp. 1–119. Springer, Heidelberg (2019). https://doi.org/10.1007/978-3-662-58611-2_1

16. Hernes, M., Bytniewski, A.: Knowledge representation of cognitive agents processing the economy events. In: Nguyen, N.T., Hoang, D.H., Hong, T.-P., Pham, H., Trawiński, B. (eds.) ACIIDS 2018. LNCS (LNAI), vol. 10751, pp. 392–401. Springer, Cham (2018). https://doi.org/10.1007/978-3-319-75417-8_37
17. Bush, P.: Tacit Knowledge in Organizational Knowledge. IGI Global, Hershey, New York (2008)
18. Nycz, M., Owoc, M.L., Pondel, M.: Business intelligence concepts for education quality management. Prace Naukowe Uniwersytetu Ekonomicznego we Wrocławiu. Informatyka Ekonomiczna 2010 I 16 I nr 104 Data Mining and Business Intelligence 47–59 (2010)

Curriculum Vitae (CVs) Evaluation Using Machine Learning Approach

Rabih Haddad[✉] ⓘ and Eunika Mercier-Laurent ⓘ

EPITA Engineering School of Computer Science, University of Reims Champagne-Ardenne,
CReSTIC, Reims, France
rabih.haddad@epita.fr
http://www.univ-reims.eu/, http://www.epita.fr/en

Abstract. Resumes or Curriculum Vitae (CVs) are still an important standard document and a decision element in evaluating the life journeys and human personalities of candidates. Its main role is to detect the eligibility of people who are applying to job vacancies or higher education programs. This research work ambitions in elaborating a system that automates the preselection of eligibility and assessment of candidates in the higher education students' recruitment process. This system will replace the tedious tasks of manual processing of CVs and will provide accurate and effective evaluation results. To achieve this requirement, the system will be implemented using a machine learning approach using different classification algorithms. The evaluation is conducted on the four main knowledge categories that build the CV: personal information, academic background, professional experience, and soft and technical skills. The output of the system will be an indicator to shortlist, discard or request more information to evaluate the candidates' eligibility. Moreover, the scores obtained for each part of the CV will be used to calibrate the indicator in each information category. Consequently, this system boosts the recruitment process of candidates and provide a reasonable decision.

Keywords: Curriculum Vitae · Data and text mining · Natural language processing · Classification · Machine learning · Naïve Bayes classifier · Support Vector Machine · Random Forest

1 Introduction

CVs are still an important standard document and a decision element in evaluating life journeys and human personalities of candidates who are applying to a specific job or pursue an academic program. This work is motivated by real need of automated processing of students applications.

International students who wish to continue their higher studies at the bachelor, or masters, or doctorate level in France should directly obtain their admission from the corresponding institution or by choosing a French institution on Campus France [4]. To apply, candidates should fill out an application form on the institution website.

© IFIP International Federation for Information Processing 2021
Published by Springer Nature Switzerland AG 2021
E. Mercier-Laurent et al. (Eds.): AI4KM 2021, IFIP AICT 614, pp. 48–65, 2021.
https://doi.org/10.1007/978-3-030-80847-1_4

The characteristics of each country and institution shape the admission system, however, there is a big percentage of commonality between these systems as they require the same traditional documentation, evaluation, information: admission and languages proficiency exams, interviews, CVs, transcripts, motivation letters, and recommendations letters. [This is the procedure that is applicable today at EPITA [2].

This is a important challenge for automated processing. In this article, a system that automates the eligibility screening and assessment of applicants in the process of recruiting higher education students will be discussed. This system might replace the tedious tasks of manually processing Curriculum Vitae and provide accurate and efficient assessment results. Considering the various forms of the CV and the needs of extracting information various classification algorithms might be used to handle this exercise. The goal of CV Analysis is to give an outcome at the current stage whether the CV fulfills the criteria to be eligible for a certain academic program. For the current experimentation, the analysis scope is applied to the candidates who are applying to pursue a Masters degree at EPITA [3].

The assessment will focus on the four main categories of knowledge that make up the CV: personal information, academic background, work experience, and personal and technical skills. Spoken languages and extracurricular activities are considered as well. The result of the system would be indicative for a shortlist, ignore or request more information to assess the eligibility of some candidates.

Based on what has been elaborated earlier and the availability of an important volume of CVs to be tested in the frame of this research, a Machine Learning approach has been selected. After research and study of the nature of information that are available and the existing algorithm, the below evaluation process will be studied. The evaluation process will be divided into several steps as follows and as in Fig. 1:

1. System Parameterization
2. Training Data Collection
3. Model Dataset Creation
4. Data Extraction and Cleansing
5. Information Extraction Using Natural Language Processing
6. Classification and Final Output Prediction

Fig. 1. Evaluation process

2 Literature Review

The evaluation process that is presented in this paper, is mainly based on data mining and text mining. Data mining is the process of finding discrepancies, patterns, and correlations in large data sets to predict outcomes. With a wide array of technologies, this information can be used to apply in many life sectors. Methods of data mining can be decision trees, associations rules, segmentation algorithms, nearest neighbors' algorithm, and neural networks [8].

In data mining data available is used in databases to identify unknown, important and useful combinations and structures and patterns. The concepts and methods of data mining can be applied in various fields like marketing, medicine, engineering, web mining, etc. Educational data is a new emerging data mining technique that can be applied to many fields including education. This new emerging field, called educational data mining, concerns the development of methods for discovering knowledge from data from educational settings.

One of the researches, which has been already done on CV evaluation using text mining and the related techniques, is mentioned here [9]. Many works exist that mention information extraction application on CV, but the evaluation of such CVs is completely absent. For example, in one of the papers that has been recently published in Research-Gate, the study included on how to extract information from conceptual pattern from CV. The aim was to perform only the below tasks out of it:

– Identifying information to be extracted
– Preparation of linguistic and ontological resources for applying IE tools in Polish language
– Preparing tools to extract relevant information from texts
– Applying selected tools on the test document collection
– Validation of the results.

This might facilitate the task of preparing the CV text prior to being processed and evaluated, however, it will not address the main task of conducting the evaluation. Another work has been done in this regard and presented in the Journal of Critical Reviews [5]. It establishes clear and efficient registration procedures by integrating strategies of web dragging, content extraction and regular language management. This makes the registration process basic and successful by offering the possibility of transferring the course material for the required skill during the work. Additionally, it provides a scheduled suggestion for the activity seeker when individual abilities are coordinated with the activity station. This is done using the cooperative separation account, in addition to improving the additional space for specialist collaboration. On the business side, it uses the web crawler to generate a set of business responsibilities and basic requirements. On the activity seeker side, when the CV is published, word separation and letter splitting are stopped. After content segmentation, enrollment is based on training, an understanding of the job, abilities, personality traits and grade frequency. Finally, a framework is proposed that the next age at which the level of education meets the prerequisites of the profession. This approach is a bit general and its output is abstract, making it difficult to give a valid or coherent evaluation indicator.

Hence, in this work, further experimentation aligned with the methodologies is presented in order to get more adjourned results.

3 Proposed System

As mentioned earlier, a Machine Learning approach is used in this paper to conduct the evaluations of CVs. This approach is be based on the steps that were mentioned in the first section of this article. A detailed elaboration of each step is presented below and the CV evaluation process architecture is presented in Fig. 2.

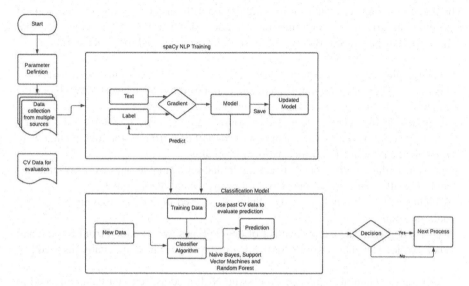

Fig. 2. CV evaluation process architecture

3.1 System Parameterization

The first step that was conducted is to train the evaluation algorithm using historical CVs and using some existing datasets. It is an essential exercise to guarantee the accuracy of results. This can be done by determining the parameters to evaluate the CV quantitatively. The parameters are considered based on their usability and their helpfulness in providing the quality of the CV. For instance, technologies practiced by the applicant is an important attribute to evaluate in the CV and has a weighted value of 5 points for this type. This step helps to identify the parameters against which the CV is evaluated. The weightings for each of its parameters were given based on its impact on the desirable qualities of the candidate. It also helps to extract only the relevant information from the CV. A decision table as shown in the Fig. 3 has been established to help in providing the overall score of the CV which can then be processed in the classification algorithms to determine the outcome of the candidate.

Technologies (Java , Python, Php etc..)	>5	>=3 and <=5	>=1 and <=3
Points	3	2	1

Fig. 3. Decision table

3.2 Sample Data Collection for Training

The process of data collection for training the algorithm is very essential as the trained algorithm can effectively determine the accuracy of the results. Therefore, a relevant data source has been used. Below is the list of data source used for various criteria:

- Technologies known: data source of Stack Overflow [11] questions and answers has been used. There are over a million records of questions and answers covering a wide range of technologies in various text combinations.
- Program specific criteria: various data sources are available in Kaggle [6] for each specific program type. Also, a manual insertion of data from historical CVs that were processed earlier at EPITA International Programs.
- Extracurricular activity: There is a Kaggle dataset available with over 666 hobbies and manually updating hobbies have not been covered in the above list.
- Languages: Only French and English are considered in our case making the related dataset simple.
- Type of degrees: The exhaustive list of degree types was obtained from Kaggle and Data World. The abbreviations for the degree types have been manually inserted [7].

To train the Natural Language Processing NLP models, relevant data is needed to identify and quantify the parameters. By having comprehensive Datasets like stack-overflow questions and answers, the gaps in the matching patterns are easily identified. This data collection process is repeated for each of the parameters defined previously. The more comprehensive the dataset is the more efficient is the named entity recognition model obtained through NLP training. This step was done by keeping in mind the objective of obtaining accurate models.

These steps are also summarized in Fig. 4.

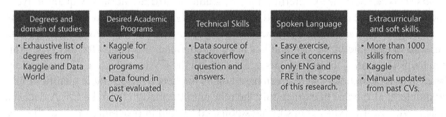

Fig. 4. Data collection samples

3.3   Dataset Creation for Testing the Trained Model

This step is to create a CV Dataset. Around 1000 CVs were randomly selected from the database of CVs available at EPITA from candidates applications. The CVs selected were based on the following criteria:

– The candidate whose CV has been selected should have applied for any of the international programs that are available.
– The admission process of the file should have been completed; therefore, the final status of the application is already known.
– Have a good combination of Accepted and Rejected CV's along with the combination of CVs of different programs that the candidates applied for.

In the previous step, specific parameter dataset has been used to be able to train each model independently. Then the collected CVs are trained in the desired context. The model is trained to learn words in the context of a CV, for example, Tesla is a company and not a physician. For this reason, the training data should always be representative of the data to process. A model trained in romantic novels will likely perform badly on legal text. This also means that in order to know how the model is performing, and whether it's learning the right things, not only training data is needed but we also evaluate data. If the model is tested only on data used in the training, chances are that it might not be generalizing. To train a model from scratch, are at least needed a few hundred examples for both training and evaluation. This step contributes to the evaluation data of the training data provided in step 2.

3.4   CV Extraction and Cleaning Data

The main objective of this step is to parse information from a CV using Natural Language Processing and find the keywords, cluster them onto parameters based on their keywords. This information extraction process involves extracting structured specific information from unstructured or semi-structured natural language (in the form of text). The data extracted is then fed to the NLP tools like spaCy [15] for example for text categorization. PDF miner [12] has been used to parse the text from PDF files and the parsed result is cleaned by various methods using RegEx patterns to remove unwanted text and special characters and split the text in different lines.

Most text data contains a lot of words that are not actually useful. These words, called stopwords, are useful in human speech, but they do not have much to contribute to data analysis. Hence stop words and lemmatizing should be performed on the selected text. For example, words like connect, connection, connecting, connected, etc. aren't exactly the same, they all have the same essential meaning: connect. The differences in spelling have grammatical functions in spoken language, but for machine processing, those differences can be confusing, so we need a way to change all the words that are forms of the word connect into the word connect itself. Spacy has a built-in way to break a word down to its lemma by calling the method *lemma* to produce the lemma for each word after analyzing.

Because in CVs data formats that are used are not completely unstructured, it is still quite challenging to take them into the structured format as there is no set in stone rule for writing a CV. As a result, many possible ways of representing qualifications in a CV has been established so far such as chronological CV and functional CV. Beyond these two types, there are many other formats and many people follow their own unique style to make their CV stand out from other ones. Additionally, there is a tendency of adding visual elements to a CV to make it more interesting to visualize. Opposed to many of the visual elements just being there for aesthetic purpose, there are exceptional cases when someone uses visual elements like graphs or charts to represent important information such as their skills because creating and interpreting graphs or charts encourages critical thinking.

As in most of the cases, these graphs are included in image formats, there is no definitive way to process them without using image processing techniques. Hence, these CVs will be kept out of consideration in the frame of this work as it is beyond the scope, therefore PDF Miner [12] is used as a tool for extracting information from PDF documents. Unlike other PDF-related tools, it focuses entirely on getting and analyzing text data. It includes a PDF converter that can transform PDF files into text format.

3.5 Information Extraction using Natural Language Processing

The cleaned text is passed to Natural Language Processing Algorithm to tokenize the text and identify the phrases and entities in the text. There are various of library options to use and spaCy is chosen as it is designed specifically for this type of applications and it understands a large volume of text. It can be used to build Information Extraction or Natural Language understanding systems or to pre-process text for Deep Learning. The objective is to train the model against reference annotation. Training is an iterative process in which the model's predictions are compared against the reference annotations in order to estimate the gradient of the loss. The gradient of the loss is then used to calculate the gradient of the weights through back-propagation. The gradients indicate how the weight values should be changed so that the model's predictions become more similar to the reference labels over time as shown in Fig. 5.

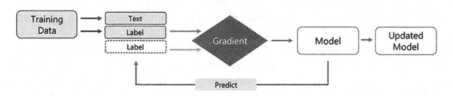

Fig. 5. Model training

The main idea is to train and obtain the model for each of the parameters that form a certain CV. For example, it could be applied on the Programming Language, Extra-Curricular Activities, Qualification or Degree, Spoken Language, English Language Test, Program Specific Criteria, etc. The result obtained by processing the CV data of each of the trained model is then passed on to the trained classification model to predict the outcome.

For elaboration, an example of applying the model to programming lan- guage is presented. To obtain a consistent Named Entity Recognizer model for the programming language, the model is trained with a comprehensive list of language including the various patterns it could appear in (eg: php3.4, php7, GoLang, GoLang). In order to do that a large Dataset is needed based on which the model is trained. Through this research, it was found that Stack Overflow provides a dataset for its question and answers which can be downloaded from Kaggle. Now the dataset is ready spaCy Matcher pattern is used to identify and train the programming languages in each question.

The matching algorithm should follow the steps mentioned in the below figure. It starts by writing exhaustive matcher pattern rules to cover all the criteria for the programming languages, hobbies, languages, degree types in order to obtain the model to be used in the CV evaluation. This algorithm is presented in Fig. 6.

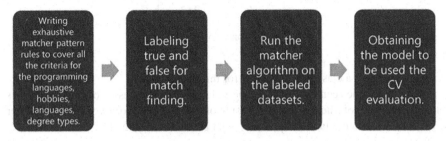

Fig. 6. Matcher algorithm

Based on various samples testing with Stack Overflow questions dataset over multiple iterations, an exhaustive list of programming languages (like php, java, python, C), was after obtained as well as patterns across programming language (like php3.4,php7, python3). An interesting scenario for the programming language obtained here was for "GO Lang" since "go" can be a verb in a lot of sentences. The part of speech feature of NLP library is used to help us distinguish the programming language GO from the verb GO. This observation also shows that using NLP along with Regex (Regular Expression) helps efficiently train the algorithm. Once the matcher patterns are defined, labelling is used to evaluate the effectiveness of the pattern. In order to do this, a copy of the Questions Dataset is manually prepared and added in additional column Label. Then this column is manually marked to 1 if a programming language is found for that question and 0 if not. This was done for over 650 records and tested. On running the labelled csv (comma separated values) against the patterns defined, identification of any mistake made in pattern definition was done as well as the pattern to accommodate the changes. The statistical analysis of this model can be determined through the generation of the confusion matrix and classification report. A confusion matrix is a table that is often used to describe the performance of a classification model (or "classifier") on a set of test data for which the true values are known. The confusion matrix itself is relatively simple to understand, but the related terminology can be confusing. Below is an example of a confusion matrix that has been created for this example.

A classification report is used to measure the quality of predictions from a classification algorithm. How many predictions are True and how many are False. More specifically, True Positives TP, False Positives FP, True Negatives TN and False Negatives FNare used to predict the metrics of a classification report.

Figure 7 shows an example of a confusion matrix that has been created for this example.

n=165	Predicted: NO	Predicted: YES	
Actual: NO	TN = 50	FP = 10	60
Actual: YES	FN = 5	TP = 100	105
	55	110	

Fig. 7. Confusion matrix

Figure 8 shows a classification report for this example.

Precision can be seen as a measure of a classifier's exactness. For each class, it is defined as the ratio of true positives to the sum of true and false positives. Said in another way, "for all instances classified positive, what percent was correct?".

	precision	recall	f1-score	support
0	0.77	0.86	0.81	37584
1	0.84	0.75	0.79	37577
accuracy			0.80	75161
macro avg	0.81	0.80	0.80	75161
weighted avg	0.81	0.80	0.80	75161

Fig. 8. Classification report

A recall is a measure of the classifier's completeness; the ability of a classifier to correctly find all positive instances. For each class, it is defined as the ratio of true positives to the sum of true positives and false negatives. Said another way, "for all instances that were actually positive, what percent was classified correctly?". The F1 score is a weighted harmonic mean of precision and recall such that the best score is 1.0 and the worst is 0.0. Generally speaking, F1 scores are lower than accuracy measures as they embed precision and recall into their computation. As a rule of thumb, the weighted average of F1 should be used to compare classifier models, not global accuracy.

Support is the number of actual occurrences of the class in the specified Dataset. Imbalanced support in the training data may indicate structural weak- nesses in the reported scores of the classifier and could indicate the need for stratified sampling or re-balancing. Support doesn't change between models but instead diagnoses the evaluation process. Moving further after obtaining satisfactory results from the above steps, the programming model is ready to get trained by constructing the model as per the NLP requirement. The obtained trained data is shown in Fig. 9.

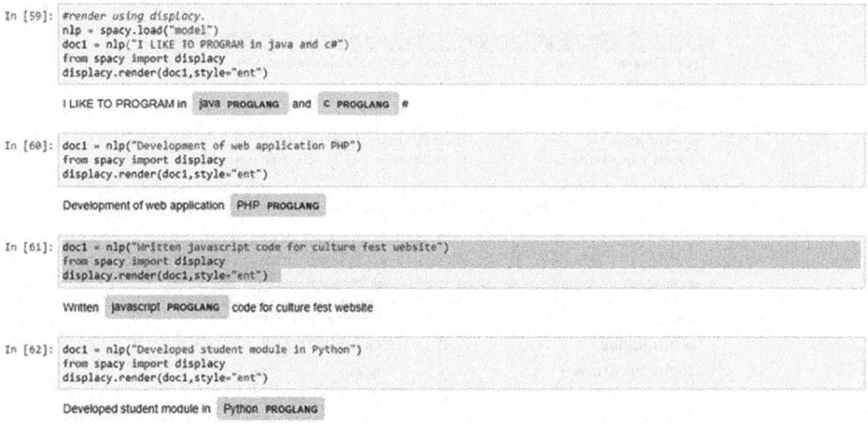

Fig. 9. Trained data

This exercise has been repeated for all parts of the CV (Extra-Curricular activities, English Language Test, Program Specific Criteria...).

This step will provide us with a custom Named Entity Recognition model using spaCy statistical modelling for each parameter that will later be used for information extraction (IE) that seeks out and categorizes specified entities in a body or bodies of texts of the CV. The generated model can recognize a wide range of named or numerical entities, which include qualification, extracurricular activities, language, program specific criteria and English language test. The result obtained by processing CV data to each of the trained models is fed in the trained classification model to predict the outcome.

3.6   Classification and Final Output Prediction

The role of the classification model is to draw some conclusion from observed values. Given one or more inputs a classification model will try to predict the value of one or more outcomes. Outcomes are labels that can be applied to a dataset. For example, when filtering emails "spam" or "not spam", when looking at transaction data, "fraudulent", or "authorized". Similarly, in our case, for a given result set of Programming Languages, Extra-Curricular Activities, Qualification, Spoken Language, English Language Test and Program Specific criteria the classification model should be able to predict the final outcome. It aims to provide pattern recognition based on previously obtained results.

Data is segregated in 2 main Datasets: the training test that is used to train the model to recognize the patterns in the given data for suitable predictions and the test set that contains the previously predicted value. The model is trained using several Machine Learning algorithms and the one with the least error will be chosen as a classifier. In order to classify the data obtained after the CV evaluation under the accepted and rejected categories, a sample of over 500 CVs has been man- ually evaluated based on the parameters mentioned above. An example of the manual attribution on an accepted and refused CV is mentioned in the Figs. 10, 11 and 12.

Parameter	Points	Reason
Type of Degree	1	Bachelor in Information Management
Technologies	2	C, C++, Java
Languages Known	1	English
Competitive Entrance	1	TOEFL
Extra-Curricular	1	Football, Cricket, games, music
Program Related criteria	1	IT Entrepreneurship, Supply chain management

Fig. 10. Shortlisted CV

Parameter	Points	Reason
Type of Degree	1	Bachelor of Technology
Technologies	0	None mentioned
Languages Known	1	English
Competitive Entrance	0	None mentioned
Extra-Curricular	0	None mentioned
Program Related criteria	0	None mentioned

Fig. 11. Refused CV

Fig. 12. Accepted/refused CV

This step provides three classification models for predictive modeling. In ma- chine learning selecting the best hypothesis for a given data is the most interesting part. The accuracy obtained in general is most for Random Forest classifier. Therefore its result is used to determine the final outcome for the CV. Then it is only needed to provide the parameters weighting to the model to predict the final outcome. In a typical supervised learning workflow, evaluation of various combinations of feature sub-spaces, learning algorithms, and hyper-parameters is done before selecting the model that has a satis-factory performance. As mentioned above, cross-validation is a good way for such an assessment in order to avoid over-fitting to the training data.

4 Experimentation

This part of the article is dedicated for the experimentation of the CV evaluation. The experimentation will be dedicated to the CV Information Extraction, the training process, and the classification process using 3 different algorithms as follows:

1. Naïve Bayes Classifier
2. Support Vector Machine SVM
3. Random Forest

The classification is done after finalizing the 5 steps that are mentioned in the previous sections as all of them serve to conduct the classification experiment to obtain the desired outcomes.

4.1 Naïve Bayes Classifier

Naive Bayes classifiers are a collection of classification algorithms based on Bayes' Theorem [10]. It is not a single algorithm but a family of algorithms where all of them share a common principle, i.e., every pair of features being classified is independent each other. The Dataset is required in two parts namely feature matrix and the response vector as explained below:

– Feature matrix: it contains all the vectors(rows) of Dataset in which each vector con-sists of the value of dependent features. In the above Dataset, features are 'Program-ming Language', 'Extra-Curricular Activities', 'Language', 'Qualification', 'Work Experience' and 'Test'.
– Response Vector: it contains the value of class variable (prediction or output) for each row of the feature matrix. In the above Dataset, the class variable name is 'Result'.

The fundamental Naive Bayes assumption is that each feature makes an *independent* and *equal* contribution to the outcome. Bayes' Theorem predicts the probability of an event occurring given the probability of another event that has already occurred. Bayes' theorem is stated mathematically as the following equation:

where A and B are events and P(B) is different from 0.

$$P(A|B) = \frac{P(B|A)P(A)}{P(B)}$$

- Basically, the probability of event A is to be predicted, given the event B is true. Event B is also termed as evidence.
- P(A) is the priori of A (the prior probability, i.e., Probability of event before evidence is seen). The evidence is an attribute value of an unknown instance (here, it is event B).
- P(A—B) is a posteriori probability of B, i.e., probability of event after evidence is seen.

With regards to the used Dataset, Bayes' theorem is applied in the following way:

$$P(y|X) = \frac{P(X|y)P(y)}{P(X)}$$

where, y is class variable and X is a dependent feature vector (of size n). where: To add classification, an example of a feature vector and corresponding class variable can be: (refer 1st row of dataset)

X = (0 (Programming Language), 0 (Extra Curricular), 1 (Languages), 1 (Program Specific Criteria), 1 (Qualification), 0 (Test), 1 (Work Experience)) y = Yes

$$X = (x_1, x_2, x_3, \ldots x_n)$$

For simplicity data from each label is assigned to be drawn from a simple Gaussian distribution. The likelihood of the features is assumed to be Gaussian, hence, conditional probability is given by:

$$P(x_i|y) = \frac{1}{\sqrt{2\pi\sigma_y^2}} exp\left(-\frac{(x_i - \mu_y)^2}{2\sigma_y^2}\right)$$

The used dataset involves predicting the CV result given individual parameters like Technologies, Degree, Language, Extra-Curricular activities and Program Specific criteria. It is therefore a multi-class classification problem. There are around 40 observations with 6 input variables and 1 output variable. A sample of the input variables is listed below:

Using sci-kit learn, it is now possible to train and test the model prediction for Gaussian Naïve Bayes as shown in the Fig. 13.

['1', '1', '1', '0', '1', '0', 'Accepted'],

['1', '2', '2', '0', '1', '0', 'Accepted'],

['1', '3', '1', '0', '1', '1', 'Accepted'],

['1', '2', '1', '0', '1', '0', 'Accepted'],

['2', '1', '1', '0', '1', '1', 'Accepted']

['1', '1', '1', '0', '1', '1', 'Accepted'],

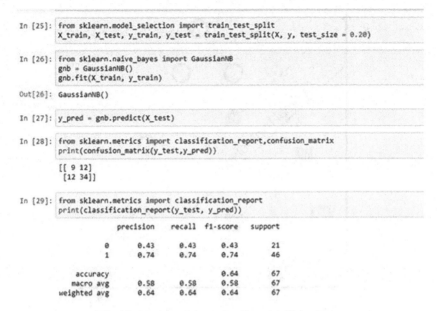

```
In [25]:  from sklearn.model_selection import train_test_split
          X_train, X_test, y_train, y_test = train_test_split(X, y, test_size = 0.20)
```

```
In [26]:  from sklearn.naive_bayes import GaussianNB
          gnb = GaussianNB()
          gnb.fit(X_train, y_train)
```

```
Out[26]:  GaussianNB()
```

```
In [27]:  y_pred = gnb.predict(X_test)
```

```
In [28]:  from sklearn.metrics import classification_report,confusion_matrix
          print(confusion_matrix(y_test,y_pred))

          [[ 9 12]
           [12 34]]
```

```
In [29]:  from sklearn.metrics import classification_report
          print(classification_report(y_test, y_pred))

                        precision    recall  f1-score   support

                    0       0.43      0.43      0.43        21
                    1       0.74      0.74      0.74        46

             accuracy                           0.64        67
            macro avg       0.58      0.58      0.58        67
         weighted avg       0.64      0.64      0.64        67
```

Fig. 13. Model training using Gaussian Naïve Bayes

It was observed that the algorithm generates a Reject response if it matches a similar combination of already existing rejected candidates and Accepted otherwise.

4.2 Support Vector Machine (SVM)

The objective of the support vector machine algorithm [13] is to find a hyperplane in an N-dimensional space (N—the number of features) that distinctly classifies the data points as shown in the Fig. 14.

To separate the two classes of data points, there are many possible hyperplanes that could be chosen. The objective of this paper is to find a plane that has the maximum margin, i.e., the maximum distance between data points of both classes. Maximizing the margin distance provides some reinforcement so that future data points can be classified with more confidence.

Hyperplanes are decision boundaries that help classify the data points. Data points falling on either side of the hyperplane can be attributed to different classes. Also, the dimension of the hyperplane depends upon the number of features. If the number of input features is 2, then the hyperplane is just a line. If the number of input features is 3, then the hyperplane becomes a two-dimensional plane. Support vectors are data points that are closer to the hyperplane and influence the position and orientation of the hyperplane. Using these support vectors, the margin of the classifier is maximized. Deleting the support vectors changes the position of the hyperplane. These are the points that help build the SVM.

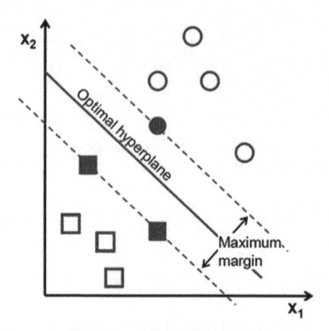

Fig. 14. Support Vector Machine (SVM)

In the SVM algorithm, maximizing the margin between the data points and the hyperplane is looked for. The loss function that helps maximize the margin is hinge loss.

$$c(x, y, f(x)) = \begin{cases} 0, & \text{if } y*f(x) \geq 1 \\ 1 - y*f(x), & \text{else} \end{cases}$$

The cost is 0 if the predicted value and the actual value are of the same sign. If they are not, then calculate the loss value is then calculated. A regularization parameter is added to the cost function. The objective of the regularization parameter is to balance the margin maximization and loss. After adding the regularization parameter, the cost functions looks as below.

$$\min_{w} \lambda \|w\|^2 + \sum_{i=1}^{n} (1 - y_i(x_i, w))_+$$

Below, the implementation of SVM in python is depicted using the scikit library using Sigmoid Kernel as it was more accurate compared to linear, polynomial linear and the Gaussian kernels:

It was observed that the algorithm generates an Accept response in almost all test cases.

4.3 Random Forest Classifier

Random Forest is a supervised learning algorithm [1]. The "forest" builds, is an ensemble of decision trees, usually trained with the "bagging" method. The general idea of the bagging method is that a combination of learning models increases the overall result.

Random forests also offers a good feature selection indicator. Scikit-learn provides an extra variable with the model, which shows the relative importance or contribution of each feature in the prediction. It automatically computes the relevance score of each feature in the training phase. Then, it scales the relevance down so that the sum of all scores is 1.

This score choose the most important features and drop the least important ones for model building (Fig. 15).

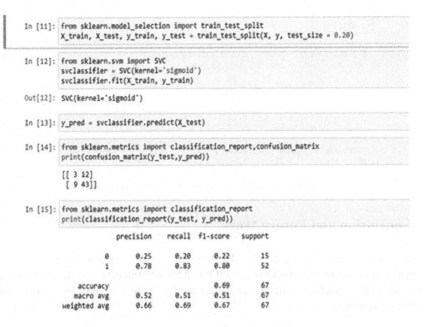

Fig. 15. Model training using SVM

Random Forest uses GINI importance or mean decrease in impurity (MDI) to calculate the importance of each feature. Gini importance is also known as the total decrease in node impurity. This is how much the model fit or accuracy decreases when you drop a variable. The larger the decrease, the more significant the variable is. Here, the mean decrease is a significant parameter for variable selection. The Gini index can describe the overall explanatory power of the variables. Figure 16 shows the implementation of Random Forest classifier using scikit learn [14].

```
In [67]: from sklearn.ensemble import RandomForestClassifier
         rfc = RandomForestClassifier(random_state=0)
         rfc.fit(X_train, y_train)

Out[67]: RandomForestClassifier(random_state=0)

In [68]: y_pred = rfc.predict(X_test)

In [69]: from sklearn.metrics import classification_report,confusion_matrix
         print(confusion_matrix(y_test,y_pred))

         [[ 5  7]
          [ 8 47]]

In [70]: from sklearn.metrics import classification_report
         print(classification_report(y_test, y_pred))

                       precision    recall  f1-score   support

                    0       0.38      0.42      0.40        12
                    1       0.87      0.85      0.86        55

             accuracy                           0.78        67
            macro avg       0.63      0.64      0.63        67
         weighted avg       0.78      0.78      0.78        67
```

Fig. 16. Model training using random forest

5 Conclusion and Future Work

As the CV evaluation is a part of a decision support system that we applied to the admission of international students in the French Higher Education systems, the results obtained in the actual classifier is cross-validated with results from the online video interviews results.

References

1. Data Camp: Understanding random forests classifiers in python. https://www.datacamp.com/community/tutorials/random-forests-classifier-python
2. EPITA: Epita international. https://www.epita.fr/en/apply-online/
3. EPITA: Epita masters. https://www.epita.fr/en/degree-programs-english/
4. CAMPUS France: Institutional. https://www.campusfrance.org/en/institutions
5. Ashish, S., Ganesh, K., Ritvik, J.: A novel job portal with resume evaluation system based on text mining and NLP techniques. J. Crit. Rev. **7**, 1234–1236 (2020)
6. Google: Kaggle. https://www.kaggle.com/
7. Google: Stackoverflow. https://www.kaggle.com/stackoverflow/stackoverflow
8. Dufour, J.C.: Aix-Marseille University. https://sesstim.univ-amu.fr/sites
9. Piskorski, J., Kaczmarek, T., Kowalkiewicz, M.: Ainformation extraction from CV (2015)
10. Machine Learning Mastery: Classification. https://machinelearningmastery.com/classification-as-conditional-probability-and-the-naive-bayes-algorithm
11. Stack Overflow: Stack overflow NLP. https://stackoverflow.com/
12. Python: Pdfminer. https://pypi.org/project/pdfminer/

13. Towards Data Science: Support vector machine—introduction to machine learning algorithms. https://towardsdatascience.com/support-vector-machine-introduction-to-machine-learning-algorithms-934a444fca47
14. Scikit Learn: Machine learning in python. https://scikit-learn.org/
15. SpaCy: Industrial-strength NLP. https://spacy.io/

University Students' Research on Artificial Intelligence and Knowledge Management. A Review and Report of Multi-case Studies

Mieczysław L. Owoc[1]([⊠]) [iD] and Paweł Weichbroth[2] [iD]

[1] Wrocław University of Economics and Business, 118/120 Komandorska Street, 53-345 Wrocław, Poland
mieczyslaw.owoc@ue.wroc.pl
[2] Faculty of Electronics, Telecommunications and Informatics, Department of Software Engineering, Gdańsk University of Technology, 11/12 Gabriela Narutowicza Street, 80-233, Gdańsk, Poland
pawel.weichbroth@pg.edu.pl
http://www.ue.wroc.pl/en/, https://pg.edu.pl/en/home

Abstract. Leading technologies are very attractive for students preparing their theses as the completion of their studies. Such an orientation of students connected with professional experiences seems to be a crucial motivator in the research in the management and business areas where these technologies condition the development of professional activities. The goal of the paper is the analysis of students' thesis topics defended in the last 10 years in business informatics and computer science in two selected universities in Poland. Our study relies on a detailed review and analysis of qualitative data, obtained from a literature review and multi-case-study research. In the case of the artificial intelligence domain, we have identified six areas of research, namely: general AI, machine learning (ML), natural language processing (NLP), artificial neural networks (ANNs), expert systems, and hybrids. In the case of the knowledge management domain, we have recognized eleven areas of research, regarding the following sectors: e-government, technology, space exploration, social media, manufacturing, healthcare, finance, entertainment, education, e-commerce, and business. Future research will be directed toward extending the scope by including other regions and universities as well as identifying and analyzing students' motivational factors, associated with research pro jects and higher education.

Keywords: Artificial intelligence · Knowledge management · Students' research · Students' theses

1 Introduction

A fascination with new technologies is typical nowadays among young people. For some, it is essential for communication, exchanging media files, participating in games or just

E. Mercier-Laurent et al. (Eds.): AI4KM 2021, IFIP AICT 614, pp. 66–81, 2021.
https://doi.org/10.1007/978-3-030-80847-1_5

informing the "world" about their current events [1]. For more ambitious students, leading technologies can be connected with their strong interest in personal development and professional life. Especially students learning information and communication technologies (ICT) are strongly motivated to become familiar with practical solutions in various sectors. Therefore the implementation of ICT for example in business or management can be considered as an interesting research area during the preparation of their thesis oriented on important computer methods. Very often artificial intelligence (AI) and knowledge management (KM) are selected as the fields of studies finally defined as bachelor's or master's theses.

Potentially, investigations of students very often lead to prototypes of solutions that are directly connected with AI methods and direct or indirect references to KM areas [2, 3]. Therefore the understanding of the importance of these solutions among young people is widely known. Besides, topics of research representing both of the mentioned areas are strongly supported by scientific societies awarding the best thesis of students in specially organized competitions (for example Polish Artificial Intelligence Society [4], and Business Informatics Scientific Society [5]).

The goal of this paper is to summarize and classify the current state of university students' research on artificial intelligence and knowledge management. With regard to this objective, we put forward the following research question: **What topics have been the subject of university students' research in the area of artificial intelligence and knowledge management?** Our study relies on a snowballing literature review, in which we adopted the procedure elaborated by Wohlin [6], as well as the case study in which we followed the guidelines provided by Gagnon [7].

The paper is structured as follows. The second section outlines the theoretical background of the study. The third section reflects the state of the art of the research on a students' thesis; the differentiation of studies connected with ICT is discussed and various forms of defining students' research are analyzed. The next part, which is an attempt to grouping students' works with the taxonomy of subjects presented in the proposed thesis. The next two sections demonstrate an overview of student theses oriented on AI and KM from two public universities and two nonpublic higher education institutions. The findings are given in the last section.

2 Background

It is claimed that the term "artificial intelligence" (AI) was first introduced at a conference at Dartmouth College, which took place in 1956 in New Hampshire [8]. At that time, the participants represented a broad range of interests, from the abstraction of content from sensory inputs, complexity theory, language simulation, neural nets, the relationship of randomness to creative thinking, to learning machines. The conference laid the foundations for a great vision which has affected research and development in almost every human activity.

In general, artificial intelligence is "the enterprise of constructing an intelligent artefact" [9]. However, this definition still needs to be further explained. In general terms, intelligence is defined twofold as (1) "the ability to learn or understand or to deal with new or trying situations, and (2) "the ability to apply knowledge to manipulate one's environment or to think abstractly as measured by objective criteria (such as tests)" [10].

In spite of the recognition of the term "artefact," the exact denotation is still not clear due to the fact of a plethora of different understandings of the term and due to a putative usage [11]. For some, an artefact is "an object made by a human being, typically one of cultural or historical interest" [12], while in the context of computer science it is "a specific bundle of hardware and software that is assembled to fulfil information needs" [13].

Despite a short history of debates, discussions and polemics, there is still no standard definition of intelligence [14]. Having said that, one can also assume the existence of a deep passage along with the notion of artificial intelligence. However, some ideas have been introduced which have brought better understanding to this field. For example, the science of artificial intelligence (AI) might be defined as "the construction of intelligent systems and their analysis" [15], or "the study of systems that act in a way that to any observer would appear to be intelligent" [16].

In many cases, AI techniques are adapted to solve simple or complex problems that are internal to more complex systems. While the former may concern the solution of the traveling salesman problem, the latter may be associated with the effort of programming the Sophia, the world's most advanced rationale robot with human traits [17]. In other words, while some systems are designed to solve particular problems, others, in contrast, are designed to behave in an intelligent way.

This separation has its reflection in two different approaches in design, so-called "weak AI" and "strong AI". The former is "the art of making computers do smart things" [18], while the latter is the art of constructing objects with mental capabilities and functions that mimic the human brain. In the case of strong AI, the definition is not narrowed to the computers where so far objects are associated with robots or humanoids. However, as stated above, since the society of researchers cannot even accurately formulate the definition of intelligence, its further classification seems to be even more obscure.

Artificial intelligence has its roots in computer science and draws from engineering, mathematics, psychology and philosophy. In the beginning, the scope solely covered the problems of developing computational methods with a consistent approach toward each problem. These problems are those which people can solve, with more or less mental effort, but the solutions of which they cannot verbalize and describe in detail. On the other hand, a properly designed and implemented method reduces or even eliminates all the risk associated with human errors [19].

Nowadays, the development of artificial intelligence is associated with machine learning [20], neural networks [21], evolutionary computing [22], image recognition [23], natural language processing [24, 25], and robotics [26, 27]. Moreover, a new multidisciplinary paradigm has been introduced, namely Ambient Intelligence (AmI), combining Norman's so-called Invisible Computer and Ubiquitous Computing [28]. AmI supports the design of the next generation of AI systems that intends to add novel means of communication between the human, machine and surrounding environment in a responsive and non-intrusive way [29].

3 Student Research Projects and Theses

There are several majors of studies oriented on specialized education and the development of abilities of ICT to create and implement. Besides faculties closely connected with computer science education, there is a huge potential in terms of usability of computers in decision-making processes. Business and the broadly represented management and social sciences studies create an opportunity for students to merge domain economic knowledge with applying intelligent technologies in their future professional life. Perceiving a problem that appears during the implementation of these technologies can be very inspirational from a student's perspective. The preparation of students for research work can be initiated according to one of the following variants:

- Students more familiar with ICT and having some professional experience can independently define an area of research and sometimes even formulate their bachelor's or master's thesis;
- For students without the above abilities, a supervisor prepares a list of topics that can be discussed with particular students and with the supervisor supporting the definition of a research field, and the final thesis is formulated as a result of stronger cooperation.

Obviously, in both cases, the students are obliged to perform a literature study finished through the preparation of a report reflecting their understanding of the topic. Basically, apart from the presentation of the theoretical background of the defined problem, practical solutions are formulated. The first theoretical chapter(s) are completed as a result of the literature review – so interpretations of AI and KM are discussed and extended by crucial classification typical for both areas. The "empirical" part refers to one of the treatments of the solution:

- investigation of the real impact, stressing of usability of AI methods or KM. approaches implemented in the selected institutions or sectors;
- development of an application (rather as a prototype) supporting the determined area(s) with the employed AI methods or KM approaches;
- comparison or analysis of potentially useful AI methods or KM approaches in terms of a survey emphasizing the solution context (for example, hybridization of the applied techniques or effectiveness of the proposed improvement).

The research devoted to the student's work on AI and KM subjects has reached a moderate interest. The list of the available trends in this investigation can be expressed as follows:

1. Artificial Neural Networks (Deep Learning).
2. Autonomous Cars.
3. Biometrics.
4. Computer Vision (including Image Processing and Recognition).
5. Expert Systems.
6. Fuzzy Logic.
7. Neural Networks.

8. Robotics.
9. Natural Language Processing.
10. Smart multi-agent systems.
11. Bayesian Networks.

There are many perspectives of the more global approach to AI as the leading technology nowadays. A more systematic way of presenting the technology landscape is depicted in Fig. 1. Embracing traditional AI methods (neural networks, pattern recognition, machine learning), they are connected with more modern approaches expressed as the AI technology landscape.

These topics, just to name a few, find their application in such areas as:

– Air Traffic Control.
– Construction and Manufacturing.
– Energy Sector.
– Software Engineering.
– Internet of Things.
– Medical Diagnosis.
– Remote Sensing.
– Telecommunication.

All the mentioned areas can potentially be considered as applications for students preparing their thesis.

4   Clustering of Students' Research

There is no doubt that active learning methods are commonly recognized as very effective and provide opportunities for students on their self-progress [31]. At least three forms of students' activities can be strictly connected with this concept. The first, which is not very popular but can appear during the earlier stages of studies, is participation in a students' scientific circle. It is a good model for organizing groups of more ambitious students interested in certain specific problems, where experienced researchers from a university support their work. Second, students can be asked to work on real scientific projects; tutors knowing the students' capabilities can formulate special tasks for them as part of the project. Compared to the previous two, the third is obligatory and relates to preparing a student's thesis as the result of their research agreed with the supervisor. In this section, we focus on the third one; remembering in all cases the leader of the research should respect the motivation and interest of the students.

We assume the majority of students are free to define their thesis but support and final acceptance by the supervisor is obvious. Therefore students try to express their direction in the research defining the area of interest and at least the crucial keywords and/or proposed research methods. Considering research in the areas of artificial intelligence, some trends and interests can be formulated in different ways. Initially, the main areas can be identified with artificial intelligence methods and techniques and presented in Fig. 2.

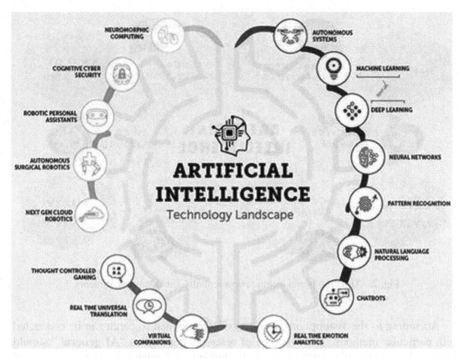

Fig. 1. Artificial intelligence technology landscape. Source [30].

Not all of the methods and techniques mentioned are acceptable to students. This is mainly due to the educational profile of the universities being taken into account in the research; practical references (in the sense of selecting a field from among the economic sciences) should be correlated with the usefulness of AI methods and techniques in the area of finance, management, etc. Therefore, we eventually excluded from the list Robotics, Computer Vision and Cognitive. computing.

The second reason for defining their research area refers to the type of investigation. There are not many discussions about the research types addressed to students. Some of the proposals are formulated very broadly. For example, White itemizes the following list [32]: qualitative, quantitative, analytical, persuasive, cause and effect, experimental, survey, problem-solution, report research), while others are rather oriented on a specific area of study.

McCombes argues that one can consider applying the following types of research [33]: basic vs applied, exploratory vs explanatory, or inductive vs deductive research. Especially the last one seems to be closer to students' approaches in business informatics nowadays. After the analysis of the topics elaborated by the students in the selected university, we decided to follow McCombes' approach with some modifications.

Therefore **basic research** is presented as a tendency to analyze the usability, effectiveness, or implementation AI methods, while **applied research** has been represented as the development of prototypes for the final solution in the selected areas. The results of clustering the topics of the bachelor's and master's theses are depicted in Fig. 3.

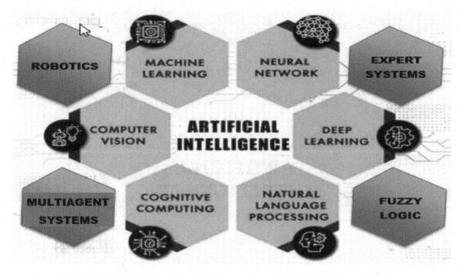

Fig. 2. AI methods and techniques potentially considered by students.

According to the assumptions, basic as well as applied research can be connected with particular methods. The first type of research, denoted as **"AI general,"** should be identified with topics without a clearly defined AI method; the last one declared as **"hybrid research,"** means theses with more than one AI method considered in the research.

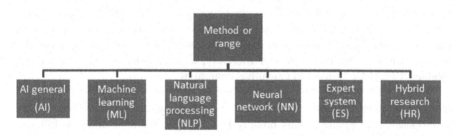

Fig. 3. Research approaches in Students' theses.

The second group of theses are related to problems of Knowledge Management [34–37]. This research area was mostly selected by students of master's degree level. The general concept of formulating topics by students is expressed in Fig. 4. Several aspects could be considered in the paper but three main perspectives should be underlined: **Knowledge Management**, as the approach oriented on global services of knowledge structures in some sense overlapping **Knowledge Engineering** [38, 39], and generated knowledge bases mostly through **Data Mining** algorithms [40].

To summarize, the final clustering of topics in the KM part can be divided into two groups; all more globally defined research is represented as Knowledge Management;

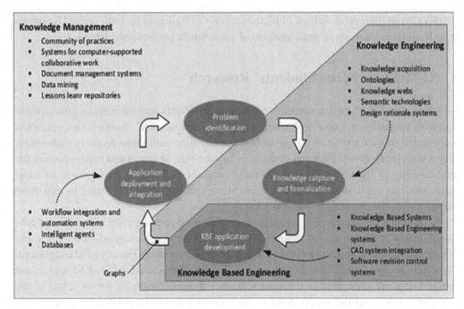

Fig. 4. Knowledge Management perspectives potentially considered by Students [41].

the others with clearly defined algorithms (mostly due to the experimental characteristics of the research) are termed Data Mining.

The last element of the students' formulated theses is connected with suggested areas of application. The potential list of sectors is proposed in Fig. 5. The list is partially changed, compared to the one presented earlier.

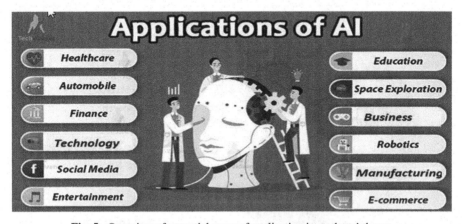

Fig. 5. Overview of potential areas of application in students' theses.

It is very natural to define the direction of the research in accordance with the major of study. So, such areas as technology, business, finance, manufacturing, and e-commerce are obvious in their proposals of implementation of intelligent technologies. The others arise from their interests or anticipations of their future professional life [42].

5   AI Methods in the Students' Research

As it was mentioned earlier, students can potentially formulate their thesis after discussion with a supervisor, knowing his/her area of scientific research. Some-times, scientists propose list of new topics or advise to become familiar with those recently elaborated. Either way, there should be a real consensus between the students and supervisors in the final labeling of the thesis. This is the most common practice in universities; in some cases, students participating in some scientific activities can be motivated to join these interests with the ongoing or past projects.

In this paper, research on the topics connected with theses covering the AI and KM disciplines was performed on students of the Wroclaw University of Economics and Business defending their works in the last ten years mostly in the Faculty of Management, Computer Science and Finance. About 120 theses represented AI + KM topics and detailed data are presented in the next sections; about 60% of the theses relate to the bachelor's level and the others refer to the master's level. The criteria to qualify the theses to the earlier proposed groups involved the titles, keywords and summaries of the works. We followed the earlier proposed differentiation of AI methods and types of the theses; therefore particular were combined with the preparation of solution prototypes (so developing applications) or with general research in the method (identified with the basic investigation).

Types of bachelor's theses are presented in Fig. 6; the division of works oriented on developing prototypes or focusing on more general research was maintained.

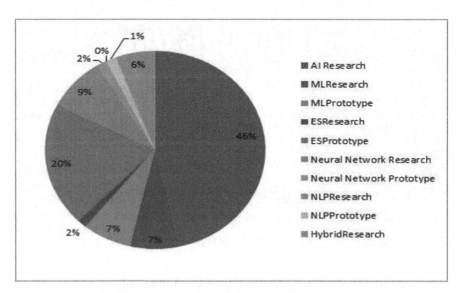

Fig. 6. Bachelor's theses presenting AI methods.

About half of the theses were devoted to fundamental research without specification of the dominant AI method. A relatively significant number of bachelor's theses were connected with the creation of prototypes of expert systems and topics on machine learning and neural networks with the preparation of prototypes and more general research.

The next implementation aspect of the research relates to applying earlier demonstrated AI methods in different sectors. The results are depicted in Fig. 7. The biggest number of bachelor's theses was oriented on technology with the crucial importance of general research in AI. The next area of AI method applications in bachelor's theses was manufacturing with the increasing role of neural networks.

The second group of theses, prepared as master's work, represent the same – as previously – AI methods. The results of the topic analysis are a bit different compared to the bachelor's level. The biggest number of authors prepared their theses on AI basic research (it was not so dominant) but the next two groups preferred machine learning and neural networks methods.

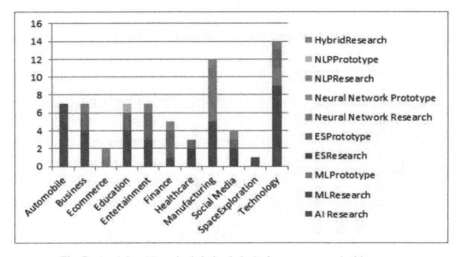

Fig. 7. Applying AI methods in bachelor's theses connected with sectors.

The finance area was considered by students as the main sector in their more practical-oriented topics (preparing prototypes and performing basic research) using mostly machine learning and neural networks. The next two sectors represent technology and business. It is also worth stressing recently appeared works connected with entertainment, automobiles and space exploration.

The presented charts inform us about the significant and increasing importance of AI topics. Recently, the number of bachelor's as well master's theses have been relatively meaningful in all faculties.

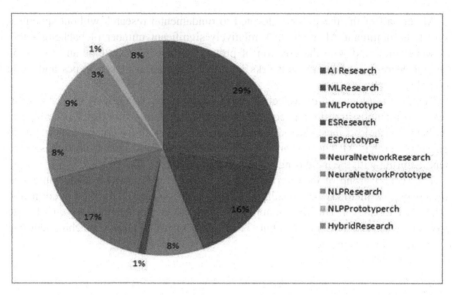

Fig. 8. Master's theses presenting AI methods.

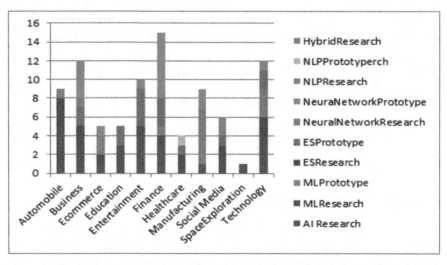

Fig. 9. Applying AI methods in master's theses connected with sectors.

6   Knowledge Management in the Students' Research

Knowledge management as a topic of research is very often strictly connected with AI methods. But in the case of students' theses, their topics were formulated and analyzed rather separately. It is also worth stressing that a KM orientation in students' works has been observed at the master's level. KM topics were very seldom formulated at the bachelor's level. According to the previous assumptions, two main groups of topics have been considered in this section: broadly defined Knowledge Management and formulated as supporting knowledge discovering technology, commonly known as **Data Mining** [43, 44].

The participation of these two topics is presented in Fig. 10. During the whole period of the elaborated theses, almost 75% of students defined some problems rooted in Knowledge Management. The rest of the students tried to solve problems using different Data Mining algorithms (especially recently).

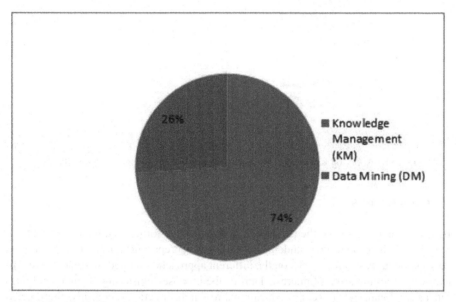

Fig. 10. Students' theses presenting Knowledge Management and Data Mining.

Knowledge Management in higher institutions is identified with surveys and the analysis of applying this concept in academic society [45–47]. On the other hand, students' experiences (especially obtained during professional work) are always connected with the concepts of knowledge acquisition or discovery. In the case of the investigated students, they tried to propose some solutions addressed to the defined areas. The list of sectors presented earlier changed: instead of the automobile sector, the government appeared.

In Fig. 11, students' topics connected with KM and DM are presented with these topics being applied in different sectors. Two main sectors appeared as leaders in implementing both approaches: Business and Technology. As previously, the Finance area and e-commerce with manufacturing represent the sectors of applying KM and DM in students' master's theses.

To sum up, the importance of knowledge management and data mining were confirmed in different sectors; most of the topics covered almost all earlier presented in the theses on artificial intelligence.

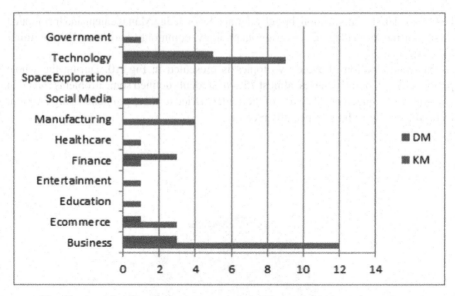

Fig. 11. Applying Knowledge Management and Data Mining in students' theses.

7   Conclusions

Based on the results from the performed study, we have formulated the following find-ings. Firstly, investigation of students' research when preparing their theses is performed very incidentally and rarely. Secondly, different approaches applied by students are typ-ical when defining areas of interest. Thirdly, the proposed clustering of students' topics reflects regional and university educational/research directions. Fourthly, the defined topics in the theses cover the majority of actual trends in AI and KM which seems to be the main determinant along with the supervisors' suggestions, students' motiva-tions, professional experiences, and current trends in the IT sector. Last but not least, active student participation in research projects and scientific circles facilitates the topic formulation of the theses and enhances their self-learning.

Further research will cover two areas. First, we plan to extend the study by investigat-ing other regions and universities. Second, we aim to explore the students' motivational factors associated with research projects and higher education.

References

1. Giuntini, F.T., et al.: How do i feel? Identifying emotional expressions on facebook reactions using clustering mechanism. IEEE Access **7**, 53909–53921 (2019)
2. Owoc, M.L., Weichbroth, P.: Dynamical aspects of knowledge evolution. In: Mercier-Laurent, E., Boulanger, Danielle (eds.) AI4KM 2017. IAICT, vol. 571, pp. 52–65. Springer, Cham (2019). https://doi.org/10.1007/978-3-030-29904-0_5
3. Weichbroth, P., Brodnicki, K.: The lemniscate knowledge flow model. In: 2017 Federated Conference on Computer Science and Information Systems (FedCSIS), pp. 1217–1220. IEEE (2017)

4. PSSI: Polish artificial intelligence society (2021). https://pssi.org.pl/en:membership
5. NTIE: Naukowe Towarzystwo Informatyki Ekonomicznej (2021). http://sartosfera.pl/ntie/
6. Wohlin, C.: Guidelines for snowballing in systematic literature studies and a replication in software engineering. In: Proceedings of the 18th International Conference on Evaluation and Assessment in Software Engineering, pp. 1–10 (2014)
7. Gagnon, Y.C.: The Case Study as Research Method: A Practical Handbook. PUQ (2010)
8. Anyoha, R.: The history of artificial intelligence (2017). http://sitn.hms.harvard.edu/flash/2017/history-artificial-intelligence/
9. Ginsberg, M.: Essentials of artificial intelligence. Newnes (2012)
10. Merriam-Webster Dictionary: Intelligence (2021). https://www.merriam-webster.com/dictionary/intelligence
11. Méndez Fernández, D., et al.: Artefacts in software engineering: a fundamental positioning. Softw. Syst. Model. **18**(5), 2777–2786 (2019). https://doi.org/10.1007/s10270-019-00714-3
12. Lexico: Artefact (2021). https://www.lexico.com/definition/artefact
13. IGI Global: What is it artifact (2021). https://www.igi-global.com/dictionary/it-artifact/15828
14. Legg, S., Hutter, M.: Universal intelligence: a definition of machine intelligence. Mind. Mach. **17**(4), 391–444 (2007)
15. Hutter, M.: Universal Artificial Intelligence: Sequential Decisions Based on Algorithmic Probability. Springer, Heidelberg (2004). https://doi.org/10.1007/b138233
16. Coppin, B.: Artificial Intelligence Illuminated. Jones & Bartlett Learning (2004)
17. The Economic Times: Sophia, world's first humanoid citizen, focuses on saving the planet, plans to conquer mt everest (2018). https://economictimes.indiatimes.com/magazines/panache/sophia-worlds-first-humanoid-citizen-focuses-on-saving-the-planet-plans-to-conquer-mt-everest/articleshow/63409249.cms?from=mdr
18. Waldrop, M.M.: Man-made minds: The promise of artificial intelligence (1987)
19. Marcinkowski, B., Kuciapski, M.: A business process modeling notation extension for risk handling. In: Cortesi, A., Chaki, N., Saeed, K., Wierzchoń, S. (eds.) CISIM 2012. LNCS, vol. 7564, pp. 374–381. Springer, Heidelberg (2012). https://doi.org/10.1007/978-3-642-33260-9_32
20. Aristodemou, L., Tietze, F.: The state-of-the-art on intellectual property analytics (IPA): a literature review on artificial intelligence, machine learning and deep learning methods for analysing intellectual property (IP) data. World Patent Inf. **55**, 37–51 (2018)
21. Zurada, J., Karwowski, W., Marras, W.S.: A neural network-based system for classification of industrial jobs with respect to risk of low back disorders due to workplace design. Appl. Ergon. **28**(1), 49–58 (1997)
22. Korczak, J., Hernes, M., Bac, M.: Collective intelligence supporting trading decisions on FOREX market. In: Nguyen, N.T., Papadopoulos, G.A., Jędrzejowicz, P., Trawiński, B., Vossen, G. (eds.) ICCCI 2017. LNCS (LNAI), vol. 10448, pp. 113–122. Springer, Cham (2017). https://doi.org/10.1007/978-3-319-67074-4_12
23. Brzeski, A.: Parameters optimization in medicine supporting image recognition algorithms (2011)
24. Boiński, T.M., Ambrożewicz, A., Szymański, J.: Knowledge base suitable for answering questions in natural language (2014)
25. Waloszek, A., Waloszek, W.: A model for describing and classifying sentiment analysis methods (2017)
26. Ambroziak, A., Kłosowski, P.: Autodesk Robot Structural Analysis: Podstawy obliczeń. Politechnika Gdańska (2010)
27. Ficht, G., Piotrowski, R.: Micromouse robot-technical design and construction (2012)
28. Remagnino, P., Hagras, H., Velastin, S., Monekosso, N.: Ambient intelligence: a gentle introduction (2005)

29. Teixeira, M.S., Maran, V., de Oliveira, J.P.M., Winter, M., Machado, A.: Situation aware model for multi-objective decision making in ambient intelligence. Appl. Soft Comput. **81**, 105532 (2019)
30. Messika, E.: Mapping the world artificial intelligence landscapes (2017). https://medium.com/@eytanmessika/mapping-the-world-artificial-intelligence-landscapes-223f752efa4
31. Owoc, M.L., Weichbroth, P.: A note on knowledge management education: towards implementing active learning methods. In: Mercier-Laurent, E. (ed.) AI4KM 2018. IAICT, vol. 588, pp. 124–140. Springer, Cham (2020). https://doi.org/10.1007/978-3-030-52903-1_10
32. White, S.: Different types of research and research skills (2020). https://www.allassignmenthelp.com/blog/research-skills/
33. McCombes, S.: The main types of research compared (2019). https://www.scribbr.com/methodology/types-of-research/
34. Mach, M.A., Owoc, M.: Knowledge granularity and representation of knowledge: towards knowledge grid. In: Shi, Z., Vadera, S., Aamodt, A., Leake, D. (eds.) IIP 2010. IAICT, vol. 340, pp. 251–258. Springer, Heidelberg (2010). https://doi.org/10.1007/978-3-642-16327-2_31
35. Owoc, M., Marciniak, K.: Knowledge management as foundation of smart university. In: 2013 Federated Conference on Computer Science and Information Systems, pp. 1267–1272. IEEE (2013)
36. Marciniak, K., Owoc, M.L.: Usability of knowledge grid in smart city concepts. In: ICEIS (3), pp. 341–346 (2013)
37. Owoc, M., Weichbroth, P., Żuralski, K.: Towards better understanding of context-aware knowledge transformation. In: 2017 Federated Conference on Computer Science and Information Systems (FedCSIS), pp. 1123–1126. IEEE (2017)
38. Owoc, M.L., Sawicka, A., Weichbroth, P.: Artificial intelligence technologies in education: benefits, challenges and strategies of implementation. arXiv preprint arXiv:2102.09365 (2021)
39. Hernes, M.: Consensus theory for cognitive agents' unstructured knowledge conflicts resolving in management information systems. In: Nguyen, N.T., Kowalczyk, R., Hernes, M. (eds.) Transactions on computational collective intelligence XXXII. LNCS, vol. 11370, pp. 1–119. Springer, Heidelberg (2019). https://doi.org/10.1007/978-3-662-58611-2_1
40. Taniar, D.: Data Mining and Knowledge Discovery Technologies. IGI Global (2008)
41. Johansson, J., Elgh, F.: Applying connectivism to engineering knowledge to support the automated business. In: 24th ISPE International Conference on Transdisciplinary Engineering, Singapore, 10 July to 14 July, 2017. pp. 621–628. IOS Press (2017)
42. Nouri, J., Larsson, K., Saqr, M.: Identifying factors for master thesis completion and non-completion through learning analytics and machine learning. In: Scheffel, M., Broisin, J., Pammer-Schindler, V., Ioannou, A., Schneider, J. (eds.) EC-TEL 2019. LNCS, vol. 11722, pp. 28–39. Springer, Cham (2019). https://doi.org/10.1007/978-3-030-29736-7_3
43. Weichbroth, P.: Odkrywanie reguł asocjacyjnych z transakcyjnych baz danych. Prace Naukowe Uniwersytetu Ekonomicznego we Wrocławiu, pp. 301–309 (2009)
44. Pondel, M., Korczak, J.: A view on the methodology of analysis and exploration of marketing data. In: 2017 Federated Conference on Computer Science and Information Systems (FedCSIS), pp. 1135–1143. IEEE (2017)
45. Dhamdhere, S.N.: Knowledge management strategies and process in traditional colleges: a study. Int. J. Inf. Libr. Soc. **4**(1), 34–42 (2015)

46. Zinzou, E.F., Doctor, T.R.: Knowledge management practices among the internal quality assurance network (iqan)-member higher education institutions (heis) in thailand. World J. Educ. **10**(5) (2020)
47. Owoc, M., Hauke, K., Weichbroth, P.: Knowledge-grid modelling for academic purposes. In: Mercier-Laurent, Eunika, Boulanger, Danielle (eds.) AI4KM 2015. IAICT, vol. 497, pp. 1–14. Springer, Cham (2016). https://doi.org/10.1007/978-3-319-55970-4_1

Customer Churn Prediction in FMCG Sector Using Machine Learning Applications

S. Nazlı Günesen⑩, Necip Şen⑩, Nihan Yıldırım(✉) ⑩, and Tolga Kaya⑩

İstanbul Technical University, 34467 Maslak, Sarıyer/İstanbul, Turkey
{gunesen16,senn15,yildirimni,kayatolga}@itu.edu.tr

Abstract. Non-contractual setting and many brands and alternative products make customer retention relatively more difficult in the FMCG market. Besides, there is no absolute customer loyalty, as most buyers split their purchases among several almost equivalent brands. Thereby, this study aims to probe the contribution of various machine learning algorithms to predict churn behaviour of the most valuable part of the existing customers of some FMCG brands (detergent, fabric conditioner, shampoo and carbonated soft drink) based on a real dataset obtained in the Turkish market over the two successive years (2018 and 2019). In this context, exploratory data analysis and feature engineering are carried out mostly to build many predictive models to reach consistent and viable results. Further, RFM analysis and clustering techniques with K-Means clustering are employed to generate meaningful insights for business operations and marketing campaigns. Lastly, revenue contributions of improved customer retention can be achieved, utilising actionable intelligence created by the churn prediction.

Keywords: Machine learning · Business intelligence · FMCG · Churn prediction · Customer retention · Customer loyalty · RFM analysis · K-means clustering

1 Introduction

The competitive landscape of today's marketplaces entails companies, regardless of industries they are in, to emphasize retaining their existing customers. FMCG companies face extra inconvenience in managing customer retention due to the non-contractual customer relationship setting in retail markets. Unsurprisingly, the inclination to churn is directly proportional to the switching cost. The lesser the switching cost, the higher the tendency to churn [1]. Therefore, FMCG firms experience difficulties in predicting customer churns and in taking preventive actions accordingly. Consequently, they lose their hard-gained customers to competitors since they fail to respond proactively.

A modest improvement in customer churn projection precision can yield a significant positive impact on a company's profitability. The cost of acquiring a new customer is 5 to 6 times higher than retaining the existing one [2]. There are much more substantial shreds of evidence in the relevant literature for cost rate of new customer acquisition to

Published by Springer Nature Switzerland AG 2021
E. Mercier-Laurent et al. (Eds.): AI4KM 2021, IFIP AICT 614, pp. 82–103, 2021.
https://doi.org/10.1007/978-3-030-80847-1_6

customer retention, such as 12-fold [3], 20 times [4] and even 25 times [5]. So, it is an indisputable fact that gaining a new customer is much more expensive than keeping an existing one. Moreover, only a 5% improvement in customer retention rate would result in a 25% to 95% profit increase [5].

In today's complex FMCG distribution environment, there are numerous factors causing dissatisfaction resulting in a customer churn. For example, quality defects, the inefficiency of distribution channels, new product offerings, inter-customer dynamics through social media, aggressive competitive campaigns, regulations, price changes etc. [4]. Accordingly, identifying churners who behave similarly and relevant root causes of their action enables companies to improve customer retention [6]. That's why creating accurate and comprehensible churn prediction models providing actionable business intelligence by detecting early symptoms to identify customers with a high probability to leave is a must-have practice for FMCG companies [4]. Thus, they can revise their marketing strategies proactively to address identified customers' concerns worth keeping to improve their bottom-line profits [7].

2   Literature Review

2.1   General Overview

In the last decade, the ingenuity of processing raw data to reveal hidden value inside providing actionable intelligence has been in humankind's spotlight on a global scale. The impact of analytics that is the engine of this initiative has already become mainstream and changed societies' way of living and the business world's capabilities, irrespective of the industry they are in [8].

On the other hand, the fierce competition of today's multichannel, digitalized markets entails FMCG companies to be more attentive to retaining their hardly gained existing customers to stay ahead of the game [9]. Moreover, customers can reach many alternative products offered by several competitive companies and easily switch from one to another or partition their purchases amongst a selected group of producers in a non-contractual nature of FMCG markets [10]. For this reason, they aim to make optimum use of their limited sales and marketing resources to attain the purpose of elongating the duration of their customers' engagement with their products.

However, many companies do not emphasize retaining customers adequately in their strategies and still perform traditional marketing planning processes prioritizing acquiring new customers and increasing market share. Further, they discern an increase in their churn rates 6 to 8 months later than they actually dissatisfy the customer and consequently, they are six months late to improve their performance [5]. Companies practising relationship marketing to maintain long-term relationships with existing customers, thus increasing their revenue stream, will positively impact the high customer retention rate on profitability [11].

In this context, creating actionable customer churn insight from raw data by predictive analytics based on machine learning techniques is one of the leading domains that have been frequently attempted by many researchers [12]. Nevertheless, there is still room for further research into accurate and comprehensible customer churn prediction models to interpret customers' purchasing behaviour more precisely [13].

2.2 Definition of Customer Churn

Customer churn is the customers' act of abandonment of the existing relationship with the company they currently purchase from [14]. It merely is customer movement from one company/brand to another [15]. In other words, customer churn is a customer's action discontinuing purchasing a brand in a definite time interval. It reveals an indication concerning the duration of customer's engagement with product/s of a company and, thereby, the customer's lifetime value (LV) that is projected net present value of total spending of a customer for the product during his/her entire relationship with the company [16]. LV propounds that all customers are not equally important in terms of profit potential in future. High LV customers bringing along more significant profit opportunities have to be detected, and resources need to be allocated to retain them [17].

Moreover, due to continuously increasing product choices and digital channels, well-informed and empowered consumers of today have ceased following the marketing funnel concept where they enter with a shortlist of brands in their minds and assess them to narrow options. At the same time, they move through and leave with the one brand they decided to buy [18].

On the other hand, defining the condition that classifies a customer as a churner is not easy, particularly in the FMCG sector's non-contractual setting, as most consumers purchase from several suppliers concurrently. Usually, a threshold based on the customer purchasing activity is set by a business preference, and any customer with lower purchasing activity is considered as a churner [19]. Hence, some cases categorize customers with no activity in the given time as churners [20], while others accept customers lowering their purchasing activity below the threshold as churners.

Some other studies focus only on the churning likelihood of loyal customers who look promising in their potential of future revenue contribution [21]. In this context, they evaluate partial defections in loyal customers as the early signals of total churns and focus on behaviourally loyal ones whose purchase frequency is above average and the standard deviation to mean for their successive purchases below average [22].

However, significant differences concerning volume and evolution of spending in loyal customers group and the idea of defining them as a whole, as the most valuable group based on the duration of their lifecycle (LC), are only questionable. For this reason, churn analysis should also consider the customers who are not classified as loyal since they purchased a large number of products over a short period in the past, but then reduced or discontinued their purchasing (hence, denominated as "butterfly") because they have a high monetary value in the past [23].

Consequently, estimating a recently acquired customer's future LC slope to predict future spending evolution based on the initial purchase information provides valuable qualitative insights to reshape marketing strategy [23]. Classifying churners with a threshold is not always meaningful, and the evolution of customer purchasing patterns is also a significant factor [19].

2.3 Substantiality of Customer Churn

Today's consumers are more demanding and need to be responded with a more customized treatment [24]. Companies spend significant effort to attract new customers.

However, the total spending of an average new customer within the first year or two of his/her LC with the company just offsets the acquisition cost. On the contrary, a 5% increase in customer retention rate adds at least 3 years to the average LC of customers. Besides, only a 2% improvement in customer retention improves overheads by 10% [25].

The positive impacts of customer retention on business performance are notably referred to in the literature. A compilation of precedents to give an idea are as follows: companies that succeeded in retaining their customers do not have to spend much effort to acquire new customers, and thereby they can concentrate on concerns of their existing customers to develop stronger relations [26], cost of acquiring new clients is at least 5 to 6 times higher than that of retaining existing customers [27; 28], higher profits are generated out of customers with long LC with the brand [21], loyal customers bring along new customers by word of mouth in favour of the brand they have purchased, while churned customers might negatively influence potential customers with their biased product comments [21; 20], long-term customers can tolerate price differences and are less responsive to competitive marketing campaigns [28; 12], even a small increment in customer retention can culminate in a remarkable profit increase [26].

For an appropriate customer retention strategy, it is needed to analyse the factors motivating customers to churn. Those who are profitable to retain and continue to serve must also be identified [25]. Therefore, viable, conceivable, and accurate predictive churn models are essential to detect customers' intentions to leave and identify causes behind their churn behaviour [33]. Some recent studies performed for the FMCG sector in this context are summarized in Table 1.

Table 1. Some recent studies at a glance [relevant to customer churn prediction in the FMGC sector].

Reference	Models used	Dataset	Remarks
Buckinx et al. (2002) Using machine learning techniques to predict defection of top clients	Logistic Regression, Linear Discriminant Analysis, Quadratic Discriminant Analysis, C4.5, Neural Networks, Naive Bayes	Private Dataset: Individual records of 158,884 customers with a loyalty card (85 per cent of total customers) within ten months (# of features: 32)	Partial defection is the initial signal of total churn in future. Neural network outperforms other classification techniques in terms of both PCC and AUC metrics. The number of past shop visits and the time between past shop incidences are best performing variables concerning predictive power

(continued)

Table 1. (*continued*)

Reference	Models used	Dataset	Remarks
Buckinx et al. (2005) Customer base analysis: partial defection of behaviourally loyal clients in a non-contractual FMCG retail setting [22]	Logistic regression, Automatic Relevance Determination (ARD) Neural Networks and Random Forest	Private Dataset: Individual records of 158,884 customers with a loyalty card (85 percent of total customers) within ten months (# of features: 32)	PCC and AUC are used to evaluate classifier performance of predicting partial defection. No remarkable performance differences are observed among alternative classification methods used. RFM variables are the best predictors to be used for partial customer defection
Lessmann & Voss (2008) SupervisedcClassification for decision support in customer relationship management [29]	N/A	N/A	Extraordinary approaches (such as learning from imbalanced data and cost-sensitive learning) and algorithms are necessary to overcome complications caused by imbalanced class and cost distributions. Basic linear models may fall short of explanatoriness in complex CRM settings
Burez & Van den Poel (2009) Handling class imbalance in customer churn prediction [30]	Gradient Boosting Machine and Weighted Random Forest (with random and advanced under-sampling), CUBE Sampling Technique, Random Forest, Logistic Regression	Private Dataset: Purchase data of 32,371 customers with a 25.15% churn rate (#of features: 21)	Under-sampling can lead to improved prediction accuracy, primarily when evaluated with AUC. The advanced sampling technique CUBE does not increase predictive performance. Weighted random forest performs noticeably better than the random forest

(*continued*)

Table 1. (*continued*)

Reference	Models used	Dataset	Remarks
Miguéis et al. (2013) Customer attrition in retailing: An application of multivariate adaptive regression splines [31]	Logistic Regression and Multivariate Adaptive Regression Splines (MARS)	Private Dataset: Purchase data and demographics of 130,284 customers with a loyalty card within two years	MARS performs better than Logistic regression when variable selection procedures are not used. However, MARS loses its superiority when logistic regression is conducted with stepwise feature selection
Coussement (2014) Improving customer retention management through cost-sensitive learning	Logistic Regression Classifying Technique and Non-Sampling Based Cost-Sensitive Learning Techniques [Direct Minimum Expected Cost (DMECC), Metacost, Thresholding and Weighting]	Private Dataset: Records of 100,000 customers including transactional, socio-demographical and client/company interaction information (with 30.86% churn incidence)	Total misclassification cost, as a churn prediction evaluation measure, is a crucial metric. Cost-sensitive learners are benchmarked for different cost and churn levels in terms of indicating churn prediction reliability
Jahromi et al. (2017) Managing B2B customer churn, retention and profitability [32]	Decision Tree, Logistic Regression, Adaptive Boosting	Private Dataset: Transactional records of 11,021 business customers in a year	Adaptive boosting considerably outperforms the decision tree model concerning prediction accuracy. However, its accuracy performance superiority is negligible compared to that of logistic regression
Calciu et al. (2015) Recognising dangerous drop out incidents as opposed to accidents to improve the efficiency of triggers reducing customer churn [33]	Stochastic Model (Pareto NBD)	Private Dataset: 199,352 randomly selected customers from the top four RFM segments within 3,5 years	Drop Out Incidents (DOIs) of customers are used to estimate probability of being active and high Duration between DOIs (DDOI) are considered as the signals of potential customer churns. Allocating marketing resources on active users with risk of churn is suggested

(*continued*)

Table 1. (*continued*)

Reference	Models used	Dataset	Remarks
Sulistiani & Tjahyanto (2017) Comparative analysis of feature selection method to predict customer loyalty [34]	Random Forest	Private Dataset: Consumer questionnaire (# of respondents: 386, # of features 26)	Feature selection methods can considerably affect the prediction accuracy of random forest algorithm. The Chi-square feature selection method improved random forest accuracy up to 83.2%
Shoaib (2018) Customers' churn prediction in a retail store through machine learning algorithms [35]	Logistic Regression, KNN, Decision Tree, Random Forest, XG Boost	Private Dataset: 880,000 transactions of 180,000 customers within two months	XG boost, random forest and decision tree are the best performing classifiers, respectively. K-means clustering technique is used for segmentation. Churn probability is found higher for the high-value customer segment

3   Data Preparation

3.1   Dataset

A real-life dataset obtained through field research for four selected FMCG brands (detergent, fabric conditioner, shampoo and carbonated soft drink) over the two successive years [2018 (P1 period) and 2019 (P2 period)] was used. These nineteen features are included: age, gender, marital status, location, education, job status, region, duration of consumption, point of purchase, basket value, the basket of goods, purchase value of the brand, purchase value of the product category, the quantity of the brand purchased, the quantity of the product category purchased, frequency of buying, recency of buying, number of equivalent brands consumed, and purchasing points used.

3.2   Sampling

Instead of focusing on the entire customer base, we selected the most profitable (valuable) and behaviourally loyal customers. For determining this segment for each brand, we designated the first 2/3 of customers by their purchasing value in P1 and P2 periods.

Afterwards, we identified the customers-in-common included in the selections of both successive years, and we nominated them as the valuable customer base. For example, the detergent brand number of the first 2/3 of customers in terms of purchasing value is 8414 out of 12622 in P1 and 8738 out of 13105 in P2, and the number of customers who are common in both periods is 3936. In this way, we selected the heavy buyers in common in the top 2/3 of customers regarding purchasing value for the P1 and P2 periods to sample the detergent brand's valuable customers.

3.3 Loyalty Definition

Loyalty was defined based on the threshold of the ratio of the brand's quantity purchased to the quantity of the product category purchased. The valuable customers whose loyalty threshold are higher than 0.33 in the P1 period were accepted as loyal. By using the loyalty threshold for elimination, 616 detergent customers out of 3936, valuable customers were identified as loyal. In this way, 466 laundry softener customers, 937 shampoo customers, and 2200 carbonated soft drink customers were selected as samples representing loyal customers.

3.4 Churn Definition

In a non-contractual setting of the FMCG market, customers can easily switch from one brand to another or partition their purchases amongst a selected group of products. For this reason, churn must be defined carefully by paying regard to purchase tendency. In this context, we divided loyal customers into two groups: (1) Customers whose loyalty ratio is between 0.33 and 0.5 in the P1 period are accepted as churn if their loyalty ratio is 0 (no purchase from that brand) in the P2 period. (2) Customers whose loyalty ratio is higher than 0.5 in the P1 period are accepted as churn if their loyalty ratio in the P2 period is at least 0.5 less than their P1 loyalty ratio. To exemplify, 0.2 and lower P2 loyalty ratio will be accepted as a churn while greater than 0.2 P2 loyalty ratio is taken as no-churn for a P1 loyalty ratio of 0.7.

4 Method

The procedures explained in this section were applied for all selected FMCG brands (detergent, fabric conditioner, shampoo and carbonated soft drink). However, only the procedures conducted for the shampoo brand have been presented.

4.1 RFM Analysis

At first, the shampoo customers were grouped by a cluster dendrogram after scaling the relevant data. The following output indicates eight different groups (Fig. 1).

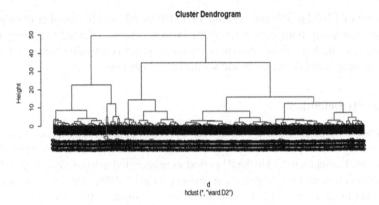

Fig. 1. Cluster dendrogram.

These groups are illustrated in the following 3D RFM scatter plot where X represents Frequency, Y represents the Recency, and Z represents the Monetary (Fig. 2).

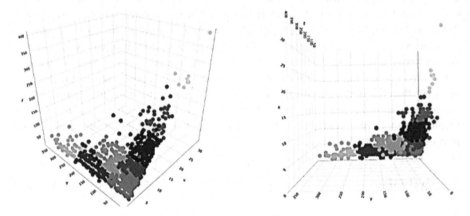

Fig. 2. 3D RFM.

4.2 Segmentation with Clustering

Three different approaches are used to determine an optimal number of clusters. According to the total within-cluster sum of squares graph, the slope starts to flatten after 8 groups. The gap statistics method predicates that at least 6 clusters would be sufficient. As a final check, the average silhouettes graph remarks that 8–9 clusters would be appropriate for customer segmentation (See Fig. 3).

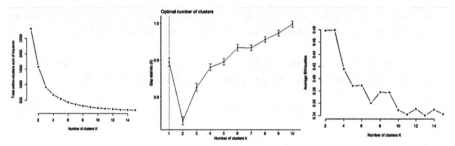

Fig. 3. The total within-clusters sum of squares graph (left), gap statistics graph (middle), and average silhouettes graph (right).

4.3 Exploratory Data Analysis, Visualisation and Feature Engineering

After trying various combinations of features, the best-performing feature set was defined as shown in Table 2.

Table 2. Table of features used.

LABEL	VARIABLES FORMULA	CATEGORY
SES_GROUP	SES_GROUP	FACTOR
PAX	PAX	FACTOR
KENT_KIR	KENT_KIR	FACTOR
PS_GENDER	PS_GENDER	FACTOR
EDU_LEVEL	EDU_LEVEL	FACTOR
AGE	AGE	FACTOR
REGION	REGION	FACTOR
DHAIRCONDITIONER	[HAIRCONDITIONER(P2)-HAIRCONDITIONER(P1)]*1.2]	NUMERIC
DFMCG	[FMCG_TOTAL(P2)-FMCG_TOTAL(P1)*1.2]/[FMCG_TOTAL(P1)*1.2]	NUMERIC
DSHAMPOOSPM	[SHAMPOO_SPM(P2)-SHAMPOO_SPM(P1)*1.2]	NUMERIC
DSHAMPOOGRC	[SHAMPOO_GRC(P2)-SHAMPOO_GRC(P1)*1.2]	NUMERIC
RPRICE	[SHAMPOOPRICE(P2)-SHAMPOOPRICE(P1)*1.2]	NUMERIC
DCOUNTDIFBRAND	[DCOUNTDIFBRAND(P2)-DCOUNTDIFBRAND(P1)]	NUMERIC

1. With as.factor() function, all character columns were transformed into factor columns.
2. {sum(is.na()} function is used to look for sum of "NA" numbers in dataset.
3. summary() shows the information about numeric and factor variables [202 CHURN, 735 NO CHURN labels in the dataset]
4. Unselect function is used to eliminate all columns, including factors to show correlations and densities of all numeric variables with ggpairs() function (see Fig. 5).

- DSHAMPOOGRC feature's distribution is not expanded because the 0 values have dominated the whole column, so these columns seem like such. Kurtosis of these features' distributions is positive and higher than the normal distribution's kurtosis.
- The Farness of the correlations shown above from 1 and −1 indicates that there is no correlation among features. The correlation value between RPRICE and DCOUNTDIFBRAND is so close to 0. This finding is surprising because they are expected to be parallel.

- The scatters between each pair show the distribution of the observations among them, and the line on them indicates the direction of observations.

5. The graph in Fig. 4 is built with the corrplot() function showing the correlations among features after scaling. Ggpairs plot is also presented in Fig. 5.

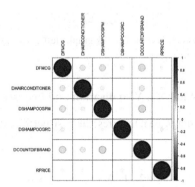

Fig. 4. Correlation plot.

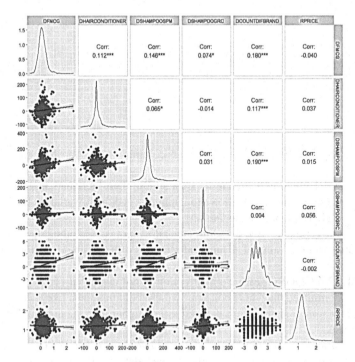

Fig. 5. Ggpairs plot.

4.4 Application of Models

In this study, various prediction models based on eight different machine learning algorithms (logistic regression, logistic regression with k fold, boosted logistic regression, linear discriminant analysis, quadratic discriminant analysis, decision tree, random forest, and extreme gradient boosting) were built, tested and optimized. Ultimately, we found the best performing machine learning technique with the highest meaningful accuracy for each FMCG brand. The accuracy comparison of all models used for each brand is given in Table 3.

The first applied method was decision tree, and before pruning; the training set accuracy, sensitivity and specificity were 81%, 21% and 98%, respectively. Upon pruning, test set accuracy was 77%, sensitivity was 10%, and specificity was 96%. The final decision tree generated after pruning was as follows (Fig. 6):

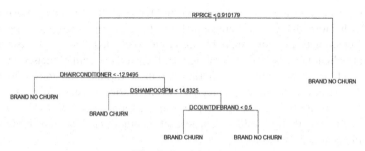

Fig. 6. Decision tree

The most dominating variable was the RPRICE, and its terminal value was calculated as 0.91. After pruning, the test set accuracy was 77%, sensitivity was 13%, and the specificity was 95%.

Table 3. Decision tree test set confusion matrix after pruning.

	BRAND CHURN	BRAND NO CHURN
BRAND CHURN	8	11
BRAND NO CHURN	53	210

Application of logistic regression made it possible to understand churn behaviour better by showing variables' contributions to the churn prediction (Table 4);

PS_GENDER, REGION, DFMCG, DHAIRCONDITIONER, DSHAMPOOSPM, DSHAMPOOGRC, RPRICE were the most contributing variables. PS_GENDERERKEK, REGIONMediterranean, DFMCG, DSHAMPOOSPM, DSHAMPOOGRC and PRICECHANGE have positive coefficients. The findings can be interpreted as all else being equal; (1) males, people living in the Mediterranean region, (2) customers with increased total FMCG expenditures, (3) customers with increased supermarket shampoo expenditures, and (4) customers with increased grocery store

Table 4. Logistic regression variable contribution.

Coefficients:	Estimate	Std. Error	z value	Pr(>|z|)	
(Intercept)	-0.474	0.620	-0.765	0.444	
PS_GENDERFemale	0.547	0.342	1.598	0.110	
PS_GENDERMale	1.770	0.624	2.834	0.005	**
REGIONBlacksea	0.766	0.512	1.495	0.135	
REGIONCentral	0.081	0.341	0.239	0.811	
REGIONEast and Southeast	0.099	0.343	0.287	0.774	
REGIONMarmara	0.374	0.295	1.266	0.206	
REGIONMediterranean	0.739	0.349	2.114	0.034	*
DFMCG	0.365	0.373	0.979	0.328	
DHAIRCONDITIONER	-0.009	0.003	-2.926	0.003	**
DSHAMPOOSPM	0.005	0.002	2.223	0.026	*
DSHAMPOOGRC	0.015	0.006	2.522	0.012	*
RPRICE	0.753	0.414	1.819	0.069	.

Signif. codes: 0 '***' 0.001 '**' 0.01 '*'   0.05 '.' 0.1 ' ' 1

shampoo expenditures are more likely to churn. Moreover, RPRICE has a positive coefficient which shows that all else being equal; when the average shampoo category price increases, customers are more likely to churn. DHAIRCONDITIONER has a negative coefficient, which indicates: all else being equal; customers with increased hair conditioner expenditures are less likely to churn. From these variables, the most critical churn factor is the increase in the product category's average price and customer's region since their coefficients are the biggest ones. The training set accuracy was 78%, sensitivity was 0.05%, and specificity was 98%. The test set accuracy was 77%, sensitivity was 0%, and specificity was 78% (Table 5).

Table 5. Logistic regression test set confusion matrix.

	BRAND CHURN	BRAND NO CHURN
BRAND CHURN	0	61
BRAND NO CHURN	2	219

The prediction power of the algorithm is also illustrated with a ROC curve (Fig. 7);

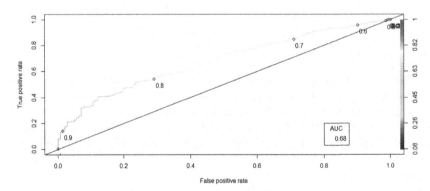

Fig. 7. ROC curve

To apply the random forest technique, the dataset was divided into test and training parts same as the decision tree method. However, in the random forest algorithm Smote-Classif() function was used to create artificial observations that belong to the "CHURN" label. When the model was performed, k-fold helped to build it with the value of 5. The other crucial concern in applying the method was to determine optimum ntree and mtry values (Fig. 8).

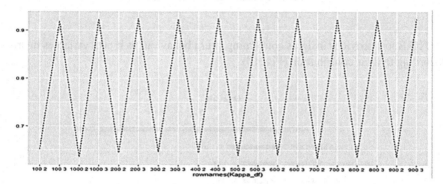

Fig. 8. Random forest classifier plot

Tuning parameter 'mtry' was held constant at a value of 3 because of the highest accuracy rate. The ntree parameter also was chosen as 1000.

Accuracy, sensitivity and specificity rates were calculated as 74%, 15% and %91, respectively (Table 6).

Table 6. Random classifier confusion matrix.

	BRAND CHURN	BRAND NO CHURN
BRAND CHURN	9	20
BRAND NO CHURN	52	201

The random forest technique gives insights about churn behaviour because it orders variables according to their contribution (Fig. 9).

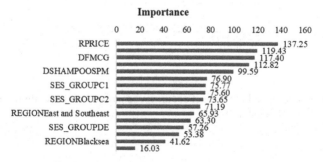

Fig. 9. Random classifier variable contribution

XG boost algorithm was another applied method, and accuracy, sensitivity and specificity rates were calculated as 87%, 17% and 93%, respectively (Table 7).

Table 7. XG boost confusion matrix.

	BRAND CHURN	BRAND NO CHURN
BRAND CHURN	4	21
BRAND NO CHURN	19	273

XG Boost provides insights concerning churn behaviour as it puts variables in order according to their contribution (Fig. 10).

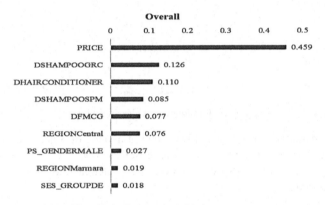

Fig. 10. XG boost variable importance

RPRICE (change in average product category price), DSHAMPOOGRC (change in grocery store product category expenditure), DHAIRCONDITIONER (change in hair conditioner expenditures) were the most important factors.

For boosted logic; the test set accuracy was 87%, sensitivity was 39% and specificity was 91% (Table 8).

Table 8. Boosted logic confusion matrix.

	BRAND CHURN	BRAND NO CHURN
BRAND CHURN	9	27
BRAND NO CHURN	14	267

QDA model calculated the test set accuracy, sensitivity and specificity as 70%, 48% and 72%, respectively (Table 9).

Table 9. QDA confusion matrix.

	BRAND CHURN	BRAND NO CHURN
BRAND CHURN	11	82
BRAND NO CHURN	12	212

LDA was another applied model and it calculated the test set accuracy, sensitivity and specificity as 87%, 0% and 94%, respectively (Table 10).

Table 10. LDA confusion matrix.

	BRAND CHURN	BRAND NO CHURN
BRAND CHURN	0	17
BRAND NO CHURN	23	277

Finally, logistic regression with k fold was applied, and the test set accuracy, sensitivity and specificity were calculated as 77%, 0% and 98%, respectively (Table 11).

Table 11. K-fold logistic regression confusion matrix.

	BRAND CHURN	BRAND NO CHURN
BRAND CHURN	0	11
BRAND NO CHURN	141	503

A summary table of the models applied for the shampoo category is illustrated in the following table (Table 12).

Table 12. Model comparison for shampoo category

Model	Accuracy (%)	Sensitivity (%)	Specificity (%)	Error Rate (%)	Precision (%)	Negative Predictive Value (%)
Decision Tree	77.305	13.115	95.023	22.695	**42.105**	79.848
Logistic Regression with k fold	76.794	0.000	**97.860**	23.206	0.000	78.106
Logistic Regression	77.660	0.000	78.214	22.340	0.000	**99.095**
Random Forest	74.468	14.754	90.950	25.532	31.034	79.447
XG Boost	**87.382**	17.391	92.857	12.618	16.000	93.493
Boosted Logic	87.066	39.130	90.816	12.934	25.000	95.018
LDA	87.382	0.000	94.218	12.618	0.000	92.333
QDA	70.347	**47.826**	72.109	29.653	11.828	95.848

4.5 Comparison of Each Model for 4 FMCG Product Categories

Accuracies of the models applied with the base rates ("NO CHURN" ratio) for all product categories are demonstrated in the following table (Table 13).

Table 13. Accuracy comparison of the models applied.

Model	Detergent Accuracy (%)	Shampoo Accuracy (%)	Carbonated Soft Drink Accuracy (%)	Fabric Softener Accuracy (%)
Decision Tree	68.280	77.305	96.369	68.794
Logistic Regression with k fold	61.628	76.794	96.491	56.308
Logistic Regression	63.441	77.660	96.067	65.957
Random Forest	62.903	74.468	93.041	64.539
XG Boost	75.000	87.382	98.951	45.098
Boosted Logic	55.435	87.066	96.970	49.020
LDA	66.304	87.382	93.939	45.098
QDA	52.174	75.393	98.718	61.765
Base	0.646	0.784	0.965	0.631

4.6 Impact of Customer Retention Improvement on Revenue

The shampoo brand has approximately 2,100,000 customers, and the number of loyal customers was estimated with the help of the method used for sampling previously. Thus, the impact of the increase of retained loyal customers' percentage was estimated for each churn improvement scenario as follows (Table 14);

Table 14. Reflection of churn improvement on customer retention.

Churn Improvement	Retention Rate	# of Loyal Customers* Retained					
		Year 1	Year 2	Year 3	Year 4	Year 5	Year 6
0,00%	78,44%	333.270	261.417	205.055	160.846	126.167	98.966
5,00%	83,44%	333.270	278.080	232.030	193.606	161.545	134.793
10,00%	88,44%	333.270	294.744	260.672	230.538	203.888	180.318
15,00%	93,44%	333.270	311.407	290.979	271.891	254.055	237.389
20,00%	98,44%	333.270	328.071	322.953	317.915	312.956	308.073

# of Total Customers: 2.100.000 *[estimated min.]*

*Loyal Customers: Customers who constitute the segment realizing the top 2/3 of annual transaction value among total customers and also whose brand volume/product category volume ratio is greater than 0,33.

To estimate the impact of improved loyal customer retention on the revenue over the next five years, we multiplied the number of loyal customers obtained above by the loyal customers' average revenue contribution in the first year (which is TL 73.16 ₺). We then corrected the amount by the annual average CPI inflation rate for the following five years. Cumulative revenues were projected and plotted for 10% and 20% customer retention improvement scenarios in the following graph (Fig. 11).

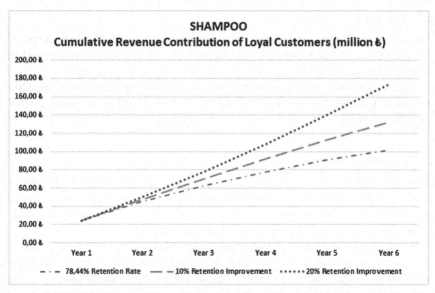

Fig. 11. Impact of retention improvement on cumulative revenue contribution of loyal customers

5 Findings and Conclusion

5.1 Findings

Findings regarding predicting customer churn for the selected detergent, shampoo, fabric conditioner, and carbonated soft drink brands are as follows:

- For most of the product categories, customers with a relatively higher number of preferred brands are less likely to churn. This might indicate strong brand positioning of the selected brands in the conscious consumer segment.
- The category price change is the most critical factor referring to increased churn potentiality for all FMCG product categories.
- Changes in the discount store, grocery store and supermarket expenditures might give initial warning signals of churn for most product categories.
- In most of the product categories, being located in the Mediterranean region has a remarkable impact on churn potentiality. This might indicate a structural difference in distribution channels as the region is a leading touristic destination. Particularly for the shampoo brand, the Mediterranean region variable is significant, together with the change in grocery store expenditures. This designation supports this argument.

5.1.1 Detergent

- Customers with larger households are more likely to churn. A deeper analysis of this segment might be instrumental for the detergent brand to improve customer retention. Targeted marketing and advertising efforts can bring along significant returns. For instance, bundling the product with baby detergents or other child products might be considered.

5.1.2 Shampoo

- When hair conditioner expenditure increases, customers are less likely to churn. This indicates that complimentary personal care products together with the shampoo should also be taken into consideration.
- Customers with increased supermarket and grocery store expenditures are more likely to churn, possibly due to the increased number of available substitute products, distribution problems, or the store's wrong shelf location.

5.1.3 Fabric Conditioner

- Discount markets, supermarkets and grocery stores are the most determinant purchasing channels, although channel effects differ according to the product's quality perception. Changing the preferred channel is decisive for churn. It may be useful to review the efficiency of product distribution channels.
- When there is a price increase, customers are less likely to churn. This might indicate that price was increased less than the customers' expectations or price increase is not a factor influencing loyal consumer behaviour for the products addressing upper segments. Moreover, this may be caused by the price-performance perception of upper segment products from the customer perspective.
- Customers located in the Central Anatolian region are more likely to churn. However, customers located in the Mediterranean region are less likely to churn. This finding might point out that fabric conditioner brand suffers from product distribution problems.
- Upper-class customers are found as more likely to churn for the fabric conditioner brand. Underlining cause may be the availability problem of the product or increased existence of substitute products.

5.1.4 Carbonated Soft Drink (CSD)

- When the alcoholic drinks expenditures increase, customers are more likely to churn. This might indicate that consumers perceive some alcoholic drinks as a substitute for CSD products. Thus, when investigating an edible product, identifying substitute products is critically important.
- Customers with increased salt expenditures are less likely to churn for the CSD brand. This indicates that analyzing the products that reflect a similar lifestyle (i.e., both salt and CSD are signs of an unhealthier lifestyle) can help foresee customers' behavioural changes.
- Upper-class customers are more likely to churn for the CSD brand. This can also be associated with the tendency of switching to a healthier lifestyle.

5.2 Conclusion

FMCG companies deal with difficulties to manage customer retention because the non-contractual setting of the FMCG market enables customers to switch to other brands easily due to the availability of many alternatives in various channels. For this reason, understanding the underlying factors of customer churn behaviour and identifying its early signals is critically essential. Although market research companies collect customer data by conducting surveys, transforming them to actionable business intelligence practices is challenging and time-consuming for FMCG companies. Needless to mention that, providing FMCG companies with solutions empowered by machine learning techniques to predict customer churn and divide customers into segments to handle accordingly will be a competitive differentiator. As a result of our analysis; analyzing customer demographics, changes in expenditures of different channels, and change in purchasing of complementary or substitute products reveals valuable insights concerning future consumer behavior and uncovers the brands' strengths and weaknesses. To sum up, using machine learning applications would enable FMCG companies to generate the best of breed customer-centric strategies and targeted marketing efforts.

References

1. Lipowski, M.: Customer churn as a purchasing journey. In: 32nd IBIMA Conference: 15-16 November 2018, Seville, Spain. Maria Curie-Sklodowska University, Poland (2018)
2. Verbeke, W., Martens, D., Mues, C., Baesens, B.: Building comprehensible customer churn prediction models with advanced rule induction techniques. Expert Syst. Appl. **38**(3), 2354–2364 (2011)
3. Abbasimehr, H., Setak, M., Tarokh, M.J.: A neuro-fuzzy classifier for customer churn prediction. Int. J. Comput. Appl. (0975 – 8887) **19**(8) (2011)
4. Vafeiadis, T., Diamantaras, K.I., Sarigiannidis, G., Chatzisavvas, K.C.: A comparison of machine learning techniques for customer churn prediction. Simul. Model. Pract. Theory **55**, 1–9 (2015)
5. Gallo, A.: The value of keeping the right customers. Harvard Bus. Rev. (2014)
6. Figalist, I., Elsner, C., Bosch, C., Olsson, H.H.: Customer Churn Prediction in B2B Contexts. In: 10th International Conference, ICSOB 2019, Jyväskylä, Finland, 18–20 November 2019, Proceedings (2020). https://www.researchgate.net/publication/338950901_Customer_Churn_Prediction_in_B2B_Contexts
7. Sulistiani, H., Tjahyanto, A.: Comparative analysis of feature selection method to predict customer loyalty. IPTEK, J. Eng. **3**(1) (2017)
8. Isson, J.P.: Unstructured Data Analytics: How to Improve Customer Acquisition, Customer Retention, and Fraud Detection and Prevention. Wiley, Hoboken (2018).ISBN 9781119129752
9. Shetty, P.P., Varsha, C.M., Vadone, V.D., Sarode, S., Pradeep, K.D.: Customers churn prediction with RFM model and building a recommendation system using semi-supervised learning in retail sector. Int. J. Recent Technol. Eng. (IJRTE) **8**(1), 3353–3358 (2019)
10. Buckinx, V., Baesens, B., Van den Peel, D., Van Kenhovel, P., Vanthienen, J.: Using machine learning techniques to predict defection of top clients. Data Mining III (2002). ISBN 1-85312-925-9
11. Ahmad, R., Buttle, F.: Customer retention: a potentially potent marketing management strategy. J. Strat. Mark. **9**(1), 29–45 (2001)
12. Coussement, K.: Improving customer retention management through cost-sensitive learning. Eur. J. Mark. **48**(3/4), 477–495 (2014)
13. Ahn, J.H., Han, S.P., Lee, Y.S.: Customer churn analysis: Churn determinants and mediation effects of partial defection in the Korean mobile telecommunications service industry. Telecommun. Policy **30**, 552–568 (2006)

14. Miguéis, V.L., Van den Poel, D., Camanho, A.S., Falcão e Cunha, J.: Modeling partial customer churn: on the value of first product-category purchase sequences. Expert Syst. Appl. **39**(12), 11250–11256 (2012)
15. Ahmad, A.K., Jafar, A., Aljoumaa, K.: Customer churn prediction in telecom using machine learning in big data platform. J. Big Data **6**(1), 1–24 (2019). https://doi.org/10.1186/s40537-019-0191-6
16. Neslin, S.A., Gupta, S., Kamakura, W., Lu, J., Mason, C.H.: Defection detection: measuring and understanding the predictive accuracy of customer churn models. J. Mark. Res. **43**(2), 204–211 (2006)
17. Griffin, J., Lowenstein, M.W.: Customer WinBack: How to Recapture Lost Customers and Keep Them Loyal. Jossey-Bass Inc., San Francisco (2001)
18. Court, D., Elzinga, D., Mulder, S., Vetvik, O.J.: The Consumer Decision Journey. McKinsey Quarterly, June 2009
19. Glady, N., Baesens, B., Croux, C.: Modeling churn using customer lifetime value. Eur. J. Oper. Res. **197**(1), 402–411 (2009)
20. Lariviere, B., Van den Poel, D.: Predicting customer retention and profitability by using random forests and regression forests techniques. Expert Syst. Appl. **29**(2), 472–484 (2005)
21. Ganesh, J., Arnold, M.J., Reynolds, K.E.: Understanding the customer base of service providers: an examination of the differences between switchers and stayers. J. Mark. **64**(3), 65–87 (2000)
22. Buckinx, W., Van den Poel, D.: Customer base analysis: partial defection of behaviourally loyal clients in a non-contractual FMCG retail setting. Eur. J. Oper. Res. **164**(1), 252–268 (2005)
23. Baesens, B., Verstraeten, G., Van den Poel, D., Egmont-Petersen, M., Van Kenhove, P., Vanthienen, J.: Bayesian network classifiers for identifying the slope of the customer lifecycle of long-life customers. Eur. J. Oper. Res. **156**(2), 508–523 (2004)
24. Meister, S.: Brand Communities for Fast Moving Consumer Goods - An Empirical Study of Members' Behavior and the Economic Relevance for the Marketer. Springer , Hamburg (2012)
25. Murphy, J.A.: The Lifebelt: The Definitive Guide to Managing Customer Retention. Wiley, Chichester (2001)
26. Van den Poel, D., Larivière, B.: Customer attrition analysis for financial services using proportional hazard models. Eur. J. Oper. Res. **157**(1), 196–217 (2004)
27. Athanassopoulos, A.D.: Customer satisfaction cues to support market segmentation and explain switching behavior. J. Bus. Res. **47**(3), 191–207 (2000)
28. Colgate, M.R., Danaher, P.J.: Implementing a customer relationship strategy: the asymmetric impact of poor versus excellent execution. J. Acad. Mark. Sci. **28**(3), 375–387 (2000)
29. Lessmann, S., Voss, S.: Supervised classification for decision support in customer relationship management. In: Intelligent Decision Support: Current Challenges and Approaches, pp. 231–253. Gabler (2008)
30. Burez, J., Van den Poel, D.: Handling class imbalance in customer churn prediction. Expert Syst. Appl. **36**(3), 4626–4636 (2009)
31. Miguéis, V.L., Camanho, A., Falcão e Cunha, J.: Customer attrition in retailing: an application of multivariate adaptive regression splines. Expert Syst. Appl. **40**(16), 6225–6232 (2013)
32. Jahromi, A.T., Stakhovych, S., Ewing, M.: The impact of personalised incentives on the profitability of customer retention campaigns. J. Mark. Manag. 1–21 (2017)
33. Calciu, M., Crie, D., Micheaux, A.: Recognising dangerous drop out incidents as opposed to accidents to improve the efficiency of triggers reducing customer churn. application to RFM customer segments of a fast moving customer goods retail chain. In: Proceedings International Marketing Trends Conference 2015 (2015)

34. Sulistiani, H., Tjahyanto, A.: Comparative analysis of feature selection method to predict customer loyalty. IPTEK J. Eng. **3**(1) (2017)
35. Shoaib, T.: Customers Churn Prediction in Retail Store (2018). https://doi.org/10.13140/RG.2.2.30545.38242

Crowdsourcing as a Tool Supporting Intra-city Communication

Łukasz Przysucha[⊠] [iD]

Wroclaw University of Economics and Business, Komandorska 118/120,
53-345 Wroclaw, Poland
lukasz.przysucha@ue.wroc.pl

Abstract. All over the world, we observe a trend of people moving from rural and poorly urbanized areas to larger cities and metropolises. This is due to the development of civilization, the need for work, and a greater quality of life. Sudden population growth in cities is associated with many problems that are often quite difficult to locate and repair. The idea of Smart City was created to improve urban processes, create a concept for the development of all areas of the city so that all elements in it are synchronized and harmonized with each other. The article compares Smart solutions from Singapore, Zürich and Wroclaw. The idea of the civic budget and the interaction between local administration, residents and stakeholders were also discussed. The author describes the concept of using crowdsourcing to acquire knowledge by city leaders, as well as the impact of these processes on the development of Smart City.

Keywords: Knowledge management · Crowdsourcing · Smart city · Knowledge acquisition

1 Introduction

Current statistics indicate the global trend of population migration from rural to urban areas [1]. In 1950, only 30% of the total population lived in cities, now it is almost 55%, while in 2050 it is over 65% of the population. Although the global population growth rate has dropped from 2.2% a year 50 years ago to 1.05% a year now, it is assumed that the earth will be inhabited by 8 billion people in 2024 and 9 billion people in 2043 [2]. It should be noted that the growth rate of inhabitants in cities is due to both the global migration trend and the population growth on Earth. Along with the increase in the population in cities as well as the size of metropolitan areas, problems arise in the efficient functioning of all elements of the city, starting from traffic jams, pollution, information chaos, ensuring an adequate amount of energy, which is distributed to various sources of obtaining it, as well as the lack of adequate living comfort caused by many other factors. In the 2000s, people began looking for solutions that would solve urban problems and improve their operation. At the beginning, IT companies IBM and Cisco invested a lot of money in projects developing the idea of a city that can be smart.

© IFIP International Federation for Information Processing 2021
Published by Springer Nature Switzerland AG 2021
E. Mercier-Laurent et al. (Eds.): AI4KM 2021, IFIP AICT 614, pp. 104–116, 2021.
https://doi.org/10.1007/978-3-030-80847-1_7

An extremely important element of every smart city is the management of information and knowledge possessed by residents and stakeholders. The city can acquire knowledge from residents and their needs in many ways. One of them is crowdsourcing which allows the knowledge of the crowd to be shared with the other party - in the case of cities, it can be local governments, presidents, mayors. In this case, the proper mechanism for distributing knowledge and information between all parties - city decision makers, residents, universities, business, as well as specific procedures allowing for effective management of this information and the needs of other parties must be extremely important.

The article consists of four parts. The first one focuses on the description of the Smart City idea. The first chapter describes Smart City, presents the history of the idea's creation and the division into usefulness and generations. The author presents areas in the standard Smart City division and examples of the Smart concept. The next chapter presents the practical use of intelligent solutions in selected cities: Singapore, Zürich and Wroclaw. It has described the mechanism of the civic budget and the mechanisms of interaction between residents, stakeholders and local authorities. The last part of the article is devoted to the description of crowdsourcing processes. The author indicates the place of crowdsourcing in the knowledge flow diagram, describes the advantages of crowdsourcing and the scope of direct impact.

2 Smart City

The idea of a Smart City is a relatively new concept implemented and used by central and local government authorities, business entities and urban residents them.

A smart city [3–5] is an urban area that uses information and communication technologies to increase the interactivity and efficiency of urban infrastructure and its components, as well as to raise awareness among residents. A city is intelligent if it invests in human capital [6], develops educational institutions, supports residents in managing knowledge and the flow of information inside the city. Recently, the aspect of civic participation and crowdsourcing has also been noticeable as an element activating both residents and other stakeholders operating in the area of a given urban agglomeration.

Smart City has its generations closely related to the development of the idea. The first person to divide Smart City into "versions" 1.0, 2.0. and 3.0 was Boyd Cohen, who dealt with the subject of Smart City and its development. Depending on the initiator of Smart City activities, three types of city development can be indicated: driven by the development and activity of technology companies located in a given metropolis, the intensification of activities of municipal authorities, which themselves are committed to creating new schemes and concepts for Smart City, and thanks to the initiatives of residents who they are the driving force behind Smart City projects (nowadays, quite a popular activity are civic budgets, which focus on drawing up investment tasks by residents and voting for them by others, and the result is the implementation of the most popular ideas).

It is worth dividing cities according to their models and generations [7]:

A. *Smart City 1.0*

Smart City 1.0 is created and inspired by technologies available in a given place and time. The initiator is a technology company that offers new technological solutions and wants to sell them. It is the simplest form of creating a smart city that does not fully solve the problems in the city. Often, offers are not dedicated to a given agglomeration, are not personalized and ultimately do not solve problems. Examples of such cities are Songdo in South Korea and Masdar in the United Arab Emirates. They are widely criticized for focusing too much on technology rather than the lives of ordinary residents.

B. *Smart City 2.0*

The Smart City 2.0 model is based on the development of the city by the administration. It is the local government that sets the pace of the city's technological development and imposes the concepts and paths of Smart City solutions. In this case, the needs of technology companies and the sale of their products are balanced, as well as the needs of residents living in the city and the usefulness of solutions implemented in the process of creating a Smart City. The final effect of the implementation and the obtained results are important. Currently, it is the most popular Smart City model in the world, but this is starting to change and the 3.0 model, which will be described in the next section, is becoming more and more fashionable. The most popular elements of this model are:

-   the use of big data,
-   use of electric public transport,
-   intelligent transport systems,
-   intelligent city lighting systems,
-   publicly available technologies such as USB chargers, free city internet,
-   city transport synchronized with electronic passenger systems.

C. *Smart City 3.0*

The Smart City 3.0 model focuses mainly on the role of citizens in shaping the city. It is a modern approach to the Smart City idea. The main factor determining the speed of urban development in this case is the involvement of residents. It is in this model that crowdsourcing can be used. First, however, it is necessary to determine how much residents can get involved and what factors should be met by the city in order to cooperate with residents to the maximum. The role of local government = creating space and opportunities to use the diverse potential of citizens. All kinds of development of interactions between city authorities, residents and stakeholders such as universities (education) and business are a manifestation of the Smart City 3.0 model.

The Smart City concept covers all areas of the city's development. Each resident lives with Smart City in a different way and with a different frequency. Below is a breakdown of the main areas of Smart City according to the Author. The table also includes the main aspects of the use of Smart City technology in given areas and examples of implemented solutions.

It is worth noting that despite the fact that all areas are completely different from the others, they are easy to combine and it is possible to create interdisciplinary solutions between modules, e.g. in the area of Smart Mobility, tracking of public transport through electronic boards was used, while in Smart Management it was proposed to create an urban resident portal. By combining these two concepts, it is possible to create a resident application that will include, functionality focusing on tracking vehicles remotely, e.g. on a phone (Table 1).

Table 1. Smart city areas.

Area name	Topics covering the area	Examples of smart concepts
Smart mobility	Sustainable transport system [8], IT systems supporting the use of urban transport, optimization of traffic in the city	Public transport tracking through electronic timetables at stops
Smart management	Activation of residents and stakeholders to participate in public life, civic programs and enabling voting and referenda, clear and transparent government actions	IT system enabling remote voting, resident's on-line portal
Smart environment	Generating environmental awareness, verifying air quality, using renewable energy sources	Systems supporting waste removal, creating parks and green areas, measuring air pollution, measuring water purity
Smart people	Investing in human capital, cooperation between residents, universities, business and the government, qualifications, knowledge management	Knowledge groups, competence bank, intra-city system of interpersonal communication
Smart business	innovation in business, creating areas of entrepreneurship and business zones, flexible labor market, low unemployment, cooperation with international entities	Investor support, lower taxes and reliefs for business, business events
Smart everyday life and communication	Health protection, universal access to culture, high level of education, tourist attractiveness	Social media for residents, smart shopping with RFID module, search people by personality

3 Selected Smart Initiatives

Nowadays, all cities in developed countries want to be Smart. There is a fashion for modern technologies, efficient transport, good, fast Internet, healthy lifestyle and clean air and the environment.

In this chapter, the author compared several smart cities and showed the paths for further development of the agglomeration.

3.1 Singapore

Singapore is number one in the Smart City category in most rankings. It has held this position for many years and is still in the lead. It is worth checking what the city has implemented and how it has improved the daily activities of its inhabitants.

The city-state that is discussed has a very developed awareness of being "smart". A lot of initiatives are created among the residents (Smart City 3.0). They are implemented in many aspects of life and serve both communication between decision-makers, stakeholders and residents as well as in the daily life of all citizens.

Smart Nation is an initiative of the government of Singapore, which focuses on the use of new technologies, networks of big data, elements of Business Intelligence for the development of civil society and the development of intra-city communication, as well as increasing the comfort of everyday life. The Smart Nation Initiative was presented by Prime Minister Lee Hsien Loong on November 24, 2014. The whole initiative is very money-consuming, but the effects are directly visible, and the government keeps statistics to improve ideas and increase use.

Below is an overview of the most important projects along with the effects of their implementation (Table 2).

Table 2. Smart initiatives in Singapore.

Project name	Description of the initiative and effects of implementation
MyTransport.SG	The application fully personalizes itself to the user's favorite services. The traveler can locate stops in real mode, get information about taxis, parking places, information about traffic jams and live traffic, information for cyclists. 140 000 commuters enjoy one-stop (personalized journey planning daily)
PayNow	A service supporting money transfers among users. It was launched by the Singapore Banks Association (ABS) on July 10, 2017. It operates on a peer-to-peer basis. It enables free transfer of funds among retail clients in real time. A mobile phone number or a NRIC / FIN number is required

(*continued*)

Table 2. (*continued*)

Project name	Description of the initiative and effects of implementation
Healthy365	Healthy 365 is a mobile application for Singapore citizens and residents. Its aim is to encourage users to a healthier lifestyle. The app connects to fitness monitoring devices. It mainly verifies the number of daily steps and the time spent on exercises. According to data from February 2019 [9], 1.7 million registrations were made in the application. It is quite popular and supports the health of a large part of citizens
Business Grants Portal	It is a website supporting businesses operating in the country. Offers a straightforward route to grant application. It is very intuitive
Smart Gravitrap	Devices support the fight against dengue, which is endemic in Singapore. The prototype attracts and catches dengue-carrying female Aedes mosquitoes looking for places to lay eggs. About 50000 traps deployed in HDB estates to monitor Aedes mosquito population
Dementia Friends	The Dementia-Friendly Singapore initiative aims to build a more caring and inclusive society for persons with dementia and their caregivers. More than 40 seniors with dementia assisted trough app community

3.2 Zürich

Another example of a Smart city classified at the top of the Smart City Index ranking is Zürich. It is at the major banking and financial centers of the world. In the Smart City Index 2019 ranking, Zürich was second, and third in the Smart City Index 2020 ranking. Below is the ranking of the top 30 places with the highest Smart City Index scores. They are cities from wealthy nations, mainly from Europe, Asia, North America and Australia (Fig. 1).

The Smart City project in Zürich focuses on 4 main aspects:

A. *Focus on target groups and action plans*
   The innovations and assumptions created are designed with long-term operation in mind. It is not only the present that counts, but also the future generations living in the agglomeration. Projects are created with target groups and specific utility in mind. People's needs and focused development are extremely important. All solutions are thoroughly analyzed beforehand and they are provided with appropriate, final acceptance.

B. *Integration of all groups of people living and working in Zürich*
   Creating a network between all groups in the city - establishing cooperation between residents and stakeholders. Promotion of cooperation between business, education, residents, local administration and cultural units working in the area of the Zürich agglomeration. With the use of technology, it is possible to increase the activation

City	Smart City Rank 2020	Change	Smart City Rating 2020	Smart City Rank 2019	Smart City Rating 2019
Singapore	1	— (0)	AAA	1	AAA
Helsinki	2	▲ (+6)	AA	8	A
Zurich	3	▼ (-1)	AA	2	AAA
Auckland	4	▲ (+2)	AA	6	A
Oslo	5	▼ (-2)	AA	3	AA
Copenhagen	6	▼ (-1)	AA	5	AA
Geneva	7	▼ (-3)	AA	4	AA
Taipei City	8	▼ (-1)	A	7	A
Amsterdam	9	▲ (+2)	A	11	A
New York	10	▲ (+28)	A	38	BBB
Munich	11	new	A		
Washington D.C.	12	▲ (+19)	A	31	BBB
Dusseldorf	13	▼ (-3)	A	10	A
Brisbane	14	▲ (+13)	A	27	BBB
London	15	▲ (+5)	A	20	BBB
Stockholm	16	▲ (+9)	A	25	BBB
Manchester	17	new	A		
Sydney	18	▼ (-4)	A	14	A
Vancouver	19	▼ (-6)	A	13	A
Melbourne	20	▲ (+4)	A	24	BBB
Montreal	21	▼ (-5)	A	16	A
Hamburg	22	new	A		
Newcastle	23	new	A		
Bilbao	24	▼ (-15)	BBB	9	A
Vienna	25	▼ (-8)	BBB	17	BBB
Los Angeles	26	▲ (+9)	BBB	35	BBB
San Francisco	27	▼ (-15)	BBB	12	A
The Hague	28	▲ (+1)	BBB	29	BBB
Rotterdam	29	▲ (+7)	BBB	36	BBB
Toronto	30	▼ (-15)	BBB	15	A

Fig. 1. Smart city index by international institute for management [10].

of residents and integration of all social groups. Appropriate use of technology can develop people's awareness to create a Smart Society.

C. *Reliability, security and openness*

Zürich focused on data security, reliability of its infrastructure and availability of information. Local administration data is publicly available, while personal data has the highest priority of security and is properly hidden. Giving reading attributes and access to appropriate groups is crucial for the development of Smart City.

D. *Investments in project development and great flexibility*

The city supports appropriate development, investments and processes that accelerate technological change. Modern applications are tested and implemented depending on the test results obtained and the final usefulness for the community. Modern solutions are introduced relatively early compared to other cities, and there are often project pilots that do not burden the budget too much, and guarantee innovation on a global scale.

"Zürich 2035 Strategies" is a strategy for the Zürich agglomeration assuming the achievement of long-term goals and appropriate development steps by 2035. The city focuses on sustainable development, adequate generation fertility, and implements appropriate programs to optimize energy management, housing policy and mobility.

Below is a diagram presenting the main questions regarding the city's functioning in 20 years (asked in 2015 when the project was launched) (Fig. 2).

Strategies Zurich 2035
basis for a Smart City Strategy

Strategies Zurich 2035

What will we live on today and tomorrow?

How do we maintain our quality of life?

How do we organise ourselves?

01 Attractive business location
02 Stable public finances

03 Sustainable growth
04 Social solidarity
05 Sustainable energy and environmental conservation
06 Digital city

07 Cooperative representation of interests
08 Internal organisation

Stadt Zürich
Open Data

cpaas.io Smart City Zürich and Open Data Zürich
14. December 2017, Seite 4

Fig. 2. Strategies Zürich 2035 [11].

Importantly, the strategy is long-term and is continued by successive local governments. What matters is the good of the city and the community, rather than the particular interests of politicians. The first question focuses on what we are doing now and what we will be doing in the future. For Zürich, the financial stability of the city and its inhabitants is extremely important. The city's financial stability and an attractive location for doing business have an impact on credibility and stability (investors decide to open companies in a city that is predictable and stable in terms of politics). The second question concerns caring for the quality of life and choosing the right paths of sustainable development, creating social sensitivity and solidarity, proper use of energy and digitization of the city. The third question "How do we organize ourself" concerns concerns the wider community surrounding the city, international contacts, perception of the agglomeration in the world, cooperation with business entities located in other cities and countries.

3.3 Wroclaw

The last example of a Smart City is Wroclaw, the largest city in western Poland. The city has been on the Smart City Index list for many years and in many rankings classifying agglomerations that implement innovative projects and focus on Smart Society. As in most Smart City, local administration policy focuses on cooperation between residents, administration and business. Education and culture can also be qualified as stakeholders throughout the scheme. The development strategy assumes 8 main pillars of Smart City:

A. *Management*
   Management consists of three elements that create a coherent whole: policy and strategies, e-government and open self-government. Thanks to the implementation of these solutions, the office is more open to citizens, the availability of its services and the time spent by citizens on activities performed in it increases.

B. *Economy*
   Projects to stimulate local entrepreneurship and increase the innovativeness of companies operating in the market, factors stimulating productivity and openness with the global market.

C. *Lifestyle*
   It is the way people function in the city and use the range of its offers, as well as the way they influence the city themselves. All other pillars influence the level of lifestyle and quality of life.

D. *People*
   Projects developing the involvement, creativity and awareness of Smart Society in society. Focus on the idea of sustainable living.

E. *Education*
   Sustainable and integrated development is not possible without investing in education and knowledge, including education of the elderly, elimination of e-excluded and entrepreneurship education.

F. *Mobility*
   The area of mobility is an integrated transport system, ICT and supporting green transport.

G. *Infrastructure*
   Projects related to the development of infrastructure and the provision of the latest technologies in this area [12, 13].

H. *Environment*
   Projects supporting the purification of the environment, smog, waste segregation, etc. It is the sustainable development of the city through proper resource management, investments in green technologies, public transport and pedestrians.

Wroclaw as a Smart City introduced the possibility of co-deciding the inhabitants about investments and undertakings in the city. Civic budget (in other words: participatory budget) - is a process that allows residents to discuss and directly influence decisions about allocating part of the public budget to projects proposed directly by citizens.

The main advantages of the Civic Budget include strengthening civic attitudes and shared responsibility for the city, showing the inhabitants the mechanisms of the city's functioning and better understanding of the inhabitants by local authorities.

4 Implementation of Crowdsourcing Processes

Due to the large development of the agglomeration, cities have problems with proper communication and information flow. Local authorities are wondering how to solve communication bottlenecks and how to meet the needs of residents. Crowdsourcing [14] is a tool that can support the exchange of information in the city. Crowdsourcing is a process by which the organization (company, public institution, non-profit organization) outsources the tasks performed traditionally by employees to an unidentified, usually very wide group of people in the form of open call. Importantly, for many years it was believed that crowdsourcing was possible only in organizations, companies, workplaces in order to obtain information from employees or collaborators. At present, it is possible to allow crowdsourcing in the Smart City area to improve communication between residents, local authorities and stakeholders. In this case, local authorities can obtain information through social media channels, websites, direct actions with residents and many other ways to facilitate communication between the two parties.

The chart below shows the place of crowdsourcing in the knowledge flow diagram (Fig. 3).

In Smart City ventures, the diffusion of knowledge between decision makers and stakeholders leads to a reduction of the information gap. Knowledge gaps in decision-makers in cities force the acquisition of knowledge from residents and stakeholders. It is implemented through crowdsourcing. In turn, crowdsourcing uses modern ICT tools that use the Internet, Social Media as well as stationary and mobile applications. Crowdsourcing forces commitment that is directly related to motivation. Commitment supports and creates the knowledge of residents, which together with the knowledge of an experienced local government creates Collective Intelligence. Crowdsourcing is a form of Collective Intelligence.

The main advantages of crowdsourcing are: [15].

1. saves time and money (the crowd generates ideas much faster and preparing a website is definitely cheaper than paying for the work of a narrow, specialized team).
2. variety of submitted projects and their originality (many perspectives and points of view).
3. obtaining information on the needs and expectations of residents.
4. creating an engaged community.
5. marketing and promotional benefits

Crowdsourcing directly affects: [16].

1. contact between residents and decision makers
2. finding an information gap in the city
3. exchange of knowledge throughout the city

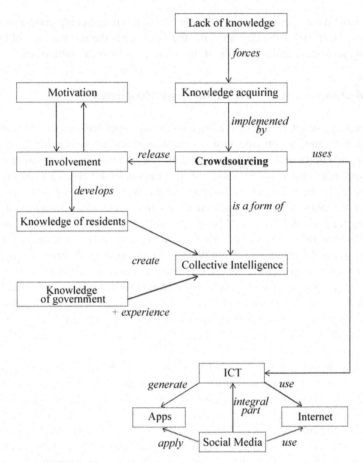

Fig. 3. The place of crowdsourcing in the knowledge flow diagram.

4. better understanding of the residents' needs
5. the ability to influence city decisions
6. creating social units

5   Conclusions

As cities develop, new problems arise. The idea of Smart City [17] is aimed at increasing the comfort of life of inhabitants living in a given agglomeration, optimization of information processes, better knowledge management, proper management of energy and available natural resources, improvement of traffic and public transport, and many others. The author focused on describing the acquisition of knowledge from the inhabitants. This process has many advantages and will certainly improve communication between residents, local decision-makers and stakeholders.

Thanks to crowdsourcing in the area of Smart City, the municipal government can save time and money when making decisions, there is a much greater variety of ideas, knowledge from the crowd results in standardization of expectations and directions, and develops originality of submitted projects. Decision-makers get information on the needs and expectations of residents. The community becomes more involved and motivated. There is a diffusion of knowledge and a full information cycle inside the city. Knowledge is sourcing, processed, modified and shared [18, 19]. An important element is bilateral exchange, interaction between decision-makers and residents.

References

1. World Migration Report. International Organization for Migration (2020)
2. RahimifardLeila, S., Sheldrick, E., Woolley, J., Colwill, M.: How to Manufacture a Sustainable Future for 9 Billion People in 2050. In: Nee, A., Song, B., Ong, S.K. (eds.) Re-engineering Manufacturing for Sustainability, pp. 1–8. Springer, Singapore (2013). https://doi.org/10.1007/978-981-4451-48-2_1
3. Dameri, R.P.: Smart city definition, goals and performance. In: Smart City Implementation. PI, pp. 1–22. Springer, Cham (2017). https://doi.org/10.1007/978-3-319-45766-6_1
4. Caragliu, A., Del Bo, C., Nijkamp, P.: Smart cities in Europe. J. Urban Technol. 18, 65–82 (2011)
5. Dameri, R.P., Rosenthal-Sabroux, C.: Smart city and value creation. In: Dameri, R.P., Rosenthal-Sabroux, C. (eds.) Smart City. PI, pp. 1–12. Springer, Cham (2014). https://doi.org/10.1007/978-3-319-06160-3_1
6. Mercier-Laurent, E.: Managing intellectual capital in knowledge economy. In: Mercier-Laurent, E., Owoc, M.L., Boulanger, D. (eds.) Artificial Intelligence for Knowledge Management, AI4KM 2014. IFIP Advances in Information and Communication Technology, vol. 469, pp. 165–179. Springer, Cham (2015). https://doi.org/10.1007/978-3-319-28868-0_10
7. Cohen, B.: The 3 generations of smart cities. In: Inside the development of the technology driven city, vol. 2 (2015)
8. Gontarz, M., Sulich, A.: The sustainable transportation solutions: smart shuttle example. In: Soliman, K.S. (ed.) Vision 2025: Education Excellence and Management of Innovations through Sustainable Economic Competitive Advantage, pp. 10833–10840. International Business Information Management Association (2020)
9. Smart Nation Singapore. www.pmo.gov.sg
10. Smart City Index. International Institute for Management Development, Switzerland (2020)
11. Grüebler, M.: Smart city Zürich and open data Zürich. In: City Platform as a Service Stakeholder Summit, p. 4 (2017)
12. Pondel, J., Pondel, M.: Stages and areas of the use of IT tools supporting the management of IT projects. Manag. Sci. Nauki o Zarządzaniu 23(1), 45–57 (2018)
13. Weichbroth, P.: Delivering usability in IT products: empirical lessons from the field. Int. J. Software Eng. Knowl. Eng. 28(07), 1027–1045 (2018)
14. Przysucha, Ł.: Implementation of Crowdsourcing as an integral element of communication engineering in the Smart City concept. In: Revista Ibérica de Sistemas e Tecnologias de Informação, pp. 97–108 (2020)
15. Aitamurto, T., Leiponen, A., Tee, R.: The Promise of Idea Crowdsourcing – Benefits, Contexts, Limitations, Nokia White Paper, 1 (30) (2011)
16. Brabham, D.C.: Crowdsourcing as a model for problem solving an introduction and cases. Converg. Int. J. Res. New Media Technol. (2008)
17. Mercier-Laurent, E.: Knowledge management &risk management in FedCSIS 2016, pp. 1369–1373 (2016)

18. Rothe, R., Rutkowska, M., Sulich, A.: Smart cities and challenges for European integration. In: Proceedings of the 4th International Conference on European Integration 2018, ICEI 2018, Ostrava, pp. 1240–1246 (2018)
19. Owoc, M. L.: Benefits of knowledge acquisition systems for management. An empirical study. In 2015 Federated Conference on Computer Science and Information Systems (FedCSIS), 1691–1698). IEEE 2015
20. Owoc, M., Weichbroth, P.: Dynamical Aspects of Knowledge Evolution. In: Mercier-Laurent, E., Boulanger, D. (eds.) AI4KM 2017. IAICT, vol. 571, pp. 52–65. Springer, Cham (2019). https://doi.org/10.1007/978-3-030-29904-0_5

The Importance of the Internet of Things for Smart Cities

Anna Reklewska[✉]

Wroclaw University of Economics and Business, Komandorska 118/120,
53-345 Wroclaw, Poland

Abstract. The concepts of Smart City and the Internet of Things have become a frequent topic of discussion in recent years. Due to the changes that take place in cities and the challenges cities face, modern solutions are sought to improve their functioning and enable their development. The aim of this paper was to demonstrate whether the Internet of Things is an essential element of a smart city. In the first part of the paper, the author focused on an introductory presentation of the basic problems of modern cities and defining the concept of Smart City. In the second part, the author focused on the Internet of Things and the description of selected technologies, with particular emphasis on their usefulness in the city. The last part of the paper showed how many elements of modern cities are closely related to the Internet of Things. The author presented real solutions implemented in smart cities, indicating that solutions based on the Internet of Things can be useful in every area of a smart city.

Keywords: Smart City · Internet of things · Artificial intelligence

1 Introduction

Modern cities are facing many challenges. There is mention of significant natural resource use and environmental protection, an aging population, management of urban services, and many others. Those cities that successfully manage to meet at least some of these needs are often called smart cities. However, it is important to consider what makes a city smart. Apart from the enormous influence of city dwellers and authorities, their creativity, skills and knowledge, the second factor is definitely technology. The main aim of this paper is to demonstrate how important the Internet of Things is for smart cities. The author of this paper decided to combine two concepts: Internet of Things and Smart City to verify whether a smart city could exist without solutions based on the Internet of Things and to present the potential benefits of their use in modern cities. In the first part of the paper, the author focused on the smart city concept, explaining its definitions. In the next section, the author presented the concept of the Internet of Things focusing in particular on the technologies used in cities. In the last part of the paper, the author focused on both concepts, showing the benefits of their combination and examples of already functioning solutions. The summary includes the issues on which the author of the paper would like to concentrate in the future.

Published by Springer Nature Switzerland AG 2021
E. Mercier-Laurent et al. (Eds.): AI4KM 2021, IFIP AICT 614, pp. 117–129, 2021.
https://doi.org/10.1007/978-3-030-80847-1_8

2 Why Do We Need Smart Cities?

2.1 The Needs of Modern Cities

Modern cities face many challenges. The constant migration of people into cities causes not only development but also numerous problems. "The future of cities" report released in 2019 by the European Commission points to the most important of these [1]:

1) Affordable housing
   The first challenge is the financialisation of housing and concerns affordability, responsibility and living conditions. For example, table number one shows how long a qualified city dweller has to work to be able to afford to buy a 60 square metre flat. These data show how many times the typical sales price is higher than the media. annual income of the household.

Table 1. Years a skilled worker needs to work to be able to buy a 60 m^2 near the city center.

City	Number of years
Hong Kong	Between 20 to 25
London	Between 13 to 17
Paris	Between 12 to 17
Singapore	Between 11 to 14
Tokyo	Between 10 to 14
New York	Between 10 to 13
Amsterdam	Between 8 to 11
Vancouver	Between 7 to 10
Sydney	Between 7 to 9
Munich	Between 7 to 9

As the table above shows, real estate markets in many large cities are difficult to access or completely inaccessible. Another report prepared by Deloitte in 2018 shows that the average annual increase in property prices in the European Union was 5% over three years [2]. The authors of the report indicate that the problem is the effects of the debt crisis or the weak and slow administration of state-building authorities (Table 1).

2) Mobility
   The mobility of people and goods is one of the fundamental determinants of urban development. In recent years, cities have been dominated by car transport, which has had a negative impact on the environment or health and has made it more difficult to move around the city through traffic jams lasting several kilometers. In order to prevent these negative effects, cities are trying to implement initiatives such as the creation of parking zones around cities or charging for entry into the city center, which should, however, be combined with investment in the development of public transport.

According to the authors of the report "The future of cities", mobility is one of the sectors that will change the most as a result of technological innovation and behavioral changes.

3) Provision of services

The nature of services in cities is constantly changing. These are mainly influenced by the widespread use of modern technology and the Internet. Nowadays, having specialised services focused on city dwellers and visitors is becoming an essential element of a city. It is expected that these changes will be even more noticeable in the future.

4) Ageing

According to "The future of cities" report, life expectancy will rise to over 88 years by 2070, while the ratio of older to younger people will double. Population ageing is a global trend, but it is a particular problem in places where the population is declining. This means that rising health care costs or pension payments will have to be covered by an ever-narrower workforce.

Table 2. Increase in a share of the population aged 65 years and over between 2009 and 2019 in selected countries [3].

Country	Increase in percentage points
Finland	5.1
Lichtenstein	5.0
Czech Republic	4.7
Malta	4.5
Netherlands	4.2
Poland	3.8
Portugal	3.8
Albania	3.7
Denmark	3.7
France	3.6
Slovenia	3.4
Serbia	3.3

Cities will have to learn to respond to these changes by also adapting their services such as health, mobility or social policies. Age-friendly cities can be characterised by age-appropriate elements such as transport, outdoor space and housing, communication and information (Table 2).

5) Urban Health

Living in a city can be linked to health in many ways. On the one hand, interconnected networks of people make it easier for diseases to spread; on the other, the fast lifestyle typical of city dwellers or environmental pollution contributes to the development of diseases of civilizations.

6) Environmental footprint

The use of natural resources puts enormous pressure on the environment and leads to irreversible consequences such as water stress, biodiversity loss or climate change. In addition, providing city dwellers with access to water, energy and food requires the use of the natural environment beyond urban borders. Most city dwellers live far from agricultural and production systems so may not be aware of the impact they have on the environment.

7) Climate action

Cities are a major factor in climate change. It is estimated that they are responsible for 75% of global carbon dioxide emissions. At the same time, rising global temperatures are causing rising sea levels, increasing weather events such as floods, droughts and storms. All these events have a costly impact on basic urban services, infrastructure, housing and human health. Only coordinated action at the global and local level can bring about positive change. Cities are beginning to see the need to innovate to protect the environment, so they are using renewable energy sources, reducing urban transport and much more.

The needs of cities identified above are not all that exists. This short description is only a starting point for further development of the topic. However, they show how many different challenges the city authorities are facing. In response, cities began to look for different solutions. The first smart cities also began to appear.

2.2 Smart City Definition

The Smart City concept is becoming more popular every year. Cities are outdoing themselves with ideas for improvements and innovations that will make their functioning even more efficient. There is actually no one proper definition of a smart city but they are often described as "high-tech", "innovative" or "green". In general, a smart city is a city that uses technology to provide services and solve urban problems, but in research and scientific sources, we can find more detailed description. One of the definitions is that "a smart city is (…) a city which invests in ICT enhanced governance and participatory processes to define appropriate public service and transportation investments that can ensure sustainable socio-economic development, enhanced quality-of-life, and intelligent management of natural resources" [4]. Another definition is "The smart city concept describes the ability for utilizing the capacity of a city/community to create and adopt solutions for overcoming challenges and seizing opportunities that help transform cities/municipalities to more prosperous and livable places for all stakeholders. The ecosystem of implemented solutions is what defines how smart a city or community is" [5]. What these and many other definitions have in common is the use of modern technology in cities and ensuring sustainability.

Some areas of the city are particularly often highlighted when talking about the smart city. The table below shows the factors of smart city with their description and examples (Table 3).

Table 3. Factors of smart cities

Defined area	Description and examples
Smart Economy	All actions that aim to strengthen the economy - Improving the attractiveness of the city, - Looking for new companies and investors, - Investing in qualified talents, - Flexibility of the labour market, - Using Information and Communication Technologies (ICT) for business
Smart Mobility	Improving the efficiency and quality of transport services and new mobility solutions - Sustainable and safe transport systems, - Innovative logistics systems, - Combining private and public transport - New forms of transportation (electric cars, bike sharing)
Smart Environment	Managing the environment to improve its quality and to ensure the well-being of cities' dwellers - Environmental protection, - Sustainable resource management, - Water management, - Managing pollution, - Reduction of waste production
Smart People	Involvement of city dwellers in its functioning and development - Level of qualification, - Creativity, - Participation in public life - Labor market opportunities, - Smart ways of education, - Lifelong learning
Smart Living	Increasing quality of life for city dwellers and visitors - Health conditions, - Cultural facilities, - Quality of education, - Smart homes, - Smart workplaces, - Social platforms, - Safety
Smart Governance	Intelligent management of public administration, connection between government and all stakeholders - city dwellers, business etc. - Transparent governance, - Political strategies, - Crowdsourcing, - Active participation in city management

As shown in the table above, the concept of a smart city can relate to many elements. It can be discussed about smart city solutions in many contexts, having in mind **the human factor** (city dwellers and visitors), **the technological factor** (smart technologies) and **the institutional factor** (governance and policy) [6].

3 Internet of Things

3.1 Internet of Things Characteristics

The term "Internet of Things" (IoT) was first used in 1999 during a presentation by Kevin Ashton at Procter&Gamble company, but the concept only began to gain popularity around 2010 [7]. Since that year, the term has increasingly featured in scientific publications and business campaigns. However, it is in vain to look for its unique, valid definition. As in the case of the 'smart city', we can find many descriptions and characteristics of the Internet of Things, but in general, it can be said that IoT is "An open and comprehensive network of intelligent objects that have the capacity to auto-organize, share information, data and resources, reacting and acting in face of situations and changes in the environment" [8]. Internet of Things can be understood as a world where almost anything can be connected and communicate in an intelligent way. Figure 1 below shows components of the Internet of Things.

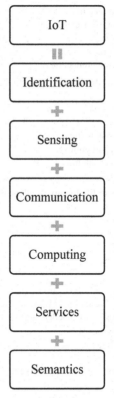

Fig. 1. Internet of Things components (Source: A. Al-Fuqaha, M. Guizani, M. Mohammadi, M. Aledhari, M. Ayyash, *Internet of things: A survey on enabling technologies, protocols, and applications*, "IEEE Communications Surveys & Tutorials" 2015)

We can identify six key elements [9]:

1) Identification

   Identification is needed to match services with their demand. We can use multiple identification methods, such as electronic product codes (EPCs) and ubiquitous codes (uCodes). Additionally, addressing IoT objects is important to differentiate between the object identifier and its address. Identification methods are used to deliver a unique identity for each object on the network.

2) Sensing

   Sensing in the context of the Internet of things means collecting data from various objects on the network and sending it to a data warehouse, database or the cloud. The collected data is then processed and analyzed to take operations based on the requested services.

3) Communication

   IoT communication technologies connect objects together to provide specific services. IoT communication protocols are communication modes that provide optimal security for data exchanged between devices. Examples of communication protocols could be WiFi, Bluetooth, IEEE or RFID. More information on specific IoT technologies can be found in Subsect. 2.2.

4) Computing

   This refers to the computing units and software applications that constitute the computing capability of IoT. Over the years, various hardware platforms have been developed to run IoT applications. In addition, many software platforms are used to provide IoT functionality.

5) Services

   The authors of the discussed classification propose to divide IoT services into four types: Identity-related Services, Information Aggregation Services, Collaborative-Aware Services and Ubiquitous Services. Identity-related Services are the most basic but also the most important because any application that wants to bring objects into the virtual world must identify them. Information Aggregation Services collect sensory measurements that need to be communicated to IoT applications. Collaborative-Aware Services use the data obtained to make decisions and react appropriately. Ubiquitous services aim to deliver collaboration-aware services at any time to anyone anywhere who needs them.

6) Semantics

   In the context of the Internet of Things, semantics refers to the ability of machines to intelligently mine knowledge to provide required services. Knowledge mining includes resource discovery and exploitation and information modelling. Semantic includes analyzing data in order to make the appropriate decisions.

The Internet of Things is an evolving concept thanks to technological developments, so more and more applications can be identified. Figure 2 shows examples of its most common applications.

As shown in Fig. 2 above, one of the applications of the Internet of Things could be smart cities, so in the following part of the paper, we will focus more on this application.

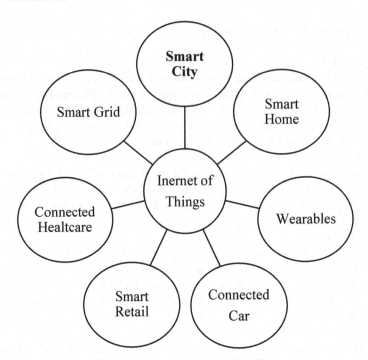

Fig. 2. Internet of Things applications

3.2 IoT Technologies for Smart Cities

The Internet of Things is a network that uses standard communication protocols, and the Internet is their convergence point. A growing number of Internet-enabled devices that can connect and communicate with each other and, as a result of the information they collect, are able to sense various situations in the environment, form their own network connections and generate entirely new information, becoming an integral part of the Internet. The selected technologies related to the Internet of Things are presented below [10].

1) Radio-Frequency Identification (RFID)
    RFID enables the communication between a powered reader and an unpowered tag, a type of electronic label with a unique identification number. The range of RFID communication significantly depends on the parameters of the reader and the size and type of tag. RFID provides applications such as smart grids, including object tracking and location, healthcare applications or parking management.
2) Near Field-Communication (NFC)
    NFC is used for two-way communication over a short distance - usually a few centimeters. Because it works two-way, it can be used to exchange data between devices. In a city, NFC can have many applications such as smartphone payments or smart energy metering.

3) ZigBee

ZigBee is a standard for self-configuring short-range radio networks, designed for use in telemetry systems, for communication between various types of sensors, monitoring devices, as well as for wireless reading of measurement results from energy meters or heat meters.

4) Wireless Sensor Networks (WSNs)

WSN is a wireless network consisting of spatially distributed devices that use sensors to monitor conditions such as temperature, sound, pressure or pollution. It consists of thousands of sensors that communicate with each other and transmit data.

5) 3G, Long Term Evolution (LTE)

3G and LTE are standards for wireless communication. 3G and LTE are common in most countries of the world. This technology was designed for wideband communications.

6) 5G

The latest mobile network standard is 5G. 5G enables a new kind of network to connect virtually all machines, objects and devices. Additionally, 5G is expected to deliver higher data rates of many Gbps, low latency, massive network capacity and increased availability. It is predicted that the 5G network could greatly influence the development of smart cities.

4 Internet of Things in a Concept of Smart City

4.1 IoT Applications for Smart Cities

The number of Internet of Things applications for smart cities is increasing successively. In general, it can be said that Smart Cities are powered by millions of connected devices. Cities are deploying sensors and devices in their areas, monitoring city activity and connecting to each other via wireless and wired networks [11]. Some examples of IoT applications in the city are listed below along with their main advantages. Listed here are those that can secure the needs of the cities identified in chapter one. The first is **traffic monitoring**. Real-time monitoring of urban traffic has benefits such as avoiding traffic jams, maintaining controlled levels of congestion and ensuring that air pollution levels are kept relatively low. Traffic volume sensors or cameras can be used here. In both of these options, real-time traffic data is made available to city managers, who can take the appropriate decisions in time if necessary. The information is often also sent to city dwellers. In addition to making immediate decisions, the data collected is also analyzed to manage the city's mobility and protect the environment. The next application is **waste management**. In the traditional way of waste collection, trucks pull up to the containers every few days or weeks, emptying the overflowing ones as well as the nearly empty ones. With modern solutions, IoT sensors can verify how full the containers are and send the information to sites that can optimize garbage truck routes based on that information. Machine learning methods that predict how full the garbage containers are based on historical data are also helpful in this case. Another example of IoT application in the city could be **smart parking management** [12]. The smart parking system sends information about free parking spaces via mobile and web applications. The data is collected from sensors or cameras that are placed in each parking space. The user can then choose the space that is best for them, and the data that the spot has been occupied updates in real-time so that other users can see it. Similar to the previously described applications, the system can not only be used for real-time operation but can also be used to monitor traffic in car parks and facilitate decisions regarding the construction of new parking spaces. The next application is the system to **support active ageing** [13]. There are more and more ways to apply the Internet of Things to support older people in cities. Interesting systems are being designed and implemented, and campaigns are being organized to encourage their use. They are based on different ideas - activating the elderly people, monitoring and promoting health lifestyle or even facilitating new friendships. One interesting proposal is described in more detail in Sect. 3.2. The last application is **public safety management** [14]. To enhance public safety, IoT-based smart city solutions offer real-time monitoring and decision-making tools. Data, in this case, comes from CCTV cameras and acoustic sensors deployed in the city, but also from social media. By analyzing these, potential crime scenes can be predicted. This will enable police to apprehend potential perpetrators or target them effectively.

The solutions indicated above are just some of the ways in which IoT-based technologies can be used in the smart city. New ideas are generated every day, and technological developments make it possible to put into practice ideas that only a few years ago seemed impossible to implement. The table below shows a number of Internet of Things-based solutions that have been used successfully in cities. The solutions are categorized into five key elements of a smart city, but "Smart People" and "Smart Living" are included in one column due to the fact that they are very similar concepts (Table 4).

Table 4. IoT based applications in Smart Cities

Smart people & smart living	Smart mobility	Smart economy	Smart governance	Smart environment
Social Network Supporting	Connected Vehicle	Energy management in Office Buildings	Civic Engagement Platform	Monitoring Air Quality
Public Place Monitoring	Car Sharing	Equipment use management systems (in factors)	Citizen Grievance Management	Smart Lightening
Security Systems	Bike Sharing			Noise pollution Monitoring

The above table indicates that although it would seem that Internet of Things-based solutions will only find their application in the **technology factor** of the smart city, they can also find their application in the other two factors - **human** and **institutional**.

4.2 Internet of Things Solutions in Smart Cities

In the last part of this paper, several real IoT-based smart city solutions will be presented, not just general concepts but actual solutions that have been successfully implemented and are in use, along with an indication of the city where they work.

1) Santander, Spain [15]
    In the city of Santander, Spain, a system designed for both city dwellers and tourists has been implemented. The application contains information on almost 3000 places such as beaches, parks and gardens, monuments, tourist offices, stores, art galleries, museums, libraries, stores, public buses, cabs, bicycles, parking spaces as well as a calendar of public events. The app provides real-time access to cameras, sends reports and weather forecasts, and includes information on public transportation making it easy to experience the city. Thanks to the popularity of the application in Spain, other cities such as Lübeck (Germany), Guilford (United Kingdom) and Belgrade (Serbia) have decided to implement it [16].

2) New York, San Francisco, Las Vegas, Chicago and other cities, USA [17]
    A system for the detection, location and analysis of gunshots and for the management of patrols has been implemented in many US cities, enabling resources to be dynamically directed to areas of greatest risk. A company offering solutions of this kind has announced that it plans to expand its operations in the near future, also in smaller US cities. The software can pinpoint the exact location of any missile fired within seconds, with street-level accuracy. Once validated, the alert is sent to dispatch centers and to field workers via any computer or mobile device with internet access - all done in less than a minute. The system can determine the type of weapon used, the number of shooters is where and how fast they are headed.

3) Tilburg, The Netherlands [18]
    In the city of Tilburg in the Netherlands, a decision was made to support elderly people on the roads. There are many busy road junctions where the time to cross the road was limited to the short period when the green light was on. This caused many problems, especially for the elderly and people with reduced mobility - many times they were only halfway across the street when the light changed to red. Now, thanks to the solution implemented in the city, such a situation is rare. The sensors in the traffic lights scan the sidewalk on both sides of the crossing, and if they "see" a waiting pedestrian who uses the discussed application, they adjust the time of the green light. The app has one of the four-time settings built-in, depending on the user's mobility level, to minimize delays for other traffic participants. The developers of the app emphasize that their system can be used not only by the elderly but also by trips, where a large group of people has to cross the pedestrian crossing at one moment.

5 Conclusion

The aim of the presented paper was to compare two popular concepts - Smart City and Internet of Things in order to verify the importance of using IoT-based solutions in the city. The first part presented the selected needs of modern cities and introduced the

Smart City concept. The second part discussed the definition of the Internet of Things and described the technology with particular emphasis on the part that can be successfully implemented and used by city dwellers, city authorities and tourists. The third part showed general examples of IoT-based solutions and real solutions from smaller and larger smart cities. The paper shows that the implemented solutions can be used not only to meet strictly technology-based needs, which can be combined with the concepts of "Smart Mobility" or "Smart Environment" but also with the other elements of a smart city – "Smart People", "Smart Living" and "Smart Governance". In the future, the author would like to focus on indicating not only the positive effects of using the Internet of Things in the city but also pointing out the challenges that appear when trying to implement them. This would include aspects such as security and privacy, technological issues related to, for example, processing and analyzing large amounts of data, high costs and finally ethical dilemmas that arise in many discussions of the implementation of modern technological solutions. By comparing the benefits of implementing the Internet of Things in a city and the doubts that may arise, it would be easier to make decisions related to the development and functioning of smart cities.

References

1. Vandecasteele, I., Baranzelli, C., Siragusa, A., et al.: The Future of Cities – Opportunities, challenges and the way forward, EUR 29752 EN, Publications Office, Luxembourg (2019)
2. https://www2.deloitte.com/content/dam/Deloitte/de/Documents/real-estate/property-index-2019-2.pdf
3. https://ec.europa.eu/eurostat/statistics-explained/index.php?title=Population_structure_and_ageing
4. Khan, Z., Anjum, A., Kiani, S.L.: Cloud based big data analytics for smart future cities. In Proceedings of the 2013 IEEE/ACM 6th International Conference on Utility and Cloud Computing. IEEE Computer Society (2013)
5. Muller, T.: *Redefining the smart city concept: a new smart city* definition. https://hub.bee smart.city/en/strategy/towards-a-new-smart-city-definition
6. Nam, T., Pardo, T.: Conceptualizing smart city with dimensions of technology, people, and institutions. In: the Proceedings of the 12th Annual International Conference on Digital Government Research (2013)
7. https://iot-analytics.com/internet-of-things-definition/. Accessed 01 Mar 2021
8. Somayya Madakam, R., Ramaswamy, S.T.: Internet of Things (IoT): A Literature Review, Vihar Lake, Mumbai, India (2015)
9. Al-Fuqaha, A., Guizani, M., Mohammadi, M., Aledhari, M., Ayyash, M.: Internet of things: A survey on enabling technologies, protocols, and applications. IEEE Communications Surveys&Tutorials (2015)
10. Talari, S., Shafie-khah, M., et al.: Review of Smart Cities Based on the Internet of Things Concept (2017)
11. Righetti, F., Vallati, C., Anastasi, G.: IoT Applications in smart cities: a perspective into social and ethical issues. In: 2018 IEEE International Conference on Smart Computing (2018)
12. Elsonbaty, A.A., Shams, M.: The smart parking management systems. Int. J. Comput. Sci. Inf. Technol. (IJCSIT) **12**(4) (2020)
13. Rocha, N., Dias, A., et al.: A Systematic Review of Smart Cities' Applications to Support Active Ageing. In: The 9th International Conference on Current and Future Trends of Information and Communication Technologies in Healthcare (2019)

14. https://www.scnsoft.com/blog/iot-for-smart-city-use-cases-approaches-outcomes
15. Hammi, B., Khatoun, R.: Internet of Things (IoT) Technologies for Smart Cities. IET Res. J. (2017)
16. Galis, A., Gavras, A. (eds.): FIA 2013. LNCS, vol. 7858. Springer, Heidelberg (2013). https://doi.org/10.1007/978-3-642-38082-2
17. https://www.globenewswire.com/news-release/2020/12/22/2149702/0/en/Smaller-Cities-Increasingly-Turn-to-Gunshot-Detection-Technology-to-Prevent-and-Reduce-Gun-Violence.html
18. https://www.theguardian.com/cities/2017/jul/12/dutch-app-elderly-hack-pedestrian-crossings

Developing a Knowledge Base on Climate Change for Metropolitan Cities

Eunika Mercier-Laurent, Guilaine Talens, and Eric Thivant[✉]

Laboratoire de Recherche Magellan, IAE Lyon, Université Jean Moulin Lyon 3, Lyon, France
eric.thivant@univ-lyon3.fr

Abstract. French Metropolitan Cities have developed their PCETs program (Territorial Climate and Energy Plan) to meet the objectives set by the European Union for 2020 and the National Climate Plan, in France. This research aim is defining and initiating a knowledge base on climate change and more specifically on WEEE (waste electrical and electronic equipment) for large Metropolitan cities such as Metropole of Lyon and Metropole of Montpellier. This Knowledge base will contain best (and bad) practices, experiences, suited metrics, collaborative measures, projects, etc., using the Knowledge Management approach exploring artificial intelligence techniques. For our methodology we work on the state of the art for building such a knowledge base, taking into account the previous works of Boulanger [1, 2], Mercier-Laurent [3–6] and Kayakutlu and Mercier-Laurent [7]. We begin to list existing materials in order to implement a knowledge base on the recycling of products starting by electronic devices.

Keywords: Knowledge base on climate change · Waste electrical and electronic equipment · Metropolitan cities

1 Introduction

Studying climate change requires to take into consideration multiple factors that influence it. Finding and understanding the degree of importance of these factors as well as their inter-influences could provide indicators on how to apply these principles in growing metropolitan cities.

Public, semi-public & private actors (research laboratories, government agencies, etc.), associations, NGOs, mobilize and participate in new discoveries in related fields and experiment; some of them involve citizens (Smart Cities, Enoll, Triple Helix, etc.).

This article proposes to define and initiate an knowledge base on climate change and more specifically on the WEEE (waste electrical and electronic equipment). We focus on large Metropolitan cities such as Metropole of Lyon or Metropole of Montpellier in order to develop such a Knowledge base. It will contain best (and bad) practices, experiences, suited metrics, collaborative measures, projects, etc., using the Knowledge Management approach based on artificial intelligence techniques [8, 9]. We will present now the state of art of KM and Ontology, then we concentrate on the SCO (Smart City Ontology).

E. Mercier-Laurent et al. (Eds.): AI4KM 2021, IFIP AICT 614, pp. 130–143, 2021.
https://doi.org/10.1007/978-3-030-80847-1_9

1.1 The Metropolis of Lyon Case Study

French Metropolitan Cities have developed their PCETs program (Territorial Climate and Energy Plan) to meet the objectives set by the European Union for 2020 [10] and the National Climate Plan, set out in the Grenelle I and Grenelle II laws in France.

In 2007, as part of its Climate Energy Plan, the Metropolis of Lyon made a commitment to reduce CO_2 emissions by 20% by 2020 (75% by 2050), to cut energy consumption by 20% and to consume 20% of renewable energies.

The Metropole of Lyon has launched a "territorial climate-energy plan" (PCET), i.e. a territorial sustainable development project, whose primary purpose is to combat climate change in 2007. The first plan was designed for the period 2010–2020. Then Lyon Metropole has voted a new plan in December 2019, called "Plan climate air energy territorial" (PCAET) for the period 2020–2030 (Table 1).

"The metropolis of Lyon is working with its 145 partners to take effective action throughout its territory: The Climate and Territorial Energy Plan, which brings together local authorities, industrial and energy producers, companies in the tertiary sector, research laboratories and associations" [11, 12].

Table 1. Lyon Metropolitan mains objectives.

3 main objectives of Lyon Metropole https://blogs.grandlyon.com/plan-climat/
– 17% renewable energy in 2030
– 43% CO_2 emissions compared to 2000
– 30% Energy consumption compared to 2000

1.2 The Metropole of Montpellier Case Study

The Montpellier Mediterranean Metropole has developed also a called "Plan climate air energy territorial" (PCAET) for the period 2020–2030 [13].

The PCAET has two objectives: on the one hand, mitigation, in order to limit the territory's impact on the climate by reducing greenhouse gas (GHG) emissions and the atmospheric pollutants produced, and on the other hand, adaptation, in order to reduce the territory's vulnerability to climate change.

The national objectives thus aim at a 33% reduction in GHG emissions from 2015 to 2030, and 85% by 2050. These objectives are defined by sector of activity. And so the Montpellier Mediterranean Metropole proposes also 14 strategic directions to address climate change mitigation and adaptation issues for reaching this goal.

2   State of Art or Related Works on KM and Ontology

Concerning our state of art, we first define what is an ontology Since 90s some researchers in Knowledge Engineering field want to develop new SCB system and propose to use ontology to resolve SCB problems [14].

Gruber [16] explains to us that "*A body of formally represented knowledge is based on a conceptualization: the objects, concepts and other entities that are presumed to exist in some area of interest and the relationships that hold among them (Genesereth and Nilsson 1987). A conceptualization is an abstract, simplified view of the world that we wish to represent for some purpose. Every knowledge base, knowledge-based system or knowledge-level agent is committed to some conceptualization, explicitly or implicitly*".

[16] continue his thinking and define the concept of ontology: "*An ontology is an explicit specification of a conceptualization. The term is borrowed from philosophy, where an ontology is a systematic account of Existence. For Knowledge-based systems, what exists is exactly that which can be represented. When the knowledge of a domain is represented in a declarative formalism, the set of objects, that can be represented is called the universe of discourse. This set of objects and the formalized relationships among them, are reflected in the representational vocabulary with which a knowledge-based program represents knowledge. Thus, we can describe the ontology of a program by defining a set of representational terms.*"

Inside the ontology, "definitions associate the names of entities in the universe of discourse (e.g. classes, relations, functions, or other objects) with human readable text describing what the names are meant to denote, and formal axioms that constrain the interpretation and well-formed use of these terms."

The definition of Studer [15] based on Gruber [16] is: "*An ontology is a formal, explicit specification of a shared conceptualization*". *'Formal' refers to the fact that the ontology should be machine understandable, excludes natural language. 'Shared' reflects the notion, an ontology captures consensual knowledge, that is, it is not private to some individual, but accepted by a group*".

We can have two different ways of thinking Ontology, the Description Logics (DL) and the conceptual graphs [18, 19].

According to Moulin [20], "*A conceptual graph is a semantic network composed of concepts and conceptual relations. Concepts are representations of objects of the application domain. A concept is characterized by two elements: a type which represents the set of all the occurrences of a given class (i.e., human, animal etc.) and a referent which represents a given occurrence of the class that is associated with the concept (i.e., John, Mary, etc.). Using CGlinear notation, a concept is specified between square brackets: [TYPE-NAME: referent].*

The concept types are classified within a type lattice whose root is the universal concept, denoted T. The type lattice supports operations on concepts: generalization and specialization of concepts; determination of the minimal common generalization and of the maximal common specialization of two concepts." (Fig. 1)

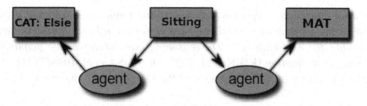

Fig. 1. Cat-on-Mat, a conceptual graphs classic example (Wikipedia: w:Ademoor)

This conceptual graphs' approach is different from the Description Logics clearly according to Nardi & Brachman [21] (Fig. 2).

"Description Logic languages are then viewed as the core of knowledge representation systems, considering both the structure of a DL knowledge base and its associated reasoning services."

"Within a knowledge base one can see a clear distinction between intentional knowledge, or general knowledge about the problem domain, and extensional knowledge, which is specific to a particular problem. A DL knowledge base is analogously typically comprised by two components—a "TBox" and an "ABox".

"The TBox contains intentional knowledge in the form of a terminology (hence the term "TBox" but "taxonomy" could be used as well) and is built through declarations that describe general properties of concepts. Because of the nature of the subsumption relationships among the concepts that constitute the terminology, TBoxes are usually thought of as having a lattice-like structure; this mathematical structure is entailed by the subsumption relationship—it has nothing to do with any implementation" [21].

$$Woman \equiv Person \sqcap Female$$

Fig. 2. TBox example of a woman can be defined as a female person

The ABox contains extensional knowledge—also called assertional knowledge (hence the term "ABox")—knowledge that is specific to the individuals of the domain of discourse. Intensional knowledge is usually thought not to change—to be "time-less," in a way—and extensional knowledge is usually thought to be contingent, or dependent on a single set of circumstances, and therefore subject to occasional or even constant change" [21] (Fig. 3).

$$Female \sqcap Person(ANNA)$$

Fig. 3. ABox states that the individual ANNA is a female person.

Description Logics is widely used in Medecine, Sofware Engineering, Digital libraries, and Web-based information systems, planning and data mining.

"Based on the relationship between Description Logics and semantic networks, a number of proposals were developed that used Description Logics to model Web structures, allowing the exploitation of DL reasoning capabilities in the acquisition and management of information [KIRK et al. 1995; DE ROSA et al. 1998]" [21].

In order to summarize the importance of the DL approach, that we will us, we can cite:

"Description Logics are responsible for many of the cornerstone notions used in knowledge representation and reasoning. They helped crystallize many of the idea streated informally in earlier notations, such as concepts and roles. But they added many new important building blocks for later work in the field: the terminology/assertion distinction (TBox/ABox), number and value restrictions on roles, internal structure for concepts, Tell/Ask interfaces, and others." [21].

Concerning the development of the Semantic Web, researchers has propose to use a new language The Web Ontology Language OWL, which extends RDF and RDFS and using DL And this is this language that we will use for this article.

3   Methodology

For our methodology we work on the state of the art for building such a knowledge base, taking into account the works of Boulanger [1, 2], Mercier-Laurent [3–6] or Kayakutlu and Mercier-Laurent [7] on that particular field, and we begin to list existing materials in order to implement in a near future a little knowledge base, on the recycling of products, particularly electronic products for these metropolitan cities (Fig. 4).

For example, Mercier-Laurent [4] has developed the concept of ontology of innovation...

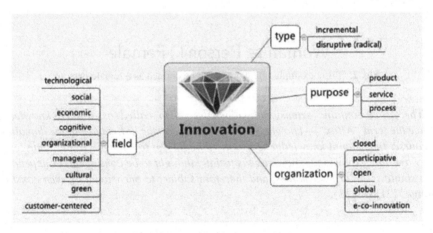

Fig. 4. Ontology of Innovation [4]

In order to build our ontology, we can use the following set of 5 criteria proposed by Gruber [17]: Clarity, Coherence, Extendibility, minimal encoding bias, Minimal ontological commitment. Clarity means that ". Coherence means "An ontology should effectively

communicate the intended meaning of defined terms. Definitions should be objective.";
For Coherence: "An ontology should be coherent: that is, it should sanction inferences
that are consistent with the definitions. At the least, the defining axioms should be logically consistent".; Extendibility: "An ontology should be designed to anticipate the
uses of the shared vocabulary. It should offer a conceptual foundation for a range of
anticipated tasks, and the representation should be crafted so that one can extend and
specialize the ontology monotonically". Minimal encoging bias "The conceptualization
should be specified at the knowledge level without depending on a particular symbol-
level encoding. An encoding bias results when a representation choice are made purely
for the convenience of notation or implementation.";

Minimal ontological commitment: "An ontology should require the minimal ontological commitment sufficient to support the intended knowledge sharing activities. An
ontology should make as few claims as possible about the world being modeled, allowing
the parties committed to the ontology freedom to specialize and instantiate the ontology
as needed".

4   Presentation of the SCO (Smart City Ontology)

Komninos et al. [22, 23] have developed a Smart City Ontology. This Ontology is
specifically built for Smart Cities, because there are a lot of ontologies existing already
and they want to propose a new ontology... The authors have reviewed the existing
ontologies for cities such as SOFIA, NOW, SCRIBE, etc. and then they define the
buildings blocks of this ontology with respect to the most cited definitions of smart
cities and structuring this ontology with the Protégé 5.0 editor, defining entities, class
hierarchy and object properties and data type properties. review also the building blocks
of smart or intelligent cities, which allows to define the class and properties of the SCO.

According to the authors: "The first version (v01) contains 10 superclasses, 708
entities, 422 classes, 62 object properties, 190 data properties, and 27 individuals from
the software application class. Additionally, widely adopted extra ontologies are used,
enriching the SCO, such as the Simple Knowledge Organization System (SKOS), a W3C
recommendation designed for representation of thesauri, classification schemes, tax-
onomies, subject-heading systems, or any other type of structured controlled vocabulary
[22]". You can see below in the graph the structure of the first level of the ontology.

In [24], smart city ontologies are presented and compared in order to be applied to
IoT ontologies. The set of criteria are mainly focused on the reusability of the ontologies.
The goal is to define a methodology to enrich smart city catalogs with the new ontologies
found. It's implemented within the LOV4IoT ontology catalog. The aim of this catalog
is to help developers in reusing existing smart city and IoT ontologies to build future
applications.

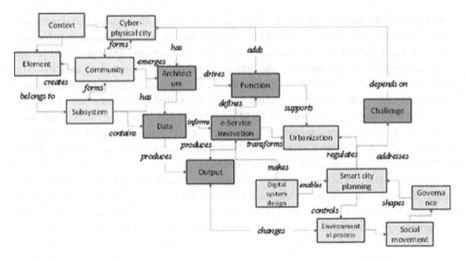

Fig. 5. A new view of the Smart City Ontology Komninos et al. [22]

Ontologies for Climate Change

Pilegi et al. [25] build an ontology to describe the climate change story from multiple perspectives, including scientific, social, political and technological ones.

In this article, several ontologies for climate are cited, ontologies to measure the impact of a changing climate on food and waterborne diseases, the impacts of agriculture on water resources, ... but there is none ontology to capture the recycling of products.

5 Developing the WEEE Ontology

5.1 Eco-design a Key Element for Innovation

Evbuomwan et al. [26] defined the eco-design like "the process of establishing requirements based on human needs, transforming them into performance specification and functions, which are then mapped and converted (subject to constraints) into design solutions (using creativity, scientific principles and technical knowledge) that can be economically manufactured and produced".

Lindhqvist [27] proposes the Extended Producer Responsibility (EPR) concept and change the classical view of PPP (the polluter pay for the pollution, from the consumer to the economic agent who produce the goods). According to the Organisation for Economic Co-operation and Development (OECD), EPR is "an environmental policy approach in which a producer's responsibility for a product is extended to the post-consumer stage of a product's life cycle" [28].

"The economic reasoning behind the EPR concept is to have producers internalise treatment and disposal cost so that they have an incentive to design products that last longer and are more easily treated after use" [28].

Definitions of the EPR System (Development of Guidance on Extended Producer Responsibility).

EPR system or EPR scheme: Any system set up by one or several producers to implement the EPR principle. It can be an individual system (or individual compliance scheme) when a producer organises its own system, or a collective system (collective compliance scheme) when several producers decide to collaborate and thus transfer their responsibility to a specific organisation (a PRO).

Producer Responsibility Organisation or PRO: Entity set up in collective EPR schemes to implement the EPR principle in the name of all the adhering companies.

Fees: Tariff paid by a producer to have its products dealt with through a PRO.

According to the WEEE Directive (2012/19/EU), there are 7 Categories of EEE:

1. Large household appliances
2. Small household appliances
3. IT and telecommunications equipment
4. Consumer equipment and photovoltaic panels
5. Lighting equipment
6. Electrical and electronic tools (with the exception of large-scale stationary industrial tools)
7. Toys, leisure and sports equipment

For each category of EEE, we should develop our own view on WEEE.

5.2 Ecosystem of the Recycling Circuit

Thanks to Mérot [29], Movilla [30] presents us the physical and financial flows of the WEEE industry below. Concerning the physical flow of the WEEE, the households bring back the old electrical and electronical to the collectivity or to the distributor. Sometimes the household bring back their old electrical or electronical tools to different actors of the Social and Solidarity Economy. Then all the actors implied ask transport operators to send their WEEE to Waste processing operators (Fig. 6).

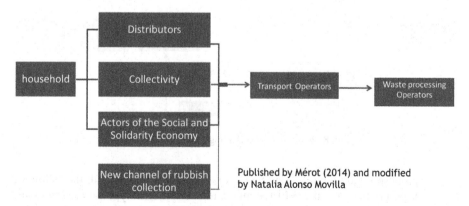

Fig. 6. Physical flows of WEEE Industry, from Mérot [29] & modified by Movilla [30]

Concerning the financial flow of the WEEE, we can see that the household pay a contribution when they buy new electronical or electrical goods to their productors. The productors then give the money to the Eco-Organization who send a participation to OCAD3E. OCAD3E then gives a financial support to the collectivities and the distributors in order to better collect Electrical and Electronical Wastes (Fig. 7).

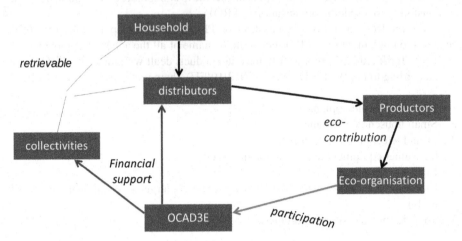

Fig. 7. Financial Flows of WEEE Indutry, from Mérot [29] & modified by Movilla [30]

Concerning the process of dismantling electrical or electronical wastes, we can say that there is three ways of dismantling, the manual dismantling & recycling process, the semi-automatic dismantling & recycling process and the final grinding. All these elements can be described in the Fig. 5 and extracted from Natalia Alonso Movilla's thesis (Fig. 8).

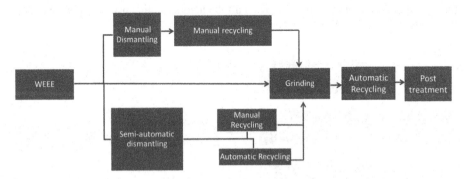

Fig. 8. Process of dismantling from Movilla [30]

We propose to add the recycling theme to this SCO ontology, with the following classes & proprieties from the WEEE domain, It takes different types of organizations, of products and ways of managing Electronics waste (Fig. 9).

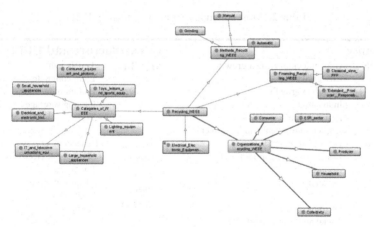

Fig. 9. Recycling WEEE with main classes with Protégé software

For the classes of Wee, we propose to use the same object relationships as for SCO:

– define relationships between class and sub-class (is_a)
– define predicates of possession (has, owns)
– define predicates of information (informs, disseminates, diffuses)
– define predicates of digital transformation (digitalize, digitize, cloudify)
– define predicates of inclusion (belongs, contains, is_located)
– define predicates of impact (creates, forms, transforms, produces, innovates, regulates, supports)
– define predicates of interaction (connects, depends_on, defines, enables, drives)
– define predicates of usage (uses, employ, operate, dismantle, recycle, grind)

Using these objects, we can define most relationships between classes. We have defined some data properties in order to complete our ontology.

6 Discussions and Conclusion

6.1 Smart Cities and Waste

We should think about integrating Waste Electrical and Electronic Equipment into SCO ontology. According to Komninos et al. [22], "Table 2 *shows the most usual types of challenges in cities, which are inherited to smart cities. They are classified into four main typical domains of cities, (1) challenges related to economy, (2) living conditions, (3) infrastructure and utilities, and (4) government*".

Table 2. Most common smart city challenges [22]

Economy		Infrastructure and Utility	
Growth	- GDP and employment growth - City growth - Suburban growth - Innovation - Extroversion - Attraction of talent and investment	**Mobility**	- Traffic jam - Long commute - Pollution due to traffic - Parking shortage - Traffic accident
Decline	- Decline of industry - Disinvestment / capital flight - Brain-drain - Urban decay / inner-city decline - Poverty - Unemployment / job loss - Social and economic divide	**Utility: energy, water, waste, internet**	-Renewable energy provision - Shortage of electric power - Energy saving - Clean water provision - Waste disposal - Aging infrastructure - Low broadband

Living conditions, quality of life		Governance	
Hous-ing	- Lack of housing - Homelessness - Slums and squatter areas - Illegal housing - Crowding / high-density area - Gentrification	**Decision-making**	- Non-transparent government - Undemocratic government - Closed government - Non-participatory government - Planning shortage
Crime	- Crime, gang activity - Violence, aggression - Vandalism - Safety and security	**System failure**	- Corruption - Political clientelism - Red tape - Fiscal crisis - Planning failure
Social care	- Public health - Social care for vulnerable group - Health in low-income neighbor-hood	**Access to services**	- A few online services - Disregard of citizen's request - Low-quality services

Climate Change		Digital system	
Environmental degradation	- Air pollution - Pollution of land - Water pollution - Natural habitat at risk	**Infrastructure**	High Speed Broadband
Greenhouse gas emission	- CO_2 emission - Methane - Other GG (nitrous oxide fluorinated gases)	**e-service analytics**	*-At various domains of services -Data*
		Digital skill	*-Shortage of digital skills*

6.2   Adding Recycling WEEE in the SCO

According to Komninos et al. [22], *"Sustainability, climate change, and recycling can be under many different classes of the smart city ontology"*.

- *Under "Environmental Context", related to natural resources (Water, Flood, Air, Land, Drought, Natural resource, Natural ecosystem).*
- *Under planning process, for processes such as: sustainable urban planning, environmental planning, green mobility plan, planning for water resources, planning for recycling.*
- *Under the class "Elements" for digital elements, smart city applications, e-services, sensor networks, energy grid, etc.*
- *It can be also a subsystem of the cyber-physical city, together with smart transport, smart energy, smart water, smart recycling, waste management, etc.*
- *Sustainability is also related to values that some entities take, (e.g. pollution is a measure of microparticles). In this case, it is a restriction.*

The same for climate change, it can be defined by restrictions related to CO2, renewable energy use, greenhouse gas emissions.

We should take time before integrating them in the classes and data properties of the Smart City Ontology. Our proposal for a new ontology of this domain, with different classes and proprieties is not yet finish. We need to continue our work with a case-based analysis & application in order to explain better our classes and the relationships between them.

References

1. Chamekh, F., Boulanger, D., Talens, G.: Web of data evolution by exploiting agent based-argumentation. In: Mercier-Laurent, E., Boulanger, D. (eds.) AI4KM 2015. IAICT, vol. 497, pp. 32–50. Springer, Cham (2016). https://doi.org/10.1007/978-3-319-55970-4_3
2. Colloc, J., Boulanger, D.: Automatic Knowledge Acquisition for Object-Oriented Expert Systems. CoRR abs/2005.08517 (2020).
3. Mercier-Laurent, E.: Platform for knowledge society and innovation ecosystems. In: Mercier-Laurent, E. (ed.) AI4KM 2018. IAICT, vol. 588, pp. 34–47. Springer, Cham (2020). https://doi.org/10.1007/978-3-030-52903-1_4
4. Mercier-Laurent, E.: The Innovation Biosphere. Wiley, London (2015)
5. Mercier-Laurent, E.: Managing intellectual capital in knowledge economy. In: Mercier-Laurent, E., Owoc, M.L., Boulanger, D. (eds.) AI4KM 2014. IAICT, vol. 469, pp. 165–179. Springer, Cham (2015). https://doi.org/10.1007/978-3-319-28868-0_10
6. Wojtusiak, J., Mercier-Laurent, E., Punihaole, C.: Introduction to the Minitrack on AI and sustainability: the use of AI in sustainability initiatives. HICSS 2020, pp. 1–2
7. Kayakutlu, D.G., Mercier-Laurent, E.: Intelligence in Energy. Elsevier, London (2016)
8. Hauke, K., Owoc, M.L., Pondel, M.: Usability of knowledge portals for exclusives in local governments. In: Mercier-Laurent, E., Owoc, M.L., Boulanger, D. (eds.) AI4KM 2014. IAICT, vol. 469, pp. 92–106. Springer, Cham (2015). https://doi.org/10.1007/978-3-319-28868-0_6
9. Przysucha, Ł.: Effective management of information processes with CMS in smart city. the concept of crowdsourcing. In: Mercier-Laurent, E. (ed.) AI4KM 2018. IAICT, vol. 588, pp. 65–76. Springer, Cham (2020). https://doi.org/10.1007/978-3-030-52903-1_6
10. European Union: Green Paper: A 2030 framework for climate and energy policies (2013). https://ec.europa.eu/clima/policies/strategies/2030_en#tab-0-1 & https://eur-lex.europa.eu/legal-content/EN/TXT/?uri=CELEX:52013DC0169
11. Métropole de Lyon, Projet de Plan Climat Air Énergie Territorial, 2018–2019. https://www.grandlyon.com/fileadmin/user_upload/media/pdf/grands-projets/concertation-reglementaire/20190524_projet-pcaet.pdf

12. Métropole de Lyon, Rapport Environnemental PCAET April 2019. https://www.grandl yon.com/fileadmin/user_upload/media/pdf/grands-projets/concertation-reglementaire/201 90429_rapport-environnemental-pcaet.pdf
13. Montpellier Mediterranean Metropole. https://www.montpellier3m.fr/climact--engagement-cit-ergie. Accessed 28 Feb 2021
14. Neches, R., et al.: Enabling technology for knowledge sharing. AI Mag. **12**(3), 36–56 (1991)
15. Studer, R., Benjamins, D., Fensel, D.: Knowledge engineering: principles and methods. IEEE Trans. Data Knowl. Eng. **25**(1–2), 161–197 (1998)
16. Gruber, T.R.: A translation approach to portable ontologies. Knowl. Acquisit. **5**(2), 199–220 (1993)
17. Gruber, T.R.: Toward principles for the design of ontologies used for knowledge sharing. Int. J. Hum.-Comput. Stud. **43**(5–6), 907–928 (1995)
18. Sowa, J.F.: Conceptual Structures: Information Processing in Mind and Machine, Addison-Wesley (1984). ISBN 0-201-14472-7
19. Sowa, J.F.: Conceptual graphs for a data base interface. IBM J. Res. Dev. **20**(4), 336–357 (1976)
20. Moulin, B.: Temporal contexts for discourse representation: an extension of the conceptual graph approach. Appl. Intell. **7**, 227–255 (1997). https://doi-org.ezscd.univ-lyon3.fr/10.1023/A:1008224616031
21. Nardi, D., Brachman, R.J.: An introduction to description logics. In: Baader, F., Calvanese, D., McGuinness, D.L., Nardi, D., Patel-Schneider, P.F. (eds.) The Description Logic Handbook, pp. 5–44. Cambridge University Press (2002)
22. Komninos, N., Panori, A., Kakderi, C.: Smart City Ontology 2.0 (2020). https://www.urenio.org/2020/12/16/smart-city-ontology-2-0/
23. Komninos, N., Bratsas, C., Kakderi, C., Tsarchopoulos, P.: Smart city ontologies: improving the effectiveness of smart city applications. J. Smart Cit. **1**(1), 31–46 (2015). https://doi.org/10.18063/JSC.2015.01.001
24. Gyrard, A., Zimmermann, A., Sheth, A.P.: Building IoT based applications for smart cities: how can ontology catalogs help? IEEE Internet Things J. **5**(5), 3978–3990 (2018)
25. Pileggi, S.P., Lamia, A.V.: Climate change TimeLine: an ontology to tell the story so far. IEEE access **8** (2020). https://doi.org/10.1109/ACCESS.2020.2985112
26. Evbuomwan, N.F.O., Sivaloganathan,, S., Jebb, A.: A Survey of Design Philosophies, Models, Methods and Systems. Proc. Inst. Mech. Eng. Part B J. Eng. Manuf. **210**, 301–320 (1996). https://doi.org/10.1243/PIME_PROC_1996_210_123_02
27. Lindhqvist, T.: Extended producer responsibility in cleaner production - policy principle to promote environmental improvements of product systems. Doctoral Dissertation, Lund University, International Institute for Industrial Environmental Economics (2000)
28. European Commission, DG Environment, Development of Guidance on Extended Producer Responsibility (EPR) (2014)
29. Mérot, A.-S.: Gouvernance et développement durable: le cas de la responsabilité élargie du producteur dans la filière de gestion des déchets des équipements électriques et électroniques. Thesis, Management Science, University Grenoble Alpes (2014)
30. Movilla, N. A.: Contribution to Design for End-of-Life approaches: taking into consideration pre-treatment practices from the WEEE (Waste Electrical and Electronic Equipment) compliance scheme. Thesis, Process Engineering. University Grenoble Alpes (2016)

Other Reference

31. Mercier-Laurent, E., Boulanger, D.: Artificial Intelligence for Knowledge Management - 5th IFIP WG 12.6 International Workshop, AI4KM 2017, Held at IJCAI 2017, Melbourne,

VIC, Australia, August 20, 2017, Revised Selected Papers. IFIP Advances in Information and Communication Technology 571, Springer (2019). https://doi.org/10.1007/978-3-030-29904-0, ISBN 978-3-030-29903-3

32. Mercier-Laurent, E., Boulanger, D. (eds.): Artificial Intelligence for Knowledge Management - 4th IFIP WG 12.6 International Workshop, AI4KM 2016, Held at IJCAI 2016, New York, NY, USA, July 9, 2016, Revised Selected Papers. IFIP Advances in Information and Communication Technology 518, Springer (2018). https://doi.org/10.1007/978-3-319-92928-6, ISBN 978-3-319-92927-9

33. Mercier-Laurent, E., Owoc, M.L., Boulanger, D.: Artificial Intelligence for Knowledge Management - Second IFIP WG 12.6 International Workshop, AI4KM@FedCSIS 2014, Warsaw, Poland, September 7–10, 2014, Revised Selected Papers. IFIP Advances in Information and Communication Technology 469, Springer (2015). https://doi.org/10.1007/978-3-319-28868-0. ISBN 978–3–319–28867–3

34. Mercier-Laurent, E., Boulanger, D.: Artificial Intelligence for Knowledge Management - Third IFIP WG 12.6 International Workshop, AI4KM 2015, Held at IJCAI 2015, Buenos Aires, Argentina, July 25–31, 2015, Revised Selected Papers. IFIP Advances in Information and Communication Technology 497 (2016). ISBN 978–3–319–55969–8

35. Mercier-Laurent, E., Boulanger, D.: Artificial Intelligence for Knowledge Management - First IFIP WG 12.6 International Workshop, AI4KM 2012, Held in Conjunction with ECAI 2012, Montpellier, France, August 28, 2012, Revised Selected Papers. IFIP Advances in Information and Communication Technology 422, Springer (2014). https://doi.org/10.1007/978-3-642-54897-0. ISBN 978-3-642-54896-3

Can Artificial Intelligence Effectively Support Sustainable Development?

Eunika Mercier-Laurent(✉) 🆔

University of Reims Champagne Ardenne, Reims, France
eunika.mercier-laurent@univ-reims.fr

Abstract. This paper describes the role AI may play in sustainability. Sustainable development is currently among the greatest challenges. Sustainability and development are apparently opposite. The current efforts to face the Planet Crisis by separate actions generate less impact than expected. The capacity of available technology and in particular Artificial Intelligence is underexplored. Eco-innovation actions focus mainly on smart transportation, smart use of energy and water and waste recycling but do not consider the necessary evolution of behaviors and focus. The concepts such as Smart, Intelligent, Innovative, Green or Wise City invented to promote existing technology transform the IT market. Most of offers consist in data processing with statistical/optimization methods. This paper explains how the AI approach and techniques combined with adequate thinking may innovate the way of facing Planet Crisis and achieving some of 17 United Nations Sustainable Development Goals.

Keywords: Artificial Intelligence · Sustainability · Sustainable development · Planet crisis · Climate change · Data obesity

1 Introduction

Many factors affect the sustainability. One of them is quick technological progress, considered as powerful engine of economy. It provides benefits for humanity, but contributes also to Planet Crisis with waste generation, energy consumption, cooling data centers and depletion of scarce metals. The majority of computers, smartphones, IoT and other electronic devices are mostly not eco-designed and even integrate a principle of planned obsolescence. Consequently they are thrown away and replaced by the latest model. Not conceived with knowledge approach, the consecutive layers of software and frequent update for various reasons increase already existing "obesity" and creating a need for more powerful computers. The combination of various communicating software requires "up-to-date" hardware to run correctly.

Despite the large introduction of Corporate Social Responsibility, some companies still practice planned obsolescence to generate more revenues [1].

Is getting huge and quick revenue compatible with Planet protection?

© IFIP International Federation for Information Processing 2021
Published by Springer Nature Switzerland AG 2021
E. Mercier-Laurent et al. (Eds.): AI4KM 2021, IFIP AICT 614, pp. 144–159, 2021.
https://doi.org/10.1007/978-3-030-80847-1_10

Main conferences devoted to climate change blame coal and automotive industry as the biggest emitters of carbon dioxide. However, they seem forgot the other influencing factors and do not study the pollution systems as a whole.

According to [2, 3] simple email without attachment generates equivalent of 4 g CO_2, annual google search 10 kg by only one person.

Social networks and various applications produce an exponential amount of data stored in data centers that need cooling. Fortunately, few apply circular energy to reduce environmental impact, but still those in Scandinavian countries and North America clearly contribute to the rise of temperature and melting of ice [4].

The third hype of AI has been triggered by marketing needs to sale more and quicker to largest public. The involved companies collect all available data in aim to elaborate the models and selected algorithms to generate "client experience" among others.

The advertisement companies explore the navigation data and "client experience" in aim pushing not always targeted advertisement to large population of the Internet users. It generates not only carbon footprint, but also visual pollution and certainly influence concentration.

Advertisement-based business model, invented by Google influences and mass media promote the "buy more" and "to have more and to show" mentality. "Buy more, throw away and buy new" are the engines of today business. The demand for data scientists, especially in marketing is increasing, which is good for employment.

This trend affected also the problem solving capacity among the AI programmers to the point that many apply Big Data + machine learning principle to solve all kind of problems even if the alternative methods, greener and smarter are available. Collection of data became a prerequisite. However, their quality should be adapted to the expected results without cheating aiming in influencing the results. Raw data need "cleaning" before processing.

In fact, the quality of data is not controlled – there is not "garbage collector" for outdated data, no verification of consistency, and no selection in function of target. For example, many organizations collect our personal data that are in various database instead of having just one (identity). By consequence the same data may be registered a dozen of times, contributing again to data obesity.

Globalization has changed the economic landscape. Opening to business and quick development of China and other Asian and South American countries offering the low labor cost increases the relocation-out from origin countries, mainly US and Europe, in search of quick and high revenues. It requires transportation across the world by ships and airplanes, which increases pollution [5]. Besides, the end-buyers have to recycle products, often of poor quality, made just for sale. Repairing costs often more than new product and requires the availability of spare pieces and related expertise.

Huge global business amplifies through communication technology, e-commerce, and transportation facilities. The each day of recent Suez Canal blockage disrupted more than $9 billion worth of goods, according to The Associated Press, citing estimates from Lloyd's List. The large number of ships stuck in one place—at the northern end of the Suez Canal in the Mediterranean Sea—caused sulphur emissions to spike in the region [6].

The knowledge of adequate techniques of AI and expertise in applying them can help finding and optimizing the local resources in aim avoiding or minimizing transportation of many goods and enhance local economy.

Despite the provided benefits, the innovation is among contributors to planet disaster, because the inventors and designers think mostly about the functionalities, shape, look, attractiveness, and few about minimizing the use of raw materials, reducing the energy consumption, providing the remanufacturing and recycling facilities and other ways to reduce environmental impacts. "Innovation" in packaging by reducing the quantity of a given product (food) in more attractive box produces more waste.

The primary eco-innovation movement claims to generate new businesses and jobs but the use of technology in the related activities is moderate, except maybe for waste sorting [7]. Instead of sorting, it is smarter to produce less waste. Corporate Social Responsibility aims in balancing environmental, economic and social impacts. The standards associated with product lifecycle management (PLM) software claim to manage environmental impact of the design [8].

The industrial renewal in Europe called Industry 4.0, initiated by German government to face Asian competition, focuses on digitalization and optimization of related processes. Therefore, eco-design is included into Industry 4.0 [9]. Future factories, such as those at Vaudreuil of Schneider Electric and Safran in France integrate a lot of AI, preserving principle of collaboration human-machine, instead of replacing humans. Cyber physical systems allow simulate and improve maintenance of existing equipment and design [10–12].

Artificial Intelligence plays already a significant role in decision support systems, optimization, simulation, but can do better at the condition to consider the mentioned elements as an ecosystem. It requires a capacity of different thinking without the barriers between fields [13], complex problem solving, art of choosing appropriate techniques and managing available knowledge and experience that apply.

After describing the concepts of sustainability, and sustainable development we give a short overview of AI techniques useful for sustainability management. This is following by discussion on how AI can help achieving some of the 17 goals of UN. The case of Smart City demonstrates AI applied to mastering of environmental impact.

The paper ends with some perspective on alternative way of doing and on the role of intelligent technology in the transformation of society.

2 Sustainability and Sustainable Development

For many sustainability means economic health. Indeed sustainability depends on how human activities are in balance with natural ecosystems and how they affect biodiversity and our biosphere [14].

Facing the Planet Crisis requires different approach that world conferences, agreements and separate actions. By the way, participants travel mostly by planes generating CO_2 instead of using available teleconferencing technology. Nobody publish the "return on investment" in terms of tangible and intangible effects of such actions.

Covid 19 however, changed the way we work; many conferences went online. Remote working generates positive impact on the environment, such as but there are also few negative often forgotten. All conferences online are recorded and stored in the data centers, nevertheless these records offer the access to knowledge to large audience.

Successive lock downs have also increased shopping online and by consequence traffic on the internet and transportation of goods.

In biological systems, sustainability means long life. Systems components influence each other and the balance of the whole system is the condition to survive. Human activities and especially greedy economic system have affected the balance of natural ecosystems [14, 15].

Sustainable development is a principle that many people claim to have invented. The definition of the European Union [16] inspired by those of Antoine de Saint Exupéry [17] is following:

"Sustainable Development stands for meeting the needs of present generations without jeopardizing the ability of futures generations to meet their own needs – in other words, a better quality of life for everyone, now and for generations to come. It offers a vision of progress that integrates immediate and longer-term objectives, local and global action, and regards social, economic and environmental issues as inseparable and interdependent components of human progress".

"Sustainable development will not be brought about by policies only: it must be taken up by society at large as a principle guiding the many choices each citizen makes every day, as well as the big political and economic decisions that have to be taken. This requires profound changes in thinking, in economic and social structures and in consumption and production patterns" [18].

Sustainable development can be considered as a process for meeting human development goals while maintaining the ability of natural systems to provide the required natural resources and ecosystem services upon which the current economy and society depend.

The current greedy economic system is not compatible with sustainable development. Burning forests to plant genetically modified soybeans or remove trees to build houses just for sale destroys unnecessarily biodiversity. In this context, sustainable development is an oxymoron – it is impossible to remain sustainable without deep understanding of our natural ecosystems (multidisciplinary knowledge) and without radical change of behaviours, objectives, values, political and economic system. Sustainable development is an attitude to learn and cultivate.

Various actions aiming in changing the way of acting and doing things have been engaged since 1960 [18]. Recently the young individuals such as for example Boyan Slat, Greta Thunberg and some NGOs are engaged in actions for planet cleaning and protection. Spreaded through social networks such actions have potential to influence behaviours. The initiatives as buy local, sharing knowledge on repairing via video and numerous applications, such as Uber, wonolo [19] and some others, connect people offering services or jobs with those who need them. It is quick and effective, but out of the current economic practices (taxes, companies...). Sometimes this way of doing raise conflicts between "traditional" and "innovative". Some platforms connecting offer and demand use AI techniques such as Case-based reasoning or deep learning for direct matching of offer and demand [20, 21].

Games and serious games (with AI) have also potential to encourage people to think and act differently. For example, the game Nega-water developed by association Du Flocon à la Vague calculates the use of water when doing daily activities [22].

Introducing the environmental principles into a design of products and services is a step forward. However, the traditional PLM tools should evolve to take into consideration a new way of doing [12] by using alternative thinking, simulators before doing and optimizers. Future Factories are supposed to evolve in this direction [10, 11].

Technology is able to provide a considerable help in eco-design, but the way of thinking compatible with such complex problem solving should evolve to global, holistic and system [14, 32]. For example, aerospace and automotive industries focus on lightening weight and reducing carbon footprint, while other related aspects such as route optimization for users are weakly considered. Current travel search engines works for their clients, not for travellers. The air transportation system "hub-and-spoke" in which local airports offer air transportation to a central airport where long-distance flights are available, need innovation to minimize the distance and related CO2 emission. The effort can be done through better collaboration between airlines. Three main alliances Sky Team, Star Alliance and One world do not accept combining the flight tickets between them for optimizing flights distance. This situation my change with Covid crisis.

The International Standard ISO 26000 provides guidelines on how businesses and organizations can operate in a socially responsible way [23]. While it constraints companies to integrate social and environmental aspects into their activities, for ex. design, they should also focus on balancing their economic performance. These guidelines are complex and it is very difficult for a small company to check and respect all these principles without losing business. The AI-based simulators can help checking and optimizing things. Such system has been prototyped in the framework on French national funded project Convergence [8] that delivered a game-based guide for SMEs aiming in guiding them in applying ISO 26000 requirements related to eco-design.

To remain sustainable, development requires a smart use of available AI techniques, not only trendy ones but also those effective for a given case. Combined with intensive use of available knowledge – individual and collective, from related domains, from the past and currently gained from experience such systems can really help minimizing impact of human activity.

3   Artificial Intelligence and Sustainability

Since years, researchers and practitioners of AI have demonstrated the AI has potential to provide valuable solutions for facing today challenges. Since 1980s, numerous applications in the fields of medicine, chemistry, industry, finance and others demonstrated that AI is able to help human in many situations [24].

3.1   Third Hype of AI

The third hype of AI triggered by marketing needs to sale more and to more people amplified collection of multisource data. Despite of GBDR the acceptation of cookies by users is mandatory to access most of websites. Before marketing, professionals in operational safety, reliability and feedback processing applied mathematical methods based on statistical analysis to sample of data. While engineering specialists understood that it is necessary to combine "data approach" with "knowledge–based AI", those of marketing were suddenly empowered by analytics and "machine learning" algorithms. As deep-learning requires big data for more accurate results the marketing specialists focus mainly on gathering more data from various available sources about customers to push them more products and services. Collected data is mined using analytics and deep learning software and the results explored commercially. This approach is not sustainable, because it requires a huge amount of data (data obesity) and consequently their storage and cooling, as well as energy for processing.

Third generation of AI includes also evolution of robots – now robots are deployed in many contexts without necessarily having a need for robot capacities. Currently many various robots replace humans including military robots and drones what raise ethical questions [25]. Very few is wondering about sustainability, eco-designing of robots, their recyclability and reparability, availability of raw materials and of electronic components to build "super-robots".

While an "automated" dialog between human and machine was proposed by Turing (famous Turing test) and Weizenbaum (Eliza, 1966), today there is a trend for having a chatbot able to answer the questions of clients and visitors. The designers of "intelligent" assistants implemented this principle. The majority of chatbots explore the ready answers recorded in (again) database. Main applications of chatbotsare described in [26].

Some research groups still follow the old dream of AI founding fathers work on Artificial General Intelligence (AGI) – a machine able to surpass human intelligence [27].

3.2 AI Patrimony

Since over 60 years, AI researchers and practitioners invented and have experimented the various approaches and techniques. The first robot Perceptron built in the late 1960s was equipped with embedded sensors, camera, and neural networks. It was able to ride on the ground and "learn" from "observation".

The knowledge-based AI introduced object programming, expert systems, natural language understanding and processing. After neural networks (1943) other machine learning approaches has been invented, such as automated generation of decision tree (ID3, 1970), Star methodology (Michalski, 1969) implemented in AQ [29]. All existing ML methods were grouped in Multi-Strategy Machine Learning (MSML) toolbox [28]. ID3 laid the foundation for data mining.

Case-based reasoning developed from the works of Roger Shank and Janet Kolodner in 1982 was latter improved by adding ID3 algorithm and dynamic induction combining the best from induction and nearest neighbors' algorithms.

Voice recognition and latter face recognition (image mining) are not new neither. Virtual reality implemented the principles of image processing in the middle of the 1990s.

The Fig. 1 presents an overview of main AI fields and available techniques.

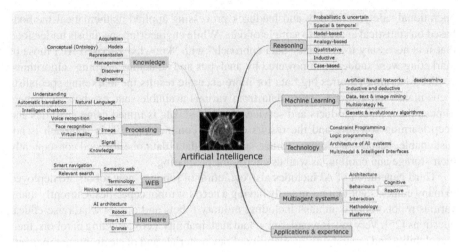

Fig. 1. Overview of main AI fields and techniques [30]

All techniques shown in Fig. 1 have been successfully experimented for various applications in many fields around the globe. Decision support systems, diagnosis and many others are now embedded in larger applications such as automated pilot, autonomous car, intelligent building, in drones, translation systems, personal assistants, security and many others.

AI introduced specific way of thinking and problem solving which is different from those related to exploring databases. For example, managing sustainability requires deep understanding of all influencing factors, relations between them and elements of context, such as policies and human behaviors. The approach such as KADS [31] combing Newell knowledge level, Chandrasekeran interaction hypothesis and Clancey generalization, requires defining of a goal and decomposing it into the tasks; each tasks corresponds to a specific reasoning model that will use available knowledge and consider the context to achieve a given goal.

Deep problem understanding (global, holistic and system thinking) facilitates the choice of right technique or combination of them in hybrid systems [32, 33]. For example, we can use constraint programming for optimizing, planning and scheduling, artificial neural networks to find similar pattern in images, text or in audio file, case-based reasoning for matching local offers of jobs and competency and in intelligent e-commerce application. Some of mentioned techniques are integrated in multi-agents systems (MAS) [34]. They have been used to study and to simulate complex systems in different application domains where physical factor are present for energy minimizing, where physical objects tend to reach the lowest energy consumption possible within the physically constrained world. Furthermore, MAS have been intensively exploited for the analysis through simulation of biological and chemical systems.

In the case of sustainability the contextual knowledge on policies in a given country, base of available actions and practice/prototyping should be considered. Taking inspiration from games [35] we can imagine building a Sustainability Support System as a simulator containing various interrelated components to evaluate the impact of decisions for policy makers, planners, organizations and companies. It can be conceived as a tool-box allowing easy configuration in function of the needs and allowing verifying various constraints before doing.

3.3 AI and Sustainability

AI affects the sustainability. Two aspects of AI should be investigated: negative and positive. Negative consists in being dependent of all forms of computers and of software sometimes unnecessarily complicated; the both quickly evolving for many reasons including planned obsolescence. Collecting and storing exponentially growing data related to web services, for marketing and other purposes can be optimized by alternative green and smart approach to programming, using the suited knowledge models, both for collecting relevant data (Fig. 2) and for guidance in "learning".

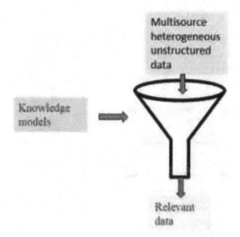

Fig. 2. Collection of data guided by knowledge models

According to Eric Thivant [36] all outdated electronic devices can be partially recycled or reused in the developing countries that lacks computers.

Repairing is a key when it is possible. However, it requires expertise and can be supported by videos or AI applications. Since over five years now, French company called Back Market has been working on revaluation of apparently outdated smartphones [37]. Repair cafés multiplies connecting people that need a service or learn reparation [38]. 3D printer services provide spare pieces if not available for sale (old equipment). Sweden government offers the tax reduction for repairing goods.

The United Nations defined the 17 Sustainable Development Goals presented in Fig. 3. Some of them can be achieved with the help of adequate AI approach and techniques.

For example the Goal 1 – "No poverty" can be partially achieved by better management of talents – from education to employment and entrepreneurship [39]. However it is related to human behaviors.

The Goal 2 "End hunger, achieve food security and improved nutrition and promote sustainable agriculture". AI can bring a contribution here by smart agriculture, combining past knowledge on crop rotation, natural fertilization and symbiosis between plants with various optimization techniques, forecasting, smart use of water, optimal gathering and distribution (local). French Research Center on Agriculture CIRAD initiated agroecology [40] that addresses this goal by combining Knowledge Management and selected AI techniques.

We have also avoid the food waste, especially in developed countries, pushed by business. Again behaviors plays a role here – it is better to explain how to do instead of giving ready food, as says an old proverb "Give a man a fish, and you feed him for a day. Teach a man to fish, and you feed him for a lifetime".

Fig. 3. United Nations sustainability goals, source http://www.gogeometry.com/mindmap/sdg-sustainable-development-goals-mind-map-10.jpg

Achieving of Goal 3 "Ensure healthy lives and promote well-being for all at all ages" requires education on how our body works and nutrition. Access to Knowledge base on healthy cooking (not just to multitude of recipes) with available local ingredients, the basic phytotherapy, gymnastic may help achieving this goal. It can be done through games combining knowledge and fun. AI brought significant contribution in health systems – early detection of serious diseases, robot surgery, diagnosis (expert systems), elaboration of vaccines and other. Artificial human "spare pieces" such as artificial pancreas [41] are already available and research on it progresses.

The well-being strongly depends on environment; it is linked with goals 11, 13 and 15.

The Goal 4 "Ensure inclusive and equitable quality education and promote lifelong learning opportunities for all" involves the distribution of knowledge via technology. While AI-supported online learning has been practiced from the late 1990s and many MOOCs are available, the Covid pandemics accelerated massive use of technology in education. Many conferences on various topics are online and often for free. What should be better developed is the early evaluation of talents via dialogue with intelligent systems, interaction human-machine during learning and adaptation of the program to the students' level. An advice system for matching talents and interests with the range of occupational possibilities including new professions created by AI may help young people selecting their dream education leading to this job. Education influences the results in achieving the other goals.

The contribution of AI to the achievement of the Goal 5 "Achieve gender equality and empower all women and girls" can be done through access to education and better management of talents, independently of gender. However, the biggest challenge here is to make evolve mentalities, accept and develop the women talents, attract girls to scientific and technical study and professions. Social networks and other communication media has a significant role to play in achieving this goal.

The Goal 6 "Ensure availability and sustainable management of water and sanitation for all" can be partially achieved by optimized use of water. There are the similarity with achieving of the Goal 7 "Ensure access to affordable, reliable, sustainable and modern energy for all". The IBM offer Smarter Planet launched in 2010 contains few optimizing tools, however it addresses the energy, water and transportation providers. Kayakutlu and Mercier-Laurent [30] addresses the energy users and propose applying of AI techniques for optimized combining of natural and fossil energy, but also making citizens aware about energy waste. The trend of bitcoin, of collecting data, posting on social networks and recent recording of conferences online is energy consuming. The addressing of this two goals requires critical thinking and capacity of finding the smartest way of performing our activities. For example a leaf blower is energy consuming, polluting and not effective.

The Goal 8 "Promote sustained, inclusive and sustainable economic growth, full and productive employment and decent work for all" remains very difficult to achieve. The biggest barrier here is human greed, desire to become rich and powerful at the expense of others and by exploring cheap workforce and people in the need. This attitude can be "corrected" by games and social networks. This goal is related to the goal 10.

The Goal 9 "Build resilient infrastructure, promote inclusive and sustainable indus-trialization and foster innovation" is rather easy but requires better organization of inno-vation ecosystems and again management of talents, promoting "local". Digital trans-formation has a significant role to play at the condition of innovating the whole process. AI way of thinking helps organizing and implementing it using the suited techniques. At this stage the evaluation of impacts should be considered.

The Goal 10 "Reduce inequality within and among countries" is very ambitious and requires other organization then those by countries. It is connected to the goal 8 and requires wisening and humility of the world leaders or emergence of new leaders before applying AI for global optimization. Achieving this goal requires having an effective global governance. Some examples of societal innovation are given in [43].

The Goal 11 "Make cities and human settlements inclusive, safe, resilient and sustainable" will be discussed in the point 4 on Smart City. This goal is linked with the goals 3, 6, 7 and 13.

The achievement of the Goal 12 "Ensure sustainable consumption and production patterns" again AI can help preventing various impacts. Eco-innovation and eco-design approaches [42] powered by AI and alternative thinking may lead to wise exploring of raw materials, even avoid using them, especially in electronic devices. Planned obsolescence has to be replaced by sustainable products and services.

The Goal 13 "Take urgent action to combat climate change and its impacts" addresses a very complex and interconnected problems. Dealing with this challenge requires a deep understanding and modeling of impacting components and their inter-relations, before planning the actions. As in constraint programming the priority of the actions and elaboration of adequate metrics to be implemented will determine the effectiveness of footprint reduction. Complex system approach [44] and AI-powered simulator may help in global governance of climate change. This goal is interlinked with the goals 3, 6, 7, 9, 14, 15 and 17.

The Goal 14 "Conserve and sustainably use the oceans, seas and marine resources for sustainable development". This challenge is also complex, as the ocean life that should remain sustainable is. Taking care of the oceans requires combining knowledge and expertise from related fields. It covers many actions such as removing plastic (Boyan Slat), absorbing harmful fish using robots [45] or preserving spaces actions. Fishing is regulated however, this can be managed by AI, not on the country or European level, but for each sea and ocean. Transportation amplified by globalization try to shorten the roads despite pollution and heat generated. This problem can be solved by influencing mentality (as Goal 10), producing and buying local sustainable goods. Researchers deploy other robots to understand the sea life in aim preserving the balance [47]. The European initiative OceanGov addresses 7 components in the related multidisciplinary working groups [46].

Achieving of the Goal 15 "Protect, restore and promote sustainable use of terrestrial ecosystems, sustainably manage forests, combat desertification, and halt and reverse land degradation and halt biodiversity loss" depends again of the way of doing business and searching for quick profit. AI may help in urbanization planning and optimizing. Desertification depends on managing local talents and increase the attractiveness. For example today the only way of getting benefits in France is investment into houses and buildings. Investors purchase the land for low prices and build houses or buildings for sale destroying biodiversity. If only we could change the innovation policies and make investment in innovation more attractive than investment in buildings, not always necessary. Again the AI based simulators have the potential to demonstrate such impacts.

Goal 16 "Promote peaceful and inclusive societies for sustainable development, provide access to justice for all and build effective, accountable and inclusive institutions at all levels". Achieving this goal require the change of behaviors at all levels and restoring the lost respect. Games may help, but it should be connected to politics, education and amplified by mass media.

Goal 17 "Strengthen the means of implementation and revitalize the global partnership for sustainable development" can be achieved by incentives such as investment in sustainable innovation. Global partnership has been already tried by various conference but without significant results. Interesting initiatives such as Earth Planet, agro ecology of CIRAD [40], numerous projects on preserving biodiversity and other prototyping actions [may serve as inspiration for the next. Knowledge base BC3 [36] was designed to group such experiences.

Smart city can be a playground for prototyping of sustainable development of not only cities but applying holistic approach – smart and autonomous villages, small and bigger cities and regions. Well defined and conceived such way of doing may help achieving several UN goals.

4 Contribution of AI - Case of Smart City

All concepts - Smart City, Intelligent City, Green and Wise City - aim in providing services to citizens of quickly growing cities. The citizens can be individual or a part of organization or company that is why holistic approach is appropriate. Actually, the raisons of this growth are job offer, access to services, to culture or immigration or search for better social conditions. Based on linear approximation in 2050 70% of world population will be living in the Megapolis [48, 49].

Another influencing factor to take into consideration is the ambition of politicians to grow their territory, to attract companies and capital in aim increasing their power and show it up. As consequence, regional economy collapses in many cases and should be reinvented using local talents and resources.

The concept of Smart City was probably born in early 2000s pushed by technology with Cisco as network provider, IBM and some others. In 2010, IBM introduced a new slogan "Smarter Planet" combining their current offer to various elements related with water, energy and transportation management.

Intelligent City tries to be different and defines integrated model of intelligent economy, green transportation, environment, governance and services for citizens [49].

The city of Nice (French Riviera) runs annually a conference on Innovative City [50]. This year AI and its benefits for the city is on the program. The other topics discussed are more traditional - mobility, energy, recycling, urbanism, wellbeing and specificities of Euro-Mediterranean area to explore. Technology is behind all items, but it lacks an overall approach for better optimization of efforts and investment.

Growing cities want to attract people and companies by offering wellbeing to citizens. Green City combines architecture, gardening and social cohesion [51, 52]. The topic of societal innovation is timely in the current changing context [43].

The Wise City of Hong Kong in collaboration with French Chamber of Commerce brings together large companies - Schneider Electric, Alstom, Veolia, Thales and KPMG - no room for small ones. KPMG claims to be integrator of all offers. They focus on improvement of living conditions: pollution, access to clean water, waste treatment, etc. Hong Kong with over 7 million of habitants produces 15,000 tons of waste daily and uses 60% more water than New York. Buildings are heavy consumers and air pollution is 53% local [53].

Schneider Electric being a partner of Wise City proposes an integrated offer, shown in Fig. 4.

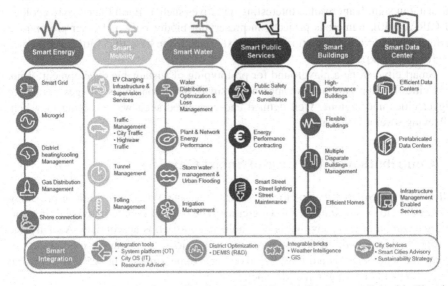

Fig. 4. Integrated services for Smart City (source https://www.slideshare.net/SchneiderElectric/schneider-electric-smart-cities-hannover-v3)

The presented offer, elaborated as a whole, improved though deployment in over hundred targeted cities includes the following components: smart energy, smart mobility, smart water, smart public services, smart buildings, smart data centers and smart integration. These components represent also the areas of Schneider expertise. Several AI techniques, for optimization, maintenance, decision support and others facilities are embedded in this offer to provide solutions tailored for the city. For example, mobility module provides the real-time monitoring of system performance and detection of problems that may occur (predictive maintenance). The collected feedback allows reducing traffic and improving the network.

The energy module is in charge of providing continuous service. In the case that apply the energy offer is composed also with available sources of renewable energy.

Another module is in charge of water management and supply. Improving public safety is possible thanks to real-time analysis of video cameras (using deeplearning).

We can notice that the offers for energy and water are a part of smart buildings. Smart buildings, IoT and home automation systems helps managing machine-to-machine connections, detection of incidents, water and energy supply and optimized use of resources.

Healthcare management includes, among others AI-bases planning and scheduling of staff and devices for better service offered to patients.

Environmental footprint assessment application collects the environmental data. After validation, they are explored for improvement of performances. Data related to "users' experience" are also collected and explored for continuous improvement.

Data Center is certainly associated with city management system and we hope there is only one for all applications proposed by partners.

This integrated city management platform designed using Knowledge Management principle connects all elements and allow information and knowledge sharing, the observation of world best practices, provides decision support and incidents management. This platform communicates with city management and citizens.

The city is also in charge of the other services that citizens may need but the above system does not allow expressing the citizen (consider in holistic perspective) ideas for new services. Considering holistic approach a Future factory is a part of the city or of the region.

AI plays multiple role in Smart city – in the above-integrated offer the optimization techniques are used to manage water and energy distribution and consumption, other techniques for diagnosis, maintenance, business intelligence, optimizing transportation, collection of garbage, planning works, meetings, events and other city activities.

However, the smart city has to be managed as the whole ecosystem in its environment and not by separate modules. Cities are concerned by economic development, but also pandemics, biodiversity, climate change, pollution, education, poverty and other UN goals.

We suggest to improve this concept by connecting several UN goals and prototyping in selected region. Some examples of such prototyping are already available, but in various context, that makes difficult finding similar example [43]. The project B3C [36] ambitions in building collaborative knowledge base of best world practices.

5 Conclusion and Perspective

Humans are the greater generators of disasters. In the context of Planet Emergency, sustainability and sustainable development is still a big challenge for humanity. Before applying technology this complex problem requires awareness about our impact and evolution of individual and companies behaviors, radical change of focus from having more to living better in harmony with nature.

AI way of thinking helps understanding better such a complex problem, finding alternative solutions. The better use of our brain capacity is mandatory.

The presented example demonstrated that AI is useful in many situations if we apply appropriate method and techniques.

AI can help managing many aspects when used appropriately, but we still need to define the right metrics for correct evaluation of the effects of our actions – individual and collective. Simulators cans help evaluating the situation, testing effect of influencing factors and consequence of decisions to take before doing. It applies in industry, city and in our lives.

The balance between the use of technology and human capacity should be preserved. Technology producers have tendency to produce software and devices that think instead of the human and take decisions for him/her. This kind of applications may replace human at the long run and reduce his cognitive capacity. That is why we have to design applications able to enhance human intelligence without switching it off.

Technology alone cannot save Planet, but can help us to be smarter.

References

1. Cueto J.: Planned Obsolescence – An Economic and Cultural Anxiety (July 2009). researchg ate.net
2. https://www.climatecare.org/resources/news/infographic-carbon-footprint-internet/
3. https://communication-responsable.ademe.fr/sites/default/files/guide-ademe-tic-quels-imp acts.pdf
4. https://nsidc.org/. Accessed Apr 2021
5. The Environmental Effects of Freight, OECD, Paris (1997)
6. https://www.dailymail.co.uk/sciencetech/article-9469541/Suez-canal-blockage-caused-spike-air-pollution.html. Accessed 14 Apr 2021
7. Waste sorting https://www.futura-sciences.com/tech/actualites/robotique-robot-dope-ia-ame liorer-tri-dechets-73184/
8. Feng, Z., et al.: Toward a systemic navigation framework to integrate sustainable development into the company. J. Clean. Prod. **54**, 199–214 (2013)
9. Dostatni, E., Diakun, J., Grajewski, D., Wichniarek, R., Karwasz, A.: Automation of the ecodesign process for Industry 4.0. In: Burduk, A., Chlebus, E., Nowakowski, T., Tubis, A. (eds.) ISPEM 2018. AISC, vol. 835, pp. 533–542. Springer, Cham (2019). https://doi.org/10.1007/978-3-319-97490-3_51
10. Future Factory Schneider Electric. https://www.youtube.com/watch?v=N2nbm5xHCjc
11. Schneider 2018–2019 Sustainability Report. https://www.schneider-electric.com/en/about-us/sustainability/
12. https://new.siemens.com/global/en/company/topic-areas/digital-enterprise/discrete-industry. html. Accessed July 2019
13. Yan, W., Zanni-Merk, C., Cavallucci, D., Collet, P.: An ontology-based approach for inventive problem solving. Eng. Appl. Artif. Intell. (2014)
14. Mercier-Laurent, E.: The Innovation Biosphere-Planet and Brains in Digital Era. Wiley, Hoboken (2015)
15. Brundtland, G.H.: Our Common Future, United Nations (March 1987)
16. European Union – sustainable development. http://ec.europa.eu/environment. Accessed July 2019
17. Antoine de Saint Exupéry: Terre des hommes (1939). https://www.argotheme.com/st_exu pery_terre_des_hommes.pdf
18. Folke, C., Holling, C.S., Perrings, C.: Biological diversity, ecosystems and the human scale. Ecol. Appl. **6**(4), 1018–1024 (1996)
19. https://www.wonolo.com/
20. Capiluppi, A., Baravalle, A.: Matching demand and offer in on-line provision: a longitudinal study of monster.com. Web System Evolution (October 2010)
21. Maher, M.L., Pu, P.: Issues and Applications of Case-based Reasoning to Design. Lavoisier, Paris (1997)
22. Nega-water. https://waterfamily.org/water-academie/
23. ISO 26000. https://www.iso.org/iso-26000-social-responsibility.html. Accessed July 2019
24. Strous, L., Johnson, R., Grier, D.A., Swade, D. (eds.): Unimagined futures – ICT opportunities and challenges. IAICT, vol. 555. Springer, Cham (2020). https://doi.org/10.1007/978-3-030-64246-4
25. Wang, A.: Ethics and regulation of artificial intelligence. In: 8th AI4KM/IJCAI 2020, Yokohama (2020)
26. Top 36 chatbot applications. https://research.aimultiple.com. Accessed 7 Apr 2021
27. AGI Society. http://www.agi-society.org/. Accessed April 2021
28. Michalski, R.S., Carbonell, T.J., Mitchell, T.M.: Machine Learning – An Artificial Intelligence Approach. Tioga Publishing, Palo Alto (1983)

29. Michalski, R.S., Tecuci, G. (eds.): Machine Learning: A Multistrategy Approach, vol. IV, Morgan and Kaufmann (1994). ISBN-13: 978-1558602519
30. Kayakutlu, G., Mercier-Laurent, E.: Intelligence in Energy. Elsevier, Amsterdam (2017)
31. Schreiber, G., Wielinga, B., Breuker, J.: KADS – A Principled Approach to Knowledge-Based System Development. Academic Press, Cambridge (1993)
32. Mercier-Laurent, E.: Rôle de l'ordinateur dans le processus global de l'innovation à partir de connaissances. HDR. Université Jean Moulin, Lyon (2007)
33. Problem Solving Methods: Past, Present, and Future, AIEDAM (Spring 2008)
34. Julian, V., Botti, V.: Multi-agent systems. Appl. Sci. **9**(7), 1402 (2019)
35. Nation States game. https://www.nationstates.net/
36. Thivant, E., Mercier-Laurent, E., Talens, G.: Developing of knowledge base on climate change for metropolitain cities. In: 8th AI4KM, IJCAI 2020, Yokohama (2020)
37. Back Market. https://www.backmarket.fr. Accessed Apr 2021
38. Repair café. https://www.repaircafe.org/fr/. Accessed Apr 2021
39. Trends and challenges for intellectual capital, chapter in intellectual capital in organizations. In: Ordonez de Pablos, P., Edvinsson, L. (eds.) Routledge (2015)
40. Côte, F., Poirier-Magona, E., Perret, S., Roudier, P., Rapidel, B., Thirion, M-C.: The agroecological transition of agricultural systems in the Global South. Editions Quæ (June 2019)
41. Artificial Pancreas. https://www.adameetingnews.org/trial-results-show-promise-of-artificial-pancreas-system/goal
42. Mercier-Laurent, E.: Innovation Ecosystems. Wiley, Brundtland (2011)
43. Mercier-Larent, E., Edvinsson, L.: World Class Cooking for Solving Global Challenges. Emerald Publishing, Bingley (2021)
44. Ouskova Leonteva, A., Abdulkarimova, U., Wintermantel, T., Jeannin-Girardon, A., Parrend, P., Collet, P.: A quantum simulation algorithm for continuous optimization (poster). In: GECCO 2020: The Genetic and Evolutionary Computation Conference, Cancun, Mexico, p. 2 (Mars 2020)
45. https://www.youtube.com/watch?v=OEIeS12TcWU. Accessed 19 June 2021
46. Ocean Gov Initiative. https://www.oceangov.eu/. Accessed Apr 2021
47. Using AI to exploring the oceans. https://www.youtube.com/watch?v=bAXveeBTZ3A
48. Duranton, G., Puga, D.: The growth of cities. OECD (2013). http://www.oecd.org/eco/growth/Growth_of_cities_Duranton.pdf
49. Ville Intelligente. http://smartgrids-cre.fr
50. https://www.innovative-city.com/
51. ICT for Societal Challenges: Digital Agenda for Europe. Publication Office of the European Union, Luxembourg (2013)
52. https://gizmodo.com/paris-as-a-green-and-sustainable-future-city-is-even-mo-1680372218
53. Wise City Hong Kong. http://wisecity.hk/

Holistic Approach to Smart Factory

Cristina Monsone[✉]

Széchenyi István University, Egyetem tér 1, Győr 9026, Hungary
monsone.cristina@sze.hu

Abstract. This article presents the key elements of the digitalization of a system, industrial and non, providing a new holistic formulation for Industry 4.0, I4.0, and a concept base of a new API system in the field of Digital Twin for industrial integrated smart solutions based on Internet of Think, IoT, devices. The general approach is also considered for "traditional" industries which come to be I4.0 and as a suitable element for virtual training and decision-making system for industrial e non -industrial customers in a vision of future application in a Virtual reality, VR, environment. In particular, this research defines a formula - CMon - representative of the digitalization of any system and the realization of an API, DTNet, able to create in real- time a Digital Twin, DT, of a single object from a video, realized through any device, using Deep Learning Techniques and then integrate it in a VR environment for a more accurate predictive analysis.

Keywords: Digital Twin · I4.0 · Artificial Intelligence

1 Introduction

The I4.0 [1, 2] panorama introduces new development and service concepts in the name of a digital transformation fostering the disruption side of the smart technologies.

This disruption is evident not only at the technological level, but, according to [3] it represents a potential way to decrease the production costs by 10–30%, logistic costs by 10–30% and quality management costs by 10–20%. There are also a number of other advantages and reasons for the adoption of this concept including, just to mention a few, a shorter time-to-market for the new products, improved customer responsiveness [4] and also optimization of environmental-friendly best practices.

Including a technological mix of robotics, sensors, connection and IoT integration, I4.0 represents a new revolution with respect to the way of traditional manufacturing products and traditional work organization, which does not exclusively imply a new process but also allows transformation of traditional industry into a smart industry in a sustainable way, following a and non-linear development as in the recent past.

The improvement provided by digitalization, in particular referring to the Smart Factory, proposing three levels [5]: smart production, smart services and smart energy. But, considering a wide application panorama, the digitalization thanks to the interconnection with machine learning technique, in particular deep learning, offers the possibility for

E. Mercier-Laurent et al. (Eds.): AI4KM 2021, IFIP AICT 614, pp. 160–176, 2021.
https://doi.org/10.1007/978-3-030-80847-1_11

advanced forecast and consequently prevention and optimization of the potential solution and best management also in other sectors, as mentioned before, like environment and health.

These innovative renewing processes and systems also bring new managed communication and service rules, firstly for workers/managers with adequate skills. In this process towards the smart factory, cloud computing, which arises from the combination of information technologies that have developed in recent decades, plays a fundamental role, covering the application of an end-to-end solution using information and communication technologies that are embedded in a cloud.

On the one hand, cloud computing can be considered mainly as a cost reduction technology, and also as a choice for quick solutions to respond to specific operational problems in the context of a global business strategy based on agility and reactivity [6].

The true value of cloud computing is how it can be used to support a global strategy designed to create business agility [7].

Companies that create a business strategy based on agility put reactivity before efficiency. This strategy emphasizes the ability to make both continuous incremental changes to products and adjustments to operating procedures so that the company can respond to the development of new economic conditions. This is where Human-Machine collaboration enters. Daughter of that digital transformation that is progressively changing habits and customs, triggering a cultural revolution on a global scale, Industry 4.0 in recent years has also become a new dimension of communication and business.

In the landscape of smart devices, another important trend for the future is the augmented humanity surrounding the AR, Augmented Reality.

In general, AR/VR devices, which initially attracted mainly private consumers, begin to enter companies to manage internal processes and customer-oriented services [8], generating much of the business market value, in the next years.

The Augmented Operator paradigm is related to the worker's technological support that is required in the manufacturing environment, which represents a challenge since the operators will face a large variety of new tasks. Industry 4.0 introduces new types of interactions between operator and machines, as well as the coexistence between human and robots/cobots, which will completely change the current industrial workforce in order to answer the changing requirements and the increasing production variability [9].

In light of the impact of these disruptive technologies, this article presents a new holistic formulation for the I4.0, considering the key elements for the digitalization of any system, for example for "traditional" industries which come to be smart, and a concept base of a new API system in the field of Digital Twin - DTNet - for industrial integrated smart solutions in a VR environment.

1.1 Components of Smart Factory: CPS and Digital Twins

The modern meaning of "Digital Twin" refers to the "Conceptual Ideal for PLM" presentation by Dr. M. Grieves published in 2002 at the University of Michigan. This term, however, originally dates back to the 1960s and was used by NASA in reference to the creation of a "terrestrial" duplicate of the systems within the spacecraft. Later it was also used as a basis for the development of computer simulations.

The two macro-elements to be connected are virtual space and real (or physical) space. This connection takes place through a "mirroring" or "twinning" process which follows the product throughout its life cycle.

In essence, it is a question of collecting all the data, information and processes of a physical element, such as a product and dividing it into a virtual version. This allows the possibility to examine and study it in all its parts and also opens up multiple possibilities for simulations and predictive analyses. The current technological evolution has been characterized in recent years by an extension from the physical world (world of atoms) to the virtual world (world of bits), thanks to the creation of static mathematical models (2D and 3D CAD drawings), models of manufacturing processes (CAM) and dynamic simulation of the behaviour of objects, machinery, plants and processes (CAE).

The I4.0 paradigm introduced the concept of integration between physical objects and their mathematical models by means of cyber-physical systems (CPS - Cyber-Physical System): computer systems capable of interacting continuously with the physical systems with which they are associated. A CPS is composed of a physical asset with computational, communication and control capabilities, which can be an object, a system or an industrial process (physical twin), to which a digital twin is associated with which it interacts. In a mono-directional way (the digital twin acquires the data produced by the physical twin, which are then analyzed and used off-line) or in a bi-directional way (the digital twin can intervene with alarms or directly on the behaviour of the physical twin if it detects abnormal or in any case optimizable behaviour).

The future will allow the development of real "digital twins", or digital representations that reflect objects, processes or systems of real-life; these can also be linked together, to create twins of larger systems, such as a power plant or a city, and in perspective, even an individual.

Digital twins allow both to monitor the activity of a plant or process and to predict its behaviour in advance. Digital twins can be created with various levels of complexity, up to a complete virtual simulation of a system, product or physical process that combines technical and managerial information on the components and processes that make up an asset, the technical characteristics of all the components, the documentation connected to the component (certifications, operating manuals, technical documents, drawings, etc.), the links between the elements of the asset and the document management systems, such as PDM (Product Data Management) and PLM (Product Lifecycle Management), production control systems such as MES (Manufacturing Execution System) or DCS (Distributed Control System), up to ERP (Enterprise Resource Planning) management systems, to integrate them in real-time with process data. The most advanced systems are based on neuronal networks and artificial intelligence algorithms that identify abnormal behaviours by comparing data from sensors with predictive models and make use of human-machine interfaces (HMI - Human Machine Interface) based on virtual reality environments and augmented reality to communicate with users immediately and immersively.

The CPS is a mechanism controlled or monitored by computerized algorithms, closely integrated with the internet and its users [10, 11]. Cyber-physical Systems (CPS) are simply physical objects with embedded software and computing power. In Industry 4.0, more manufactured products will be smart products. Based on connectivity and computing power, the main idea behind smart products is that they will incorporate self-management capabilities [12, 13]. In cyber-physical systems, the software and physical components are closely connected, each operating in different spatial and temporal scales, exhibiting multiple and distinct behavioural modes, and interacting with each other in a myriad of ways that change according to the context in real-time [12].

Through the CPS, it's possible to collect the data used in the data-mining through analytical tool working with Algorithms and relevant Model Accuracy [9–13].

The devices, equipped with intelligent sensors, allow the combination of different data into flows of useful information, as well as to monitor and optimize resources from any point in real-time, integrating control and information systems. A cyber-physical system, therefore, has computational, processing, communication and control (cyber) capabilities; integrates hardware and software objects with its own "intelligence" (smart); it consists of automated and intelligent technologies that operate autonomously and in contact with the surrounding environment (Internet of Things) which process an enormous flow of information transforming it into predictive corporate know-how (Big Data) [15] (Fig. 1).

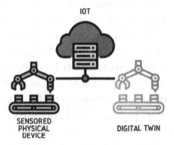

IOT

SENSORED
PHYSICAL
DEVICE

DIGITAL TWIN

Fig. 1. Digital Twin [34].

1.2 Usefulness of the Digital Twin

The usefulness of the digital twin is transversal to all manufacturing industries operating in the most diverse industrial sectors, for example, to get to intelligent buildings controlled by BIM (Building Information System) systems and Smart Cities. The sectors particularly affected by the implementation of a digital twin are design, sustainable production, quality control, performance optimization, maintenance and in general after-sales services. The main goal of a digital twin is to respond immediately to external changes to [13]:

- anticipate and prevent problems;
- resolve problems promptly, making all the necessary changes in the virtual world to ensure that the physical asset works exactly as expected;
- save time and money in the simulation, test and analysis phases and speed up time to marketing;

- improve the performance of the physical twin. The ability to monitor products during their operation allows you to check their functionality and how they are used, and allows you to continue testing in real-life situations to refine the product and update the software embedded in the product in real-time;
- the digital model can also be used to make durability tests, accelerating the scrolling of the time in order to evaluate several years of operation in a few hours. If a problem arises, time can be 'slowed down' to allow the designer to observe what happens in critical moments;
- the presence of digital twins also potentially opens up a space for third parties, such as insurance companies, SMEs and start-ups, who can develop services based on the information produced by digital twins and create an interconnected ecosystem over time.

The manufacturers of vehicles, ships and planes build digital models on which they carry out all the tests and simulations necessary to arrive at a satisfactory project (digital prototyping). When the digital model is ready, the bits are converted into atoms with various types of machines (such as 3D printers) and the prototype is obtained. This process can involve the whole logistic chain. For example, aircraft manufacturers such as Boeing send suppliers the digital specifications of the parts with which their component will interface, and these, in turn, must provide the customer with a digital representation of the component that they will have to make. The manufacturer integrates all components digitally, performs tests and simulations and, after verifying the correct functioning of the models, activates its own production and that of suppliers. With virtual commissioning, you can evaluate the behaviour of the automation of a system even before having the product assembled, verifying its goodness and consistency in advance. GE applies a dense network of sensors to its turbines (used both in wind systems and within jet engines) that communicate with the virtual Digital Twin in almost real- time. From the moment of sale, the real turbine informs its virtual copy of the current use and this allows not only to record data continuously but also to detect faults, discrepancies, forecasts of decay and resolution of problems already in the testing phase. General Electric has for some years extended the use of the digital models of its turbines (both those used in wind systems and those operating in turbo-jets) to their maintenance and control. The turbine is sold associated with its digital twin: a specific digital model of that turbine. The physical turbine contains various sensors that send all the operating data to the virtual turbine, such as rotation speed, instantaneous power, temperatures, pressures, vibrations, etc. These data allow the digital twin to simulate the operating situation and to detect any operating differences between the virtual model and the physical turbine, which trigger control mechanisms to identify and solve the problem.

Every Tesla car has a digital twin on board. Tesla receives information from hundreds of thousands of cars every day (over 2 million km per day, adding up the contributions of all cars). This huge amount of data allows you to check and solve the presence of design-dependent problems [15].

In the two examples shown, we focused on the application of the Digital Twin concept in IoT, but the applications to predictive analyses and tests that are put in place before the release of the product/service still remain to be evaluated. All those phases of conception and creation of virtual models that provide data and information that condition the subsequent decisional and project phases are relevant, especially considering the needs of a sustainable and eco-friendly production [16].

The benefits of adopting Digital Twins are innumerable and typically change according to the need and use of the company. For some companies they are linked to data collections of products already in use, for others they allow to test new designs, for still others they constitute the virtual phases of real processes.

CPS are entering mainstream use, represent a primary tool for organizations implementing IoT projects and are becoming an integral part of digital strategies. The main players in the digital twin market are large industrial groups such as General Electric, IBM, Robert Bosch, Siemens and software houses such as ANSYS, Dassault Systèmes, Microsoft, Oracle, PTC and SAP, as well as dozens of smaller companies and start-ups.

Today a fundamental requirement to create a DT is to have high-quality CAD data of all geometric objects in all phases of the planning process. Fast production scans and subsequent object recognition and identification of CAD models from a reference are required library and transfer of geometry and other object data (e.g., machine types) such as modular objects directly from the library significantly reduce scan times.

The definition of suitable interfaces allows the transfer of information in a simulation program they can be production systems and a digital twin of precision manufacturing generated - almost without manual intervention in a cloud environment [12, 14].

The general procedure for the automatic preparation of a Digital Twin as a solution involves scanning, modelling and simulation modelling. Modelling must be strongly supported by object recognition to save time which would be spent in the manual remastering phase. The object parameter (e.g., machine characteristics) are stored in the CAD library and/or in an external dataset.

Scalability is an important requirement for this approach because theoretically each of the infinite objects constructed must be recognized. Expert knowledge of construction the environment must be acquired through modules or interviews with experts and also included in the simulation process. At this time, real-time processing and recognition is a desirable option, but not a mandatory one. *For older objects that don't have 3D documentation, an alternative approach must be developed to derive a feature-based model with the recognition of singular characteristics. This is one of the challenges on this research.*

1.3   IoT

The communication path represented by the IoT and Industrial Internet of Think, IIot, which represents the interconnection of physical devices, vehicles, buildings integrated with electronics, software, sensors, actuators and network connectivity allows them to collect and exchange data. The IoT allows these objects to be detected and/or controlled remotely through the existing communications infrastructure. The utilization of these smart objects is allowing a real revolution within companies that are now always connected and leverage data to optimize their production processes [15, 16].

An Industrial Internet of Things, IIoT, object is actually a newly developed IoT device designed exclusively for its application within the fourth industrial revolution. The purpose of IIoT objects is to optimize production processes through the connection between the machines, to create useful data for an analysis center, to have a preventive check on the health of the machines in use and to control the times of industrial production [16].

A company that invests in new technologies can use both, IoT and IIoT. But the two technologies are not synonymous. The IIoT is an evolution of the IoT that allows an intelligent device to have multiple connections simultaneously and to work with a greater amount of data [16, 17].

It thus happens to direct the production towards one or another model based on the availability and the current cost of the raw materials or to make changes or customizations during the work by accepting customer inputs.

The direction is agile manufacturing: a lean supply chain and a production cycle tailored to the market as better as possible: Adidas, Toyota and many other companies in various sectors have already done. Research in academia and industry shows that retailers can achieve up to a 15%–20% increase in return on investment by introducing smart technologies [17].

In particular, as presented before, these elements closely interconnected with each other, IoT (Internet of Things) technologies and Big Data, Devices, Cloud computing, are crucial within the Smart Factory only supported by human-machine collaboration [18].

2   Research Challenge

The principle behind the integrations between digital twins is the practical application of their real twins. In operation, each component interacts with others and this entails additional aggregate data. The Digital Twins of each of these components if linked to the others and placed in simulation, can provide much more precise data on wear, failures and any other problems, using cloud-connected sensors integrated into the machines to upload operational data in real-time, producing updated virtual simulations of real machines. Producers can then use margin analysis to analyze and evaluate the performance of their products in the field. The main goal is to have a digital context running for every real-world resource in the field, with virtual replication ready to update its status thanks to data reception and analysis. *But the main challenge is the realization of a DT when the technical engineering properties are unknown and it is necessary to define all aspects to implement a smart system.*

The aim of this research is to define a "formula" for the digitalization of any system (industrial and non-industrial) - called CMon - and the parameters for an API - "DTNet", allowing the possibility to realize in real-time a Digital twin for all type of machine and a suitable definition of the proposed Digital Twin model in Virtual reality environment. The ultimate goal is also to study the potential benefits of applying knowledge management powered by adequate techniques of Artificial Intelligence proposing the new approach to Smart Factory in the context of I4.0 in a sustainable way.

The Internet of Things, as mentioned, is the key to implementing this technology. The growing convenience of sensors, the widespread use of Wi-Fi and the ability to transmit data from the cloud combine to make the application of digital modeling accessible on a large scale for a wide range of solutions and a wide audience of companies.

The formula considers the life cycle of a digital twin composed of three macro-phases, each of which is divided into further steps, each important for the purpose of a particular function (parrot) as defined in [19].

1. See

It is the phase in which a digital twin continuously updates itself to reflect the precise conditions of the environment; to do this, if necessary, it is also able to communicate with other products in the process line. In this phase we identify:

- the creation step, in which the sensors collect the data that are created in the process; these data, as already said, can be environmental or concern the production process;
- the data communication sub-phase, in which the various sensors send everything they have just detected to the data collection server.

2. Think

For the area in which it is purely used, and therefore that of IIoT, it is the most important phase because it is the one where, through machine-learning and advanced learning techniques, all possible problems are calculated that could occur in the future.

At the end of this phase, the results are shown in the real world and solutions are proposed which can be manual or automatic. In the next point, the difference between these two types of solutions will be explained. In this phase we identify:

- the aggregation sub-phase, where first and elementary processing is performed on what has been received, after which it is stored in a repository or database. The data processing phase can be done before transmitting them, or in the cloud, once they have been received in the control panel;
- the analysis sub-phase, in which the data are analysed and then displayed;
- the forecasting sub-phase, in which we try to understand the data received by searching to draw conclusions in the long run.

3. Do

It is the final phase, the one with which you interact with the production process. If the manual solution was chosen then the system says what needs to be done to make improvements after which the engineers, based on the data received and the system structure, study the proposed situation and find ways to apply it; if instead the automatic solution has been chosen then the task of applying the improvements will be fulfilled directly by the digital twin, through the actuators present in the system. It is important to note that the transition from digital to real-world occurs only through raw data or through forecasts.

In light of the previous considerations, the building blocks of the key elements of the digitalization of any system, representing the fundamental elements of the proposed formula CMon, are identified in the workflow of Fig. 2. This workflow presents the fundamentals steps of the realization of a smart system starting from the realization of a DT for an existing element of an industrial plan or an existing single industrial element especially when it's not possible to acquire the technical design project features.

In particular, it's important to highlight that the widespread use of Wi-Fi and the ability to transmit data from the cloud combine to make the application of digital modelling accessible on a large scale for a wide range of solutions and devices, included mobile-phone, it is one of key elements of the design of a DT in real-time.

The workflow has three main part
The first phase is the "Implementation" of a digital system through:

1. Realization of a Digital Twin through the proposed API, DTNet;
2. Installation of a series of sensors, distributed along the whole chain that processes the signals and allows the digital twin to capture operational and environmental data, and actuators that instead operate directly on the production process itself in order to optimize it;

The second phase considers:

3. Data collection which is part of the digital world and are nothing more than aggregations of more information received by sensors from the physical world thanks to IoT;

The third phase are the:

4. Analytical techniques that are used to analyze data and, through simulations and daily routine visualizations, produce forecasts aimed at improving the system itself;

This research defines a formula - CMon - representative of the digitalization of any system considering the fundamentals elements mentioned in the proposed workflow.

2.1 Workflow of DTNet

API

The digital representation of an object through numerical modelling and simulation techniques is certainly not a new concept: in the past decades more or less sophisticated IT tools have been developed that allow assisting designers and builders in the phases ranging from conception to production or assembly.

In the proposed model, the innovation is the realization of a DT from a video in real-time using Deep Learning techniques.

In Fig. 2 the DTNet workflow is presented.

In general, the available tools normally operate in a context of pure simulation (i.e., without any interaction with the physicality of the systems they represent), and also for this reason they are gradually less effective as the complexity of the modelled system increases. Numerical models also have limits in situations in which it is intended to observe (simulating) behaviours that are articulated over a wide time span, in which complex phenomena that can have an important impact on performance, such as wear of mechanical parts, intervene - in the real world or tools. The quality of the simulation of complex phenomena can be significantly improved if, for the realization of a DT, we use, as proposed for DTNet, CCNs, to realize a model from real-world and combining, through embedded sensors, the data from measurements made in the physical world.

In Fig. 3 we can see, for example, how a ConvNet is able to identify and recognize a computer by object detection with a high rate of accuracy from a video [20]. Now it is time to give a more accurate definition of DTNet, stating that it is the model of an object to which data exchange features are added with its correspondence in the physical world and which follows its evolution over time keeping the virtual representation updated.

Starting from this relatively generic definition, it is possible to identify some essential requirements for the physical objects of which you want to create a digital twin, as well as some functionalities necessary for the information system in charge of managing their virtual representations. It is important to note that, although the context referred to below is that of manufacturing (the one in which the concept of digital twin originated), the considerations made can be applied to any digitization process [7, 20, 22, 23].

In particular, referring to the first point, the digital representation of an object through numerical modelling and simulation techniques is certainly not a new concept: in the past decades more or less sophisticated IT tools have been developed that allow assisting designers and builders in the phases ranging from conception to production or assembly.

The innovation of this research is also the realization of an API, DTNet, able to create in real-time a DT of a single object or an element of an existing plant from a video, realized through any device, using Deep Learning Techniques and then integrate it in VR environment for a more accurate predictive analysis.

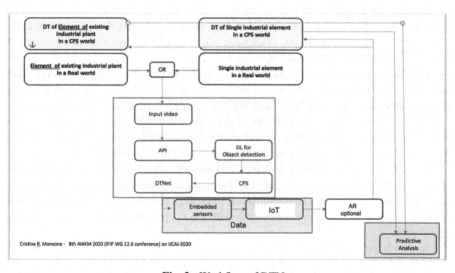

Fig. 2. Workflow of DTNet

However, the quality of the simulation of complex phenomena can be significantly improved if for the realization of a DT, we use, as proposed for DTNet, CCNs, to realize a model from real-world and combining, through embedded sensors, the data from measurements made in the physical world [7].

Fig. 3. Deep learning for DTNet: example of object detection in real-time using a mobile phone

Data

The other main component of the digitalization puzzle is the communication between the physical object and its digital twin, which must take place in the most effective way and in line with the requirements: the communication architecture in terms of protocols must therefore be precisely defined network and HW, hardware, and SW, software, interfaces. The latest generation machines have HW and SW components that allow communication with the outside world, while the older generation ones - still widely used in production plants - are not equipped in this sense.

The management of a large amount of information is a "conditio sine qua non" to optimize the production dynamics of smart factories and to ensure the passage of companies to Industry 4.0. In light of self-awareness and self-maintenance machines for industrial big data environment [21]. However, most of the time, the datasets are either too generic or too specific so you often have to create a dataset for your needs, as it will be demonstrated in the following sections [22, 23].

In light of this and thanks to the use of new technologies, data acquisition is possible not only via the internet (site, social media) but also via wireless networks, mobile devices, heat detectors and NFC in real-time [24–27]. In fact, the IoT devices play a crucial role. The sensors allow the measurement of selected physical quantities to be sent periodically to the digital twin, and actuators that enable the digital twin to be able to send data that can be translated into actions in the physical world [2].

The adaptation to the typical canons of Industry 4.0 can also be obtained for this equipment by adding sensors and processing modules (embedded systems) capable of detecting and transmitting the quantities of interest (a technique called refitting, which must be implemented without interfering with the control electronics possibly already present).

It must have as a fundamental component a database designed to manage very heterogeneous information, which can range from the master data of the machinery (static information, unchanging over time such as date of purchase, cost, manufacturer, model etc.), to the history of maintenance operations (variability relatively slow), up to the data collected in near-real-time by the on-board sensors, flows much more significant than the previous ones which generate a much greater volume of data. The structure responsible for data management is joined by one or more SW modules that make up the intelligence of the digital twin. These can include simulation tools (of the machine) and sophisticated algorithms which, being able to act on information measured in the physical world in addition to the estimated one, are able to provide extremely accurate results and information.

Prediction and Optimization
The last part of the workflow proposed is the predictive analysis phase.
Within this phase, the data collected is mainly used for two very distinct reasons:

- for current investigations, to know when a certain anomaly occurs and how to remedy it;
- for future investigations: in this case, the data are not used for a purpose that is poured into the product immediately but are used to try to anticipate what may happen in the future; anticipating malfunctions, improving over time certain features that the product offers are an example of what could concern these analyzes.

3 Proposed Approach – A Holistic View of Smart Factory

3.1 New Approach to Smart Factory in the Context of I4.0: CMon Formula to Implement Digitalization in Any System

This paper wants to define a formula – CMon (Fig. 4) - in a holistic way to identify the basic parameters for the digitalization of the industrial sector, reflecting its main characteristics:

$$H + 3D + 2C + IoT \rightleftharpoons I4.0$$

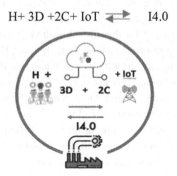

Fig. 4. CMon-formula for I40

Where:

- **H**: Human capacity/skills-Human-machine interaction
- **3D**: The 3 key-elements: data, deep learning, devices
- **2C**: Cloud computing and Communication
- **IoT**: Internet of Things.

The elements of the proposed formula are here presented in light of their main characteristics and represent the key elements to be a smart industry in light of the requirements of I4.0, following the building blocks of the workflow presented in the previous paragraph. The results are focused, in this paper, on the relationship between 3D and IoT. In particular, how built in a real-time and easy way a DT complying the needs of the digitalization of traditional industries.

Further details, including the technological and architectural choices for the information system and the methods of communication, can only be defined and tailored by analyzing the specific case of interest, through the proposed API "DTNet®".

3.2   The Definiton of the Research Parameters for DTNet

Design Phase
As presented, in the previous section, the research is focused on how to realize a tool to design a DT through Deep Learning. Here are considered the main design parameters of the proposed DGNet model.

The concept of a new product is created according to needs dictated by users and particularities of the current fashion. Even characteristics of old products affect the development of the new.

The proposed API, DTNet, is the model of an object to which data exchange features are added with its correspondence in the physical world and which follows its evolution over time keeping the virtual representation updated.

Starting from this relatively generic definition, it is possible to identify some essential requirements for the physical objects of which you want to create a digital twin, as well as some functionalities necessary for the information system in charge of managing their virtual representations. It is important to note that, although the context referred to below is that of manufacturing (the one in which the concept of digital twin originated), the considerations made can be applied to any digitization process.

As presented, in the previous section, the research is focused on how to realize a tool to design a DT through Deep Learning [27–33].

Here are considered the main design parameters of the proposed DTNet model.

The concept of a new product is created according to needs dictated by users and particularities of the current fashion. Even characteristics of traditional products affect the development of the new.

As a concept, that is, an initial development phase, it represents an initial project of how the product will be created without taking into account its software or hardware characteristics. More than anything else, we will take into account the functionalities and how the assigned tasks will have to be carried out: at each creative cycle a design will be proposed and it will be necessary to verify whether the functionality and the foreseen tasks respect in an adequate and advantageous way the user needs.

It is therefore useful to be in possession of a virtual element that acts as a support for these continuous iterations, relating if necessary, with the previous versions of the concept itself. It will therefore be necessary, as the product concept develops, that the digital twin grows hand in hand.

Another very important element that affects the design phase is the opportunity for communication of the digital twin with other digital twins in order to obtain from them information concerning them. Thanks to this particularity, it is thus possible to obtain further information concerning, for example, products already on the market in order to foresee and correct problems connected to them in advance.

However, creating a digital representation of a tool assembly for simulation purposes is far from simple.

Traditionally, to obtain the most accurate representation of a tool assembly in a CAM system, the operator must first search for the necessary information in the various supplier catalogues, then download the 3D model files and assemble them in a CAD program. This is today the only way to obtain a tool assembly in the CAM system, including all technical parameters.

It's possible to distinguish the:

- Digital Twin Prototype (DTP), which describes the prototype physical artifact and contains the information sets necessary to describe and produce a physical version that duplicates or twins the virtual version;
- Digital Twin Instance (DTI), which describes a specific physical product corresponding to which a single Digital Twin remains connected for the entire life of the product itself.

According to a Gartner study, in 2018 48% of the companies interested in the IoT are planning the use of Digital Twin, which would allow testing the solutions before they are applied and would agree in economic terms: it would save about 50% of the time and production would increase by 20%, demonstrating potential growth in short term and long term [34–38].

The model of this research, instead, consider the realization of a DT in real-time and without downloading a 3D model. The model is based on Deep Learning applied to video recognition and on the Human-Machine collaboration in a Virtual Reality environment, in particular through CCNs (Convolutional Neural networks) [27].

4 Conclusion and Future Work

Up to now, the operating and design phases, for example the industrial level, have always been conceived as two totally unrelated phases that did not need to communicate with each other. Thanks to the digital twins, it is possible to combine these phases and keep an eye – before, during and after the engineering phase – on potential weaker parts/process more carefully in order to understand where and how the problem could actually occur through the elaboration of the data collected in real-time using artificial intelligence techniques [34]. This represents a benefit for the future of the product itself and it can bring benefits to new possible products that will be created instead of recognizing the problem only once the complete product is on the market.

Up to now, moreover, the operating and design phases have always been conceived as two totally unrelated phases that did not need to communicate with each other: the data collected during this phase as well as having a benefit for the future of the product itself can bring benefits to new possible products that will be created.

During the engineering phase, parts could be identified that in the future could easily create problems to the product structure and decide to want to find a solution to this problem only once the complete product is on the market. Thanks to digital twins, it is possible to keep an eye on these weaker parts more carefully in order to understand where and how the problem could actually occur also taking into account the needs of a more sustainable and eco-friendly industrial production [39].

At the same time this large amount of data, related to the simulation models always built in the engineering phase, improves all those services that could be requested by the user, such as maintenance; in this way, intervention times and times to find the cause and solution to the problem decrease drastically, bringing benefits to the company both for evident savings in maintenance costs and for customer satisfaction.

In this research, in particular, as reported in the proposed workflow (Fig. 2), it is the combination in real-time through smart technologies of the aforementioned phases the basic parameter for the digitalization of a system, specified in the proposed formula CMon. In the proposed "smartification" the key element is the realization of a Digital Twin. In fact, the core and next step of the research will be the API realization – DTNet- for the design of a Digital Twin of any system from any device in real-time through deep learning techniques - without downloading 3D model - and potential integration in the VR environment.

References

1. Kagermann, H., Lukas, W., Wahlster, W.: Abschotten ist keine Alternative. VDI Nachrichten (16) (2015)
2. Acatech: Umsetzungsempfehlungen für das Zukunftsprojekt Industrie 4.0 – Abschlussbericht des Arbeitskreises Industrie 4.0. acatech (2013)
3. Stock, T., Seliger, G.: Opportunities of sustainable manufacturing in industry 4.0. Procedia Cirp **40**, 536–541 (2016)
4. Rojko, A.: Industry 4.0 concept: background and overview. Int. J. Interact. Mob. Technol. **11**(5), 77–90 (2017). https://doi.org/10.3991/ijim.v11i5.7072
5. Industry 4.0 after the initial hype. Where manufacturers are finding value and how they can best capture it. McKinsey Digital (2016). https://www.mckinsey.com/~/media/mckinsey/bus iness%20functions/mckinsey%20digital/our%20insights/getting%20the%20most%20out% 20of%20industry%204%200/mckinsey_industry_40_2016.ashx
6. Zhong, R.Y., Xu, X., Klotz, E., Newman, S.T.: Intelligent manufacturing in the context of Industry 4.0: a review. Engineering **3**(5), 616–630 (2017)
7. Li, B.H., Zhang, L., Wang, S.L., Tao, F., Cao, J.W., Jiang, X.D., et al.: Cloud manufacturing: a new service-oriented networked manufacturing model. Comput. Integr. Manuf. **16**(1), 1–7 (2010). (in Chinese)
8. Rüßmann, M., Lorenz, M., Gerbert, P., Waldner, M.: Industry 4.0: the future of productivity and growth in manufacturing industries. Boston Consult. Group **9**(1), 54–89 (2015)
9. Wiedenmaier, S., Oehme, O., Schmidt, L., Luczak, H.: Augmented reality (AR) for assembly processes design and experimental evaluation. Int. J. Hum.-Comput. Interact. **16**(3), 497–514 (2003)
10. Chen, F., Deng, P., Wan, J., Zhang, D., Vasilakos, A.V., Rong, X.: Data mining for the Internet of Things: literature review and challenges. Int. J. Distrib. Sens. Netw. **11**(8), 431047 (2015)

11. Monostori, L.: Cyber-physical production systems: roots, expectations and R&D challenges. Procedia CIRP **17**, 9–13 (2014)
12. Lee, J., Bagheri, B., Kao, H.A.: A cyber-physical systems architecture for Industry 4.0-based manufacturing systems. Manuf. Lett. **3**, 18–23 (2015)
13. Bagheri, B., Yang, S., Kao, H.A., Lee, J.: Cyber-physical systems architecture for self-aware machines in Industry 4.0 environment. IFAC Conf. **38**(3), 1622–1627 (2015)
14. Witten, I.H., et al.: Data Mining: Practical Machine Learning Tools and Techniques, 3rd edn. Elsevier, Amsterdam (2011)
15. Baheti, R., Gill, H.: Cyber-physical systems. In: Samad, T., Annaswamy, A.M. (eds.) The Impact of Control Technology: Overview, Success Stories, and Research Challenges, pp. 161–166. IEEE Control Systems Society, New York (2011)
16. Lee, E.A.: Cyber physical systems: design challenges. In: Proceedings of the 11th IEEE Symposium on Object/Component/Service-Oriented Real-Time Distributed Computing, May 5–7 2008, Orlando, FL, USA, pp. 363–369. The Institute of Electrical and Electronics Engineers, Inc., Piscataway (2008)
17. Tan, Y., Goddard, S., Pérez, L.C.: A prototype architecture for cyber-physical systems. ACM SIGBED Rev. **5**(1), 26 (2008)
18. Romero, D., Bernus, P., Noran, O., Stahre, J., Fast-Berglund, Å.: The operator 4.0: human cyber-physical systems & adaptive automation towards human-automation symbiosis work systems. In: Nääs, I., et al. (eds.) APMS 2016. IAICT, vol. 488, pp. 677–686. Springer, Cham (2016). https://doi.org/10.1007/978-3-319-51133-7_80
19. Pereira, A.C., Romero, F.: A review of the meaning and the implications of the Industry 4.0 concept. In: Manufacturing Engineering Society International Conference 2017, MESIC 2017, 28–30 June 2017, Vigo (Pontevedra), Spain (2017)
20. Zhong, R.Y., Xu, X., Klotz, E., Newman, S.T.: Intelligent manufacturing in the context of Industry 4.0: a review. Engineering **3**, 616–630 (2017)
21. Lee, J., Kao, H.A., Yang, S.: Service innovation and smart analytics for Industry 4.0 and big data environment. Procedia Cirp **16**, 3–8 (2014)
22. Almada-Lobo, F.: The Industry 4.0 revolution and the future of Manufacturing Execution Systems (MES). J. Innov. Manag. **3**(4), 16–21 (2015)
23. Witkowski, K.: Internet of Things, big data, Industry 4.0-innovative solutions in logistics and supply chains management. Procedia Eng. **182**, 763–769 (2017)
24. Fantana, N.L., et al.: IoT applications—value creation for industry. Internet of Things: Converging Technologies for Smart Environments and Integrated Ecosystems, p. 153. River Publishers (2013)
25. Qi, Q., et al.: Enabling technologies and tools for digital twin. J. Manuf. Syst. **58**, 3–21 (2019)
26. Ungurean, I., Gaitan, N.C., Gaitan, V.G.: IoT architecture for things from industrial environment (2014)
27. Monsone, C.R., Csápo, A.: Charting the state-of-the-art in the application of convolutional neural networks to quality control in Industry 4.0 and smart manufacturing. In: 10th IEEE International Conference on Cognitive Infocommuncations, Naples, Italy (2019)
28. Monsone, C.R., Mercier-Laurent, E., Jósvai, J.: The overview of digital twin in Industry 4.0: managing the whole ecosystem. In: 11th International Conference on Knowledge Management and Information System, Wien, Austria - Proceedings of KMIS 2019 (2019). https://doi.org/10.5220/0008348202710276, ISBN: 978-989-758-382-7
29. Monsone, C.R., Mercier-Laurent, E.: Ecosystems of Industry 4.0 - combining technology and human powers. In: Proceedings of the 11th International Conference on Management of Digital EcoSystems, Limassol, Cyprus - MEDES 2019 (November 2019)
30. Okano, M.T.: IOT and Industry 4.0: the industrial new revolution (2017)
31. Lu, B.H., Bateman, R.J., Cheng, K.: RFID enabled manufacturing: fundamentals, methodology and applications. Int. J. Agile Syst. Manag. **1**(1), 73–92 (2006)

32. Zhong, R.Y., Li, Z., Pang, L.Y., Pan, Y., Qu, T., Huang, G.Q.: RFID-enabled real-time advanced planning and scheduling shell for production decision making. Int. J. Comput. Integr. Manuf. **26**(7), 649–662 (2013)

33. Huang, G.Q., Zhang, Y.F., Chen, X., Newman, S.T.: RFID-enabled real-time wireless manufacturing for adaptive assembly planning and control. J. Intell. Manuf. **19**(6), 701–713 (2008)

34. Perrey, J., Spillecke, D., Umblijs, A.: Smart analytics: how marketing drives short term and long-term growth. In: Court, D., Perrey, J., McGuire, T., Gordon, J. (eds.) Spillecke Big Data, Analytics, and the Future of Marketing & Sales. McKinsey& Company, New York (2013)

35. Glova, J., Sabol, T., Vajda, V.: Business models for the Internet of Things environment. Procedia Econ. Financ. **15**, 1122–1129 (2014)

36. Qin, J., Liu, Y., Grosvenor, R.: A categorical framework of manufacturing for Industry 4.0 and beyond. Procedia CIRP **52**, 173–178 (2016)

37. Erol, S., Jäger, A., Hold, P., Ott, K., Sihn, W.: Tangible Industry 4.0: a scenario-based approach to learning for the future of production. Procedia CIRP **54**, 13–18 (2016)

38. Parrot. https://www2.deloitte.com/us/en/insights/focus/industry-4-0/digital-twin-techno logy-smart-factory.html

39. Adoption of the Paris Agreement: Decision 1/CP.21, in COP Report No. 21, Addendum, at 2, U.N. Doc. FCCC/CP/2015/10/Add.1 (29 January 2016)

Development of Big Data Analytics
in a Multi-site Enterprise on the Example
of Supply Chain Management

Paweł Pyda[1]([⊠]) [iD], Paweł Stefaniak[2] [iD], Helena Dudycz[3] [iD], and Bartosz Jachnik[2] [iD]

[1] KGHM Polish Copper S.A. o/COPI, KGHM Polska Miedź S.A., Lubin, Poland
pawel.pyda@ue.wroc.pl

[2] KGHM CUPRUM Research and Development Centre Ltd., gen. W. Sikorskiego Street 2-8, 53-659 Wroclaw, Poland

[3] Department of Information Technology, Wroclaw University of Economics and Business, Wrocław, Poland

Abstract. Currently, advanced data analytics in large multi-site industrial enterprises is a strategic element in making management decisions. Integrated supply chain management (SCM), machinery park management, or data analysis from industrial devices (including using Industrial Internet of Things - IIoT) requires the organization of appropriate analytical platform architecture, the selection of the analytical tools for Big Data, the implementation of advanced algorithms based on machine learning and the development of management dashboards for ongoing tracking the KPI's of assets. This article presents the issues related to the acquisition, analysis, and management of large amounts of data from various enterprise departments. These data come from multiple systems, and they are indifferent data recording standards. They are essential because they form the basis of advanced data analysis in supply chain management in multi-site enterprises. This article discusses the proposal of an analytical platform for SCM and the development of analytical processing for SCM in the multi-site industrial enterprise.

Keywords: Supply chain management · Big data · KPI · Industrial enterprise

1 Introduction

In the case of a multi-site industrial enterprise, the development of analytical systems to support decision-making should be oriented to the specific needs, limitations, and possibilities of individual business areas. The development of analytics is very often not a question of technology but the correct use of large data sets to improve the safety and efficiency of technological processes. Data and analyzes not referring to factors influencing these aspects do not bring added value.

The first decade of the 21st century saw the emergence of software for intelligent data analysis and predictive analysis (Frazzon et al. 2019; Waller and Fawcett 2013b), which contributed to a better understanding and use of data, thus improving decision

© IFIP International Federation for Information Processing 2021
Published by Springer Nature Switzerland AG 2021
E. Mercier-Laurent et al. (Eds.): AI4KM 2021, IFIP AICT 614, pp. 177–192, 2021.
https://doi.org/10.1007/978-3-030-80847-1_12

making and decision optimization by businesses (Trkman et al. 2015). In the era of global challenges, enterprises, especially large, multi-site, and production companies, have to take up the challenges they face in connection with the need for advanced data analysis. Therefore, the definition of strong hypotheses of the potential impact of advanced data analysis analytics on the technological process is crucial, so that already in the early stage of development, it is clearly focused on the increased process context awareness, support for managers in decision making and business benefits. Hence, it is essential, first of all, to identify and select key data sources, to reject irrelevant data, and to plan a data analysis process to acquire necessary information.

One of the key business areas is logistics, responsible for managing the supply chain in all production plants of the company. Supply Chain Management (SCM) is the integration of key business processes from end-user through original suppliers that provides products, services, and information that add value for customers and other stakeholders (Lambert and Cooper 2000). The primary purpose of supply chain analysis is to facilitate the understanding of all data produced by various elements of the supply chain (Wong et al. 2011). These analyses result from the management's needs for making the right decisions (Lai et al. 2018) and make it possible to extract specific hidden patterns from the data as well as acquire valuable insights. The subject of supply chain analysis is continually developing, with new technologies and methods coming into being to increase the effectiveness of forecasts, help detect weak areas, better respond to customer needs, and simulate and implement innovative solutions (Chen et al. 2015; Shafiq and Savino 2019). Having complete product information (ready capital-intensive goods, spare parts, consumables, etc.) is a crucial issue of advanced data analysis within an integrated supply chain (Vilminko-Heikkinen and Pekkola 2017). The use of advanced data analysis in SCM is a very current issue. Research in this area is discussed in more detail in: (Maheshwari et al. 2020; Tiwari et al. 2018). In the literature, the problem of analytics development for SCM is cited as marginalized. Much information is provided in a simple form, primarily due to a data sensitivity problem.

Logistics is closely related to most other business areas, especially manufacturing, finance, and purchasing. What is essential here is to ensure the flow of valuable information between all locations. It requires designing an appropriate IT infrastructure in the enterprise, including Big Data tools and analytical systems containing advanced methods and machine learning algorithms. In the papers (Dudycz et al. 2019; Pyda et al. 2019; Pyda et al. 2020), the authors presented the challenges related to the development of IT infrastructure for a multi-site industrial enterprise. A special issue is the limitations of the variety of systems, the diversity of standards for data acquisition and storage, and the quality and availability of them for the appropriate kind of end-users.

The article presents the main issues related to advanced data analysis as a critical element in supply chain management in a multi-site industrial enterprise. This article is structured as follows. Firstly, the fundamental problems and challenges of Supply Chain Management 4.0 is presented. Next, the proposal of the analytical platform and data model for SCM is described. Finally, the analytics development model for SCM in a multi-site industrial enterprise is presented. The paper ends with a summary.

2 Background of Big Data

The concept of Big Data is related to three primary attributes, i.e., large data volume, number of data diversity (structured and unstructured data), and the amount of data flowing in. For the first time in his work, these attributes were described by Laney in 2001 under the title "3D Data Management: Controlling Data Volume, Velocity, and Variety". With the growing importance and application of technology, subsequent researchers in their work developed BD's concept by defining the following attributes of veracity, value, and variability. (Schroeck et al. 2012; Demchenko et al. 2013; Gandomi and Haider 2015). In the literature on the subject, you can find further extensions of BD with additional features starting with V. Figure 1 shows the definition of the so-called 9 V's of Big Data.

Fig. 1. 9 V's of big data

The characteristics of the nine features of BD are as follows:

- Volume – how big is the volume of data?
- Velocity – how often is the data generated?
- Variety – how varied is the data?
- Veracity – how reliable is the data?
- Value – how valuable is the data?
- Variability – how often the structure of data is changing?
- Validity – how accurate is the data?
- Visualization – how challenging the data to visualize is?
- Volatility – how long the data remain valid?

The development and wide availability of technology meant that it was no longer reserved for such big players as Google, Microsoft, or Amazon. Many smaller companies have recognized BD technology's benefits and have embraced many other business areas such as finance and logistics across the entire supply chain.

With the advent of the fourth digital revolution (Industry 4.0), companies began the digital transformation processes, which increased the demand for BD technologies. The increase in the popularity of the Industry Internet of Things in the methods of automation and monitoring of devices also contributed to this.

Koot W. described in his work the use of IoT devices in supply chain management, pointing out that real-time monitoring of the flow of goods contributes to improving logistics operations (tracking, transparency, reliability) (Koot et al. 2020).

The mere acquisition and storage of large amounts of raw data in the BG environment do not yet allow for their analysis. The data must undergo a process of cleaning, validation, often integration, and writing in the form of a business data model. Making the right decisions in complex business processes as part of Supply Chain Management must be based on well-analyzed data (Speranza 2018).

Combining BD technology and advanced data analysis techniques has led to the emergence of a new definition of the term, i.e., Big Data Analyst (BDA). This concept refers to the process of data analysis in many dimensions and their visualization using dedicated tools operating in a computer cluster environment. BDA was of great interest among managers, in particular managers responsible for the supply chain management.

3 Supply Chain Management 4.0 - Basic Problems and Challenges

In (Schoenherr and Speier-Pero 2015) results of an online survey regarding the barriers to the SCM predictive analytics have been presented and supported by statistical analysis. Results show that the most critical obstacles in the implementation of SCM tools are:

- Employees are inexperienced (need to train);
- Time constraints;
- Lack of integration with current systems;
- Cost of currently available solutions;
- Change management issues (resistance to change);
- Lack of appropriate solutions for SCM;
- Overwhelming, challenging to manage.

The statistical analysis conducted in the article shows that these barriers are essential in all three groups of users: those who currently do not use analytics but plan to do so in the future already use analytics to some extent and use analytics tools to a great time. Survey results analysis also showed that SCM predictive analytics benefits were mostly seen in the more information-based decision-making process, improved supply chain efficiency and visibility, and lower overall cost of a supply chain.

Lambert and Cooper (2000) pointed out that the crucial role in the context of a successful SCM implementation is played by key people in the organization (with the division of responsibility for basic processes and auxiliary processes), the network of related processes, and the degree of their integration. According to the authors, the ineffectiveness of the supply chain is primarily influenced by the lack of coherence of activities between individual departments of the organization.

Thompson and Drucker argue that one of the most critical issues is seeking or anticipating company changes, accepting them, and responding to them to explore the possibilities of mitigating the effects of uncertainty (Thompson 1967; Drucker 1968).

According to (Azvine et al. 2007), the prosperity and further activities of an organization depend on how well it understands and interacts with the changing environment. The agile training of the enterprise allows to predict and estimate the nature and size of the change and to react to it accordingly.

Researchers and practitioners indicate that performance in conjunction with global goals throughout the supply chain depends to no small extent on close cooperation and coordination between actors in the supply chain, which in turn facilitates important decisions and formulating effective supply chain strategies (Dong et al. 2009; Cheng et al. 2010; Power 2005; Van Donk and Van der Vaart 2005; Stevenson and Spring 2009) concludes that SCM is strategic coordination between members of the supply chain to integrate supply and demand management which translates into the essence of combining internal and external systems.

Determining business requirements and customer expectations in the context of obtaining, integrating, and analyzing data and making joint and coherent decisions within the supply chain are the main challenges in the context of applying analytics for the supply chain (Sahay and Ranjan 2008).

Successful implementation of an analytical platform for processing large amounts of data for supply chain management largely depends on the support of the management board as part of the company's strategic tasks and appropriate management competencies (Dong et al. 2009).

The implementation of individual business processes as part of an integrated supply chain 4.0 depends on three key elements that an enterprise must have (Fig. 2):

- Identified and well-described processes taking place inside the enterprise along with the identification of the needs for the implementation of new processes;
- Qualified employees who have knowledge of the ongoing business processes and have the skills to use dedicated software. Management staff with the skills to identify gaps in business processes and design new ones, responding to new business needs (ideas);
- IT tools for managing the entire supply chain, appropriately selected at the stage of analysis and feasibility study of given business processes.

Due to the extensive range of functionalities offered by the software available on the market, a direct comparison of individual tools on a general level is not an easy task. According to the Business Application Research Centre (BARC) surveys, there are significant discrepancies among software properties cited as most important by industry leaders and smaller companies. However, it is understandable - leaders are large companies looking for comprehensive solutions that cover problems often unknown to smaller companies. For this reason, larger companies value software flexibility more.

The vast majority of companies participating in the surveys use this software to prepare internal reports and corporate reports. Another popular application of the software

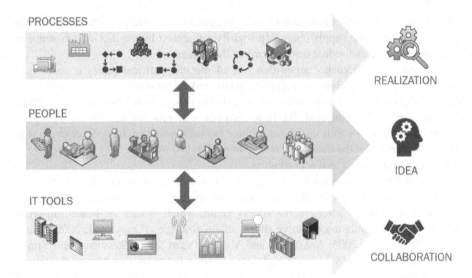

Fig. 2. Processes, people, IT tools. Source: Own work.

is the preparation of simple analyzes and ad-hoc inquiries - 70% and 78% of companies, respectively, declare using tools in this area. Less than 70% of users also use these tools to create interactive data dashboards and scorecards. The software is much less prevalent in strictly financial applications - about 1/3 of the respondents declare using it for planning and budgeting, and financial consolidation.

A widespread mistake made by organizations is trying to solve a given business problem by purchasing IT systems first and then trying to adapt them to the existing and future business processes. Such an approach very often ends with the failure of the entire project - lack of experience in handling a given software, high costs of external companies adjusting the system to support existing and new processes, or even poorly selected software that does not meet expectations.

Fulfilling the requirements in each of these three areas seems quite trivial, but in practice, it isn't easy to implement. The scope of processes often requires the introduction of appropriate organizational changes and changes in handling business processes. The area related to employees requires a proper selection of staff to carry out specific tasks, introduce dedicated training or start the process of retraining employees. The area of selecting the appropriate IT tools in large multi-plant industrial enterprises may turn out to be the most difficult. Identifying systems and data needed to support a given business process, building data flow and their integration, or building dedicated data models without experienced employees may turn out to be very difficult to implement. The success of this task may largely depend on the maturity of a given enterprise and on whether and to what extent it uses methodologies such as TOGAF in the field of managing IT architecture of the enterprise or DAMA-DMBOK Guide (Dama International https://dama.org/) – a guide containing a collection of processes in individual thematic areas (specializations) related to data management in the form of good practices.

Successful implementations of those tools may yet yield significant advantages. Below, some of the examples of implementing the SCM tools in the industry have been described.

- Schneider Electric is a company that specializes in providing digital energy management and automation solutions that uses Supply Chain Guru software, a product of Llamasoft, for demand forecasting. According to Schneider Electric, implementing the solution allowed for savings in the amount of 9.32 mln USD per year by changing the supply chain's flow.
- Siemens Building Technology is a technology partner for energy-efficient and environmentally sustainable buildings and infrastructure, using the Supply Chain Guru software. The company values the solution that is described as an integrated optimization and simulation platform with a growing community of users.
- Dematic's Warehouse Execution System (WES) is a platform that can manage all aspects of warehouse operations from receipt to shipment. The software was used by one of the American retail clothing companies. The company's goal was to create a distribution center for quick stock replenishment at 3,900 retail stores. The company said the system was able to store up to 600,000 replenishment items per day in stores, which was in line with the item's demand.

4   The Proposal of Analytical Platform for SCM

Effective supply chain management without a dedicated analytical platform is impossible in current times. Mangers should have quick access to essential data of the company's processes as well as tools and analyzes that will allow them to predict future events.

With the increase in the number of business processes inside and outside the organization that must be subjected to, the employee has the amount and size of data. Data must be obtained, cleaned, and integrated. They are finding a single source for the production of analytical and predictive models, reports, and KPIs (Govindan et al. 2018). The implementation of the tasks mentioned above is introduced with the design of the infrastructure, the implementation of IT infrastructure, and the introduction of organizational changes.

Literature studies show that many industrial enterprises have problems adapting their IT infrastructure and implementing appropriate tools for advanced data analysis (Dudycz et al. 2019).

The target architecture of the analytical platform may take various forms depending on the given enterprise. It depends on the existing IT solutions, purchased cloud services, and target expectations. There are many commercial cloud solutions on the market, such as Microsoft Azure, IBM Cloud, Amazon Web Services (AWS) - Cloud Computing Services, Oracle Cloud, Google Cloud Platform, or Open Source solutions. The target platform may be entirely based on on-premises solutions or, to some extent, be a hybrid in combination with cloud solutions from one or more vendors. As mentioned in the previous point, it is essential to identify business needs and the described processes of their implementation and map these needs to specific IT tools. At this point, we will discuss the general architecture of the analytical platform presented in Fig. 3. This model has many advantages, such as the possibility of using open-source software, which may prove very important in small companies developing their activities or larger ones who want to see the rightness of implementing a specific solution. It also has no barriers to scalability and further expansion using tools from different vendors. Its heart is a data warehouse, which can also be open-source software.

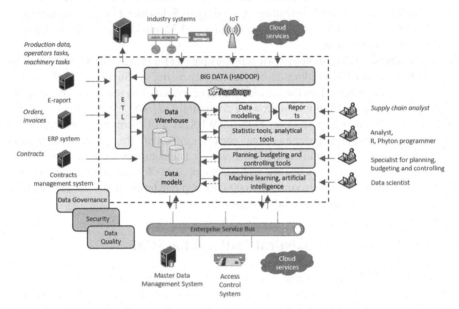

Fig. 3. An example of an analytical platform. Source: (Pyda et al. 2020)

The analytical platform is a combination of ICT infrastructure with a set of IT systems and tools that enable the acquisition, storage, processing, management, presentation, and sharing of data. The platform should be designed so that it is scalable, easy to expand, maintain and configure. It should provide the possibility of modular construction from components that will not lead to dependence on a single supplier (so-called Vendor lock-in). This issue was widely described in (Woo et al. 2018).

An analytical platform is a set of interconnected IT systems and tools between which data is transferred. We can distinguish three groups of tools that can create a platform (Fig. 4).

The first includes essential software for storing, processing, and acquiring data:

- Data warehouse - a vital element of the platform, where temporary data obtained from sources, business data, and thematic warehouses (Data marts) are stored;
- Databases - used for auxiliary purposes;
- Big Data platform for storing and processing non-standardized data based on computer clusters (e.g., Apache Hadoop);
- ETL (Extract Transform Load) tools for creating data acquisition, transformation, and loading processes.

Basic, auxiliary and support tools for business processes together with
individual users

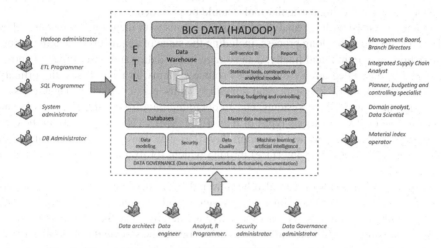

Fig. 4. Three main groups of analytical platform tools. Source: Own work.

The second group includes supporting tools:

- Data management tools;
- Data quality and consistency tools;
- Tools for data model development, documentation, and data dictionary development, often referred to as metadata management tools;
- Tools ensuring data security (authorization systems, logging, and auditing);
- Tools for the operational management of master data as the only source of master data concerning, among other things, consolidation of the customer and product data using multiple domain systems;
- Tools are supporting the use of algorithms and methods of machine learning and artificial intelligence.

The third group includes tools supporting business processes:

- Tools for creating logical data models by users, the so-called Self-service BI;
- Data reporting and presentation tools;
- Statistical tools, development of analytical or predictive models;
- Planning, budgeting, and controlling tools;
- Other dedicated tools tailored to the specific needs of the company.

Depending on the specific business requirements, the platform may consist of any combination of the components mentioned above. In the development phase, usually includes tools belonging to the first group. With the growth and complexity of data processing, tools from the second group can be incorporated. Additional applications from the third group can be added to meet new business needs.

As already mentioned in chapter two, when creating an analytical platform supporting decision-making in an enterprise, access to qualified employees fulfilling appropriate business roles and using particular tools should be provided.

Getting started with the analytical platform begins with identifying the source data that must go through a long process, including the stage of acquisition, cleaning, transformation, integration, and finally, data storage in the data warehouse. Figure 4 shows a model of data integration from various source systems. In many cases, the primary sources of data are ERP systems and domain systems, e.g., contract management systems, project management systems, etc. In obtaining data from industrial devices and systems, we deal with various types of files (CSV, XML, TXT), especially in the case of old systems as the only way to export data. The new ones provide a dedicated API (Application Programming Interface) through which, for example, we can obtain data via a data bus.

The analytical platform can also be powered by a corporate service bus that gets data from both its internal and third-party systems (websites and cloud services). When dealing with huge volumes of data, especially unstructured data, the data source is often a Big Data system. Data stored in business data models, the so-called Data marts, aggregated data, or calculated key performance indicators can be used by external applications dedicated to handling specific business processes (statistical tools, tools for building analytical models, planning and budgeting tools, machine learning, artificial intelligence, etc.). Working with these applications can be a source of data for the platform, adding value as an enrichment of the data business model. Details on the data model are presented in the next chapter.

5   The Data Model for SCM

The data model is the basis of the analytical platform. It is created by analysts and programmers using the first group's tools mentioned in the previous chapter. The life of the data model begins with the implementation of the first business process on the platform. It starts by creating physical data structures in the warehouse in the form of tables linked by relationships. Relationships usually reflect the realities of a given business area. In addition to tables with data from domain systems, dictionary tables, auxiliary tables for data processing, or tables storing aggregated data are also created. The logical data set is classified under a thematic data warehouse. When handling another business process, we save the corresponding data in the existing thematic warehouse or create a new one if the given process fits in a different thematic area. And so, for example, data related to the service of business processes in the area of project management will be saved in the thematic data warehouse under the name "Project Management," and data from the scope of purchases in the thematic data warehouse under the name "Purchasing Proceedings." An exemplary data model is presented in Fig. 5. As the supported business processes increase, our data model is extended with new thematic warehouses or the existing ones.

Additionally, thematic data warehouses may contain tables with economic and financial indicators, calculated based on implemented algorithms. They can also be fed with the results of calculations made with external tools. Depending on the needs, the data model can be extended with data from another business area or connected by a relationship with another business model. Ultimately, enterprises strive to build such a model to cover the entire supply chain and its subprocesses.

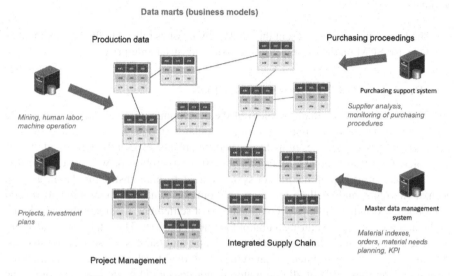

Fig. 5. An example of the data model. Source: Own work.

With a comprehensive set of consistent data located in one place, an integrated supply chain analyst can create any combination of relationships and data processing (the so-called logical data model), providing information for a specific business area.

The main expectation of the platform is to ensure quick and easy access to up-to-date, consistent, standardized, and reliable data for re-processing or presentation using reports or dashboards.

The next chapter presents the use cases of various tools based on specific data models.

6 The Analytics Development Model for SCM in a Multi-site Industrial Enterprise

The development of analytics to support the management of the supply chain requires clarifying the current needs of potential users. From the point of view of large multi-site industrial enterprise, we can distinguish:

- development of a tool for planning material needs and services (application, control tools),
- development of tools to support the planning of selected materials based on automatic procedures based on production indicators and usage standards,
- development of the SCM platform in the field of aggregate management of orders, their implementation and rationalization of warehouse management,

- creation of a platform for the exchange of information on material inventories (their age, determination of the degree of usefulness, the possibility of further distribution),
- development of controlling tools for managing costs by type in real-time (budget of the company, departments, cost execution, trend research),
- others.

The following sections present the fundamental issues related to the development of analytics for SCM on the example of multi-site industrial enterprise.

6.1 Development of Pre-processing Data Tools

As presented earlier, the main problem of the development of analytics in a multi-site industrial enterprise is the issue of various standards in data acquisition and storage. There are inconsistent names of materials between plants, especially in the field of consumables. Records of repairs, replacement of sub-assemblies, or wear of consumable parts are very often kept in flat files or systems in the form of unstructured data. Jargon, mental shortcuts, and spelling mistakes are common. One entry may refer to several components, which significantly complicates cost settlement, including the calculation of the unit cost of manufacturing a unit of the output product. The total cost for all entry activities is given, including materials, own labor, and the cost of service companies. All this limits the development of analytics, analytical teaching models, and automation of calculations. First of all, the material indexes should be unified to create a one nomenclature standard applicable in all plants. The next step is to provide tools that ensure access to crucial information on the current and historical usage of materials and refer this information to asset and infrastructure monitoring systems. The critical challenge is the development of validation tools for the correct synchronization of various data sources. One of them is the development and adjusting of Text Mining tools to the enterprise ecosystem to standardize the forms of entries, distinguish them on individual entries according to the categorization of maintenance and repair activities, and estimate the cost of materials.

6.2 Development of Data Mining Tools

At this stage, it is possible to conduct an exploratory analysis of historical data. In this regard, long-term data analysis tools should be provided to recognize how the usage of materials and stocks has changed between plants over time. Successful tracking of the variability of use, wear, and distribution of material costs in individual plants requires the development of statistical analysis methods and machine learning for pattern recognition. It is particularly important that the tool identifies seasonality and trends in data and unique regularities occurring in individual departments/plants with the possibility of flexibly setting contexts and conditions. The development of unconventional behavior detection procedures is also crucial. Thanks to this, it will be possible to answer the basic questions from the point of view of decision making and planning:

- what components and materials and on what scale are used in individual plants?
- how much did individual plants pay for the same part and from what supplier?

- where are the unique materials consumed most often, and what are the contexts?
- which warehouses/material stocks are properly managed?

6.3 Application of a Predictive Maintenance Policy in the Enterprise

Another important aspect is the access to information and the current technical condition of the machine park with the estimation of a residual lifetime for individual machines and their critical components. There is a global tendency to develop dedicated Industrial Internet of Things (IIoT) platforms with the use of low-cost sensors for monitoring the operational parameters of assets. In most cases, calculations are performed in real-time in the computing cloud. In terms of analytics, it is necessary to develop methods of fault detection in the early stages of development and KPIs. In the literature, the topic of predictive maintenance, especially technical diagnostics, is very well developed. The effectiveness of damage detection and prediction is an individual matter and depends on the type of machine component and its symptoms of incorrect operation. Therefore, it is also essential to develop reliability models, which is possible in the case of a well-prepared database of machine failures and repairs. In this respect, the multidimensional failure rate analysis and the identification of association rules are also critical. It is essential to follow the history of repairs against the background of the measured diagnostic symptoms to assess the effectiveness of the service staff's performed repair work. The above tools are necessary to estimate the future demand for individual material indexes in individual plants.

6.4 Benchmarking and Simulation Tools

Another area of analytics development is tools supporting managers in making decisions in various fields of activity. An example of proper functionality is the comparison engine in terms of reliability and costs of original parts and replacements or their respective suppliers. It is essential to access the current and historical market prices and materials offered in one place. The analytical system must be capable of multi-criteria evaluation of material suppliers so that the manager has access to supplier ranking tools when planning purchases. Besides, the critical direction is simulation tools for analyzing future orders about the state of demand and stock levels under various scenarios.

7 Summary

The article discusses the importance of advanced data analysis in SCM. The analytical platform proposal for SCM in a large enterprise was described. It consists of three groups. The first includes essential software for storing, processing, and acquiring data. The second group comprises supporting tools. At the same time, the third group contains tools supporting business processes. The proposed enterprise analytical platform model for SCM is characterized by flexibility, allowing it to connect to compatible commercial and open source systems. The data model for SCM has also been proposed. This data model is the basis of the analytical platform. The areas important for the development of advanced data analysis for SCM in a multi-branch industrial enterprise were also discussed. They are the development of pre-processing data tools, development of data mining tools, application of predictions to diagnostics of device maintenance, benchmarking, and simulation tools.

Further works will concern the construction of a model of production data to be ultimately associated with the integrated supply chain model. It is assumed that this will allow the identification and analysis of the correlation between production plans and orders for materials and services. Research into advanced data analysis in multi-site industrial enterprises will also be continued. This research will also include the development of assumptions for constructing a data and service management center, including trends resulting from the concept of Industry 4.0 and Reference Architecture (RAMI). This should include not only a look from the IT angle but - first and foremost - from the perspective of business processes. Each analytical solution must be primarily focused on business benefits, based on hypotheses concerning the potential impact on the operations and business areas.

References

Azvine, B., Cui, Z., Majeed, B., Spott, M.: Operational risk management with real-time business intelligence. BT Technol. J. **25**(1), 154–167 (2007)

Chen, D.Q., Preston, D.S., Swink, M.: How the use of big data analytics affects value creation in supply chain management. J. Manag. Inf. Syst. **32**(4), 4–39 (2015). https://doi.org/10.1080/07421222.2015.1138364

Cheng, J.C.P., Law, K.H., Bjornsson, H.: A service oriented framework for construction supply chain integration. Autom. Constr. **19**(2), 245–260 (2010)

Dama International. https://dama.org/

Demchenko, Y., Grosso, P., de Laat, C., Membrey, P.: Addressing big data issues in scientific data infrastructure. In: 2013 International Conference on Collaboration Technologies and Systems (CTS), San Diego, CA, USA, pp. 48–55 (2013). https://doi.org/10.1109/CTS.2013.6567203

Dong, S., Xu, S.X., Zhu, K.X.: Information technology in supply chains: the value of IT-enabled resources under competition. Inf. Syst. Res. **20**(1), 18–32 (2009)

Drucker, P.F.: Comeback of the entrepreneur. Management Today, 23–30 April 1968

Dudycz, H., Stefaniak, P., Pyda, P.: Advanced data analysis in multi-site enterprises. basic problems and challenges related to the IT infrastructure. In: Nguyen, N.T., Chbeir, R., Exposito, E., Aniorté, P., Trawiński, B. (eds.) ICCCI 2019. LNCS (LNAI), vol. 11684, pp. 383–393. Springer, Cham (2019). https://doi.org/10.1007/978-3-030-28374-2_33

Frazzon, E.M., Rodriguez, C.M.T., Pereira, M.M., Pires, M.C., Uhlmann, I.: Towards supply chain management 4.0. Braz. J. Oper. Prod. Manag. **16**(2), 180–191 (2019). https://doi.org/10.14488/BJOPM.2019.v16.n2.a2

Gandomi, A., Haider, M.: Beyond the hype: big data concepts, methods, and analytics. Int. J. Inf. Manag. **35**(2), 137–144 (2015). https://doi.org/10.1016/j.ijinfomgt.2014.10.007

Govindan, K., Cheng, T.C.E., Mishra, N., Shukla, N.: Big data analytics and application for logistics and supply chain management. Transp. Res. Part E: Logist. Transp. Rev. **114**, 343–349 (2018). https://doi.org/10.1016/j.tre.2018.03.011

Koot, M., Mes, M.R.K., Iacob, M.E.: A systematic literature review of supply chain decision making supported by the internet of things and big data analytics. Comput. Ind. Eng. **154**, 107076 (2020). https://doi.org/10.1016/j.cie.2020.107076

Lambert, D.M., Cooper, M.C.: Issues in supply chain management. Ind. Mark. Manag. **29**(1), 65–83 (2000)

Lai, Y., Sun, H., Ren, J.: Understanding the determinants of big data analytics (BDA) adoption in logistics and supply chain management. Int. J. Logist. Manag. **29**(2), 676–703 (2018). https://doi.org/10.1108/IJLM-06-2017-0153

Maheshwari, S., Prerna Gautam, P., Jaggi, C.K.: Role of big data analytics in supply chain management: current trends and future perspectives. Int. J. Prod. Res. (2020). https://doi.org/10.1080/00207543.2020.1793011

Power, D.: Supply chain management integration and implementation: a literature review. Supply Chain Manag. **10**(4), 252–263 (2005)

Pyda, P., Stefaniak, P., Dudycz, H.: Development assumptions of a data and service management centre at KGHM S.A. In: Mining Goes Digital: Proceedings of the 39th International Symposium 'Application of Computers and Operations Research in the Mineral Industry' (APCOM 2019), 4–6 June 2019, pp. 569–577 (2019). https://doi.org/10.1201/9780429320774

Pyda, P., Dudycz, H., Stefaniak, P.: A model of enterprise analytical platform for supply chain management. In: Hernes, M., Wojtkiewicz, K., Szczerbicki, E. (eds.) ICCCI 2020. CCIS, vol. 1287, pp. 363–375. Springer, Cham (2020). https://doi.org/10.1007/978-3-030-63119-2_30

Sahay, B.S., Ranjan, J.: Real time business intelligence in supply chain analytics. Inf. Manag. Comput. Secur. **16**(1), 28–48 (2008)

Schoenherr, T., Speier-Pero, C.: Data science, predictive analytics, and big data in supply chain management: current state and future potential. J. Bus. Logist. **36**(1), 120–132 (2015)

Schroeck, M., Shockley, R., Smart, J., Romero-Morales, D., Tufano, P.: Analytics: The real-world use of big data. 19 Martin Berner, Enrico Graupner, Alexander Maedche The Information Panopticon in the Big Data Era (2012).http://www-935.ibm.com/services/us/gbs/thoughtleadership/ibv-big-data-at-work.html. Accessed 10 Dec 2013

Shafiq, M., Savino, M.M.: Supply chain coordination to optimize manufacturer's capacity procurement decisions through a new commitment-based model with penalty and revenue-sharing. Int. J. Prod. Econ. **208**, 512–528 (2019). https://doi.org/10.1016/j.ijpe.2018.12.006

Speranza, M.: Trends in transportation and logistics. Eur. J. Oper. Res. 830–836 (2018). https://doi.org/10.1016/j.ejor.2016.08.03

Stevenson, M., Spring, M.: Supply chain flexibility: an inter-firm empirical study. Int. J. Oper. Prod. Manag. **29**(9), 946–971 (2009)

Thompson, J.: Organization in Action. McGraw-Hill, New York (1967)

Tiwari, S., Wee, H.M., Daryanto, Y.: Big data analytics in supply chain management between 2010 and 2016: insights to industries. Comput. Ind. Eng. **115**, 319–330 (2018). https://doi.org/10.1016/j.cie.2017.11.017

Trkman, P., Budler, M., Groznik, A.: A business model approach to supply chain management. Supply Chain Manag. Int. J. **20**(6), 587–602 (2015). https://doi.org/10.1108/SCM-06-2015-0219

Van Donk, D.P., Van der Vaart, T.: A case of shared resources, uncertainty and supply chain integration in the process industry. Int. J. Prod. Econ. **96**(1), 97–108 (2005)

Vilminko-Heikkinen, R., Pekkola, S.: Master data management and its organizational implementation. J. Enterp. Inf. Manag. **30**(3), 454–475 (2017). https://doi.org/10.1108/JEIM-07-2015-0070

Waller, M.A., Fawcett, S.E.: Data science, predictive analytics, and big data: a revolution that will transform supply chain design and management. J. Bus. Logist. **34**(2), 77–84 (2013a)

Waller, M.A., Fawcett, S.E.: Click here for a data scientist: big data, predictive analytics, and theory development in the era of a maker movement supply chain. J. Bus. Logist. **34**(4), 249–252 (2013b). https://doi.org/10.1111/jbl.12024

Wong, C.W.Y., Lai, K., Cheng, T.C.E.: Value of information integration to supply chain management: roles of internal and external contingencies. J. Manag. Inf. Syst. **28**(3), 161–200 (2011). https://doi.org/10.2753/MIS0742-1222280305

Woo, J., Shin, S.-J., Seo, W., Meilanitasari, P.: Developing a big data analytics platform for manufacturing systems: architecture, method, and implementation. In. J. Adv. Manufact. Technol. **99**(9–12), 2193–2217 (2018). https://doi.org/10.1007/s00170-018-2416-9

Analysing Natural Gas Prices for Turkey in the Light of a Possible Hub

Hakan Nalbant[1]([envelope]) [ID], M. Ozgur Kayalica[2] [ID], Gülgün Kayakutlu[3] [ID], and Gizem Kaya Aydın[4] [ID]

[1] Enerjisa Uretim, Beşiktaş, 34330 Istanbul, Turkey
nalbanth@itu.edu.tr

[2] Energy Institute, Faculty of Management and TEGAM, Istanbul Technical University, Maslak, 34467 Istanbul, Turkey
kayalica@itu.edu.tr

[3] Energy Institute and TEGAM, Istanbul Technical University, Atasehir, 34746 Istanbul, Turkey
kayakutlu@itu.edu.tr

[4] Faculty of Management, Istanbul Technical University, Macka, 34367 Istanbul, Turkey
kayagizem@itu.edu.tr

Abstract. Turkey has an important geopolitical position with short distances to the regions of the largest natural gas reserves. It is a country that depends on importing this energy resource from Russia, Iran and Azerbaijan through pipelines, and LNG suppliers. Being very close to high demanding countries, Turkey has yet the chance to play an important role in transferring gas from reserves to the demand sites. That is why the natural gas market in Turkey can complete the liberalization by defining an international gas hub in the global gas trade system. In this respect, the pricing of large trading volumes will be an issue for the near future. This paper aims to underline the importance of hub pricing through structuring a virtual hub in Turkey. Hence, the current outlook of the global natural gas markets and Turkey's position in this business are presented in detail.

Keywords: Natural gas market · Hub pricing · Gas demand · Gas transportation

1 Introduction

The global need for natural gas has been increasing gradually. Countries maintain active relations to trade and meet the demand of this strategic resource. While there are many countries on the consumer side, there is imperfect competition on the producer side due to the limited number of countries. The most important issue would probably be setting the price of gas. Once seen as an undesirable and dangerous by-product of oil production, natural gas was flared into the atmosphere. In time, its market value was acknowledged. This is followed by a state-of-the-art pipeline network. Since it was not clear how to value natural gas when it was first started, it was associated with the prices of petroleum products. However, the increasing demand for gas, which has increased as of today, has enabled the gas to be recognized very well by the supply and demand points. This

E. Mercier-Laurent et al. (Eds.): AI4KM 2021, IFIP AICT 614, pp. 193–212, 2021.
https://doi.org/10.1007/978-3-030-80847-1_13

makes the pricing approach based on oil inadequate. For this reason, commercial centres have been established to measure the value of gas, especially in the USA and Northern European countries. After all, the price of natural gas is determined by the balance of supply and demand as a result of commercial activities carried out in these centres.

Turkey is a natural gas import-dependent country. It responds to the domestic gas demand through oil-based long-term contracts. Turkey is close to the geographical area of rich natural gas reserves. With its growing economy, its thirst for natural gas is constantly increasing. Besides, given its geopolitical location, Turkey is close to countries that need gas, especially to Europe. All these could be seen as sufficient conditions to nominate Turkey as a strong gas-hub.

In 2019, Turkey has imported 35% of its total gas from Russia, 16% from Iran, 17% from Azerbaijan, 11% from Algeria, 5% from Nigeria, and 16% as spot LNG from primarily Qatar and other countries (EPDK 2019). While natural gas imported from Russia, Iran, and Azerbaijan comes within the scope of long-term agreements over pipelines, it is taken as LNG from other countries. There is a long-term purchase agreement with Algeria and Nigeria in LNG purchases. Although it is accepted that the use of natural gas will reduce environmental problems like air pollution caused by coal and oil combustion, the high share of natural gas imports from several countries can be seen as a significant risk to Turkey (Biresselioglu et al. 2019). The 1.3 billion cubic meter agreement signed with Nigeria in 1995 expires in October 2021, and the 4.4 billion cubic meter agreement signed with Algeria in 1988 expires in October 2024. For gas coming from pipelines, a total of 10.6 billion cubic meters of agreement, covering Russian and Azeri gas, expires in 2021, the agreement for 16 billion cubic meters of Russian gas in 2025, and the agreement for 9.6 billion cubic meters of Iran gas in 2026. Following the end of the duration of the agreement, Turkey's natural gas trade will have significant flexibility. Thus, a period of opportunities will be entered to open up new resources and create a competitive market. In light of the agreements that will end, this study will prepare an infrastructure to create a trade centre by making predictions until 2025 in the natural gas market. Thus, in this study, two main scenarios have been identified in light of the current market structure in Turkey. In both cases, estimates of natural gas prices were made monthly until the end of 2025.

As the article contains the predictive and prescriptive analytics of Turkey becoming a Global Natural Gas Hub in terms of projections for gas prices, this study is the contin-uation of our initial article (Nalbant et al. 2020). Moreover, this current study meets a need to present the dynamic pricing structures that will precise the future scenarios for using Natural Gas to respond to the increasing power demand.

Scenario 1

In the early days of the natural gas industry, there were huge capital investments into gas field development and pipeline construction operations. Hence, the supplier had to carry these costs as a significant financial burden and risk. To mitigate total risk on the supplier, "take or pay" and destination clauses were introduced and agreed upon by both parties (Osicka and Ocelik 2017). Turkey is also a country that is a net importer of natural gas. It realizes most of the gas it purchases through long term contracts with indexed pricing structure from neighbouring countries subject to conditions such as "take or pay". This scenario investigates how the price is affected under business as usual conditions. Using the time series methods, it is estimated what the gas import prices will be at the end of 2025.

Scenario 2

The second scenario estimates the price of Turkish imported gas as if there is a natural gas hub. We aim to analyse the dynamics of the prices that could be affected by many factors in the presence of such a natural gas hub. Once again, the estimation targets 2025.

Free market prices are determined by supply and demand forces. Therefore, assuming that Turkey is a trade hub, we analyse the impact on prices. Also, the factors that may affect the prices within a hub environment are identified.

Then, these factors were evaluated by Vector Autoregressive Analysis (VAR) and machine learning techniques. The results of medium-term forecasting were obtained by taking into consideration their effects on gas prices. Thus, Turkey's reference price based on supply and demand dynamics on a global scale has tried to be put forward.

2 Background

In 1995, the efficiency of US Natural Gas markets was questioned. Also, the comparison of the New York Mercantile Exchange (NYMEX) price calculations were compared to the Kansas City Board of Trade (KCBOT) contracts, the second merchandiser in the USA. It was observed that the prices were getting apart in time (Herbert and Kreil 1996). It is then seen that Henry Hub in Louisiana was not good enough in price forecasts for the USA and Canadian natural gas markets. Further econometric analysis showed that the difference is not only due to transportation costs. Pipelines and scarcity of the spot markets caused the need for more than one natural gas price in the USA and Canada. Hence, the confidence in future market price calculations got weaker in time. A cointegration analysis of USA, Japan, and Europe showed that local markets group in themselves (as pipe and LNG) but there is an evident dominance of existing long-term contracts and high impact of the traditional oil-index price formula (Siliverstovs et al. 2005). Following the achievements of this study, a comparison of the price forecast performance of the markets and the economic models was studied. Wong-Parodi et al. (2006) compares the Short-Term Outlook Model of the US Energy Information office and the Henry Hub future market price forecasts statistically and demonstrates the success of the future market.

With the impact of increasing renewable energy investments, a new vision among the European researchers came up to have more integrated and more efficient energy markets with multiple hubs (Geidl et al. 2007). Agent-based control of multiple carriers would not only allow the reductions in market operations costs but also increase the mitigation of carbon emissions. Further analysis of multi-source multi-product energy markets has increased the need for multiple-hubs (Hemmes et al. 2007). It is only in the last decade that multi-hub dispatch management is analysed. Robustness of the energy dispatch and the impacts of the wind energy-optimized by using multi-agent systems is suggested as modern management of multiple hubs by Moeini-Aghtaie et al. (2014).

European policies to combine the energy markets have also encouraged the increasing research on multiple hubs. Causality among the European gas price time series at the points where cross-border connections of pipelines and trading occur at the same time was studied by Gianfreda et al. (2012) to analyse the possibilities of the integrated European energy market. The five markets that were studied in this study were not found at all related even the natural gas is imported from the very same countries. Italian and Dutch markets were relying on the German prices. In 2013, Germany made the critical policy change "energiewende" in favour of distributed energies which allowed bioenergy to influence the natural gas markets, hence 2 trading hubs are started (Burger and Weinmann 2014).

European hubs have started influencing the other markets of the Globe. After the Fukushima explosion, Japan has also started discussing changes in the local energy market considering the regional price constructions based on energy security by the region (Tanaka 2013). Shale gas discoveries in the USA have also strengthened the effectiveness of multiple hubs for energy security in the Globe, which is clearly shown by North American analysis of Kobek et al. (2015). Xunpeng (2016) studies the influences of Europe on East Asia and concludes that the hubs will not be successful unless the liberalization of the market is completed.

In the last five years, the European research is focused on combining the electricity markets and the heating markets in Europe. With the influence of this important change, more domestic conditions are studied like the impacts of infrastructure state and storage (Santibanez 2017). The new research trend is to study the influence of electric cars on natural gas prices as in Nikoobakht et al. (2020).

Prices formed in natural gas trade centres remain under the influence of more than one factor. Various methods are used to interpret how these factors affect, and at what levels prices are sensitive to these factors. For example, Mishra (2012) revealed the factors affecting natural gas prices and then estimates gas prices using ARIMA, which is one of the linear time series methods. Salehnia et al. (2013) used regression models to estimate Henry Hub short-term-spot natural gas market prices. This study is the first user of the Gamma test for the best selection of parameters in the calibration of models. After determining the factors affecting the prices occurring in the hub in the Netherlands, they developed a linear equation and tried to reveal the relationship between prices and related factors. Misund and Oglend (2016) used vector autoregressive analysis to investigate the causes of fluctuations in gas prices in England. In another Henry Hub-market price forecasting study, Ceperic et al. (2017) used neural networks and Support Vector Machine (SVM) machine-learning algorithms. Mulder et al. (2016) and Naderi et al. (2019) combined the statistical methods with the machine learning algorithms and conducted studies to estimate crude oil and gas prices. In this study, the authors introduced a new approach by trying methods such as genetic algorithm, artificial neural network (ANN), and ARIMA to achieve the optimum combination by using a meta-heuristic bat algorithm. Herrera et al. (2019) compared the performance of traditionally used econometric models in price estimates using neural networks and random forest models. As the outcome of the study, they argued that the random forest method was particularly successful in the monthly price estimate of energy commodities. Su et al. (2019) also discussed the performance of ANN in comparison to SVM, gradient boosting machines (GBM), and Gaussian Process Regression (GBR), and Henry Hub's performance in the monthly forecast of spot gas prices. Wang et al. (2020) compared the daily gas price estimation performance to the hybrid machine-learning model using the support vector regression (SVR) and long-term and short-term memory network (LSTM) models.

3   Methodology and Data

In the literature, it has been observed that studies for only gas price estimation are not very common. In general, it has been studied alongside other fossil fuels such as oil and coal or has been addressed in areas such as gas consumption, electricity generation, and electricity price estimation. Based on the estimated monthly average natural gas import prices between January 2011 and December 2019, and by using EViews 10 and R software, in the first scenario, the forecast was made using linear (ARIMA) and non-linear time series (TAR). Autoregressive moving averages models (ARIMA) are the time series estimation and forecasting method, also known as Box and Jenkins (1970) models. In these methods, the aim is simply to predict the future value of the variable from the past values of the series and past estimation errors. Threshold Autoregressive Regression model, which is one of the nonlinear time series methods, contain regime change information, unlike linear time series models. When the threshold variable takes different values, it provides different modelling and policy recommendations (Dodge 2003).

For the second scenario in which we assume that Turkey is a natural gas hub, following Mulder et al. (2016), the study investigates the correlation between gas prices and various independent variables for the relevant periods using the vector autoregressive (VAR) model. Vector autoregression is an econometric model that generalizes univariate AR models and provides development and interdependence between multiple time series (see Enders 2003). Stacking Regressor is a machine learning method for forming linear combinations of different predictors to give improved prediction accuracy. The idea is to use cross-validation data and least squares under non-negativity constraints to determine the coefficients in the combination (Breiman 1996). Moreover, the model is also used to forecast the prices in this scenario.

Data for monthly natural gas import prices for 108 months from January 2011 to December 2019 are taken from Beyazgül (2016). The day ahead markets in Turkey form and announce natural gas prices in TL/MWh (EPIAS 2020c), therefore, this study uses $/MWh as the price unit for average monthly prices, which allows the validation and correction of the data. Figure 1 provides the time plot. According to this graph, it is clear that the decrease in imported gas prices in 2015 increased again after 2016 when it bottomed out. The reason for this decrease is that Brent oil prices, which were at the level of $110 in June 2014, declined rapidly to $50 in early 2015 and to $27 in early 2016. With this decrease in oil prices, natural gas prices and import amount started to decrease rapidly in late 2014.

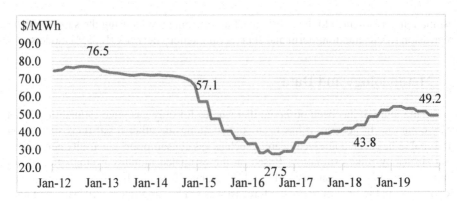

Fig. 1. Time plot of imported gas price in Turkey.

A review of the literature survey allowed the determination of the criteria that can have an impact on natural gas prices. These are briefly presented below.

Oil Price ($/Barrel): Since oil prices have an important effect on gas trade in the world, Brent oil prices are included in the analysis. For example, Serletis and Rangel-Ruiz (2004) found that there are a common trend and cycle in prices after the liberalization of the oil and gas markets in the USA. Asche et al. (2006), in their study, state that the existence of a single market for the major energy sources in England can be mentioned, and the prices in this market are determined by global oil prices. The monthly values of this variable for the years 2011–2019 are taken from the US Energy Information Administration (EIA) website (EIA 2020a).

Coal Price ($/Ton): Both the domestic and imported coal are still important inputs for the power market, i.e., coal is a close substitute for natural gas. Bachmeir and Griffin (2006) stated that there may be a weak cointegration between oil, natural gas, and coal prices, which is why it is not acceptable to have a single energy market for major sources around the world, but it can be claimed when evaluated in a very long term. Besides, Manzur and Seiflou (2011) found that there is a long-term relationship between crude oil, natural gas, and coal prices in the US energy market, but natural gas prices have no deterministic effect on oil prices in the short term. Coal price data are taken from Turkey's largest coal importer with a monthly Reuters database for Colombia's coal prices over the years 2011–2019.

Carbon Emission (€/ton): Emission Trade Scheme (ETS) aims to force industries that cause pollution by utilizing the CO_2 trade system to buy carbon credits to create an effective tax for carbon emission, and thus, encourage industries to adopt cleaner technologies. The objective is to limit global warming to 2 °C, develop energy efficiency, increase the roles of renewable energy sources, strengthen the carbon market, and provide a transparent and competitive domestic energy market (Kocaslan 2011). Unfortunately, there is no active carbon market yet established in Turkey. However, in the medium-term due to carbon market's expected existence, this variable is included. Meanwhile, since there are no reliable prices yet in Turkey, European carbon emission prices between the years 2011–2019 are included in the analysis (Business Insider 2020).

Heating Degree Days (HDD): Demand for natural gas in Turkey, especially because of the intensity of household consumption, is increasing in the cold season (Energy Market Regulatory Authority – EPDK 2017). The values of Heating Degree Days (HDD) were compiled from the calculations and data published regularly by the Turkish State Meteorological Service (MGM 2020) for each province on an annual and monthly basis. These values were calculated monthly for Turkey for the years 2011–2019.

Herfindahl-Hirschman Index (HHI): Herfindahl-Hirschman index (HHI) is widely used to demonstrate the degree of competition in a market. HHI is an indicator for understanding the depth of the market and is calculated by the formula $\boldsymbol{HHI} = \sum_{i=1}^{n} S_i^2$ (Mulder et al. 2016). Here, S_i, represents the country i's market share in total gas imports, and n represents the total number of countries in which imports are realized. Therefore, it is an indicator of a market structure and also points to the measurement of the effective power of firms in the markets. This variable, when long-term contracts and spot market purchases are concerned, reveals how many different countries Turkey imports natural gas from and in what volumes. Especially considering the diversity of supply alternatives in a gas trading hub is very critical. To include this variable in the multivariate time series analysis, monthly natural gas sector reports published by EPDK (2020) have been examined one by one, and the list and import amounts of the countries imported in the relevant month have been compiled. Finally, with the help of the specified formula, the Herfindahl-Hirschman index value was calculated monthly for the years 2012–2019.

Industry Index: According to the EPDK report, the industry sector realizes 21.69% of the total gas consumption (EPDK 2019). Acaravcı and Reyhanoğlu (2013) emphasized that there is a long-term relationship between energy prices and variables of BIST-100 index, oil prices, natural gas prices, and industrial production index. The industry sector is also accepted as a variable within the scope of this analysis since it is a very important indicator in the development of the country's economy and a significant factor in the demand fluctuations of gas. The industrial production index (2015 $=$ 100) for this purpose has been taken monthly from the Turkstat (2020) database for 2011–2019, free of season and calendar effects.

Natural Gas Storage Amount (Sm3): Natural gas storage facilities serve as a very important supply source. Because, firstly, when the demand is very high, it will contribute to the supply security by providing sufficient gas supply to the network, and secondly, it will provide an abundance of gas to trade the gas in the free market. These facilities are usually filled in summer periods for use in the winter months. While the amount of gas stored above the seasonal normal decreases the prices in a gas hub, the storage below the seasonal normal has an increasing effect on the prices (Mulder et al. 2016). The total amount of gas stored in Turkey has been compiled monthly for the 2011–2019 period from EPDK (2020) monthly reports.

Hydroelectric Energy Production (GWh): Turkey is a country with an important source of hydrology. Due to the energy supply security in the country, both reservoir and run of river type power plants are actively used for electricity generation. According to TEIAS Installed Capacity Report-2019, Turkey's total installed capacity by the end of 2019 is 91,267 MW. Hydroelectric Power Plants (HEPPs) with a total of 682 plants constitute 31% of this installed power (TEIAS 2019a). According to TEIAS, a total of 304,251.6 GWh of electricity was generated at the end of 2019, 29% by hydroelectric plants with a total production of 58 450 GWh (TEIAS 2019b). This variable was included in the analysis since the production performance of hydroelectric power plants can directly affect the working order of the gas power plants and as a natural consequence, it may change the demand for gas. Historical production data of HEPPs were compiled by reviewing both EPIAS (2020a) and related sector reports monthly for 2011–2019.

Wind Energy Production (GWh): Increasing investments in renewable energy suggest that it can help alleviate the threat of high gas prices in the short and long-term. Increasing renewable energy distribution by replacing gas-fired production is expected to reduce natural gas demand and consequently put downward pressure on gas prices (Wiser and Bolinger 2007). Wind energy investment in Turkey has gained pace especially since 2007. With the commissioning of an average capacity of 700 MW each year, a total of 7,591.2 MW wind power plant (WPP) installed power was reached at the end of 2019 (TEIAS 2019a). Again, according to the data published by TEIAS, the contribution of WPPs to electricity production in 2019 was around 7% (TEIAS 2019b). In 2017, a capacity of 3000 MW was allocated to investors through tenders and two other tenders were held within the scope of the "2 GW of renewable resource areas" study. For all these reasons, it has been found appropriate to include WPPs as a renewable energy source in this study. The past production data of WPPs were compiled by reviewing both EPIAS (2020a) and related sector reports monthly for 2011–2019.

Solar Power Generation (GWh): By diversifying natural gas and oil suppliers, increasing the use of alternative renewable energy sources such as wind and solar energy, it can be possible both to reduce foreign dependency on oil and natural gas and to reduce energy costs (Gokırmak 2017). The first tender for the realization of the licensed stations for solar energy in Turkey took place in 2014. Following this, Solar Power Plant (SPP) investments gained great momentum with the unlicensed electricity generation plants, which were initiated so that investors can meet their internal consumption primarily. As of the end of 2019, the total SPP installation, which was almost non-existent before 2014, contributed approximately 3% to the electricity generation of the country with 6.901 power plants and total installed power of 5.995.2 MW. Following its strategic goals, Turkey allocated a 1 GW solar power capacity in the first quarter of 2017. Based on the expanding pattern of solar power capacity both in and out of the country, this parameter is also taken as a variable. Data on SPP production was compiled from the related sources published (production data for 2011–2019 were reviewed monthly from both EPIAS (2020b) and related industry reports).

Natural Gas Price in the Importer Country ($ per Million Metric): De Vany and Walls (1993) indicated that natural gas prices in different markets are integrated. Opening the access to pipelines leads to increased competition and thus, makes the prices converge to each other. According to EPDK reports, Russia is Turkey's biggest natural gas provider. Therefore, natural gas prices in this market should be also in the model (the data for the 2011–2019 period is retrieved from the Russian Natural Gas Monthly Price Reuters database).

4   Scenario Analysis

Analysis Based on Scenario 1: This scenario investigates how the price is affected under business as usual conditions. Before starting the analysis of natural gas prices with time series, firstly, logarithmic transformation was applied to the variable to ensure the variance stationary, and secondly, its stationarity was examined by unit root tests. Based on the results of the unit root tests, the first-degree difference was found to be stationary according to 5% (Augmented Dickey-Fuller: -2.13 and Phillips-Perron Test: -11.02). Accordingly, the logarithmic differentiation state of the variable is used. Next, the correlogram of this variable was examined to switch to ARIMA modelling over this value (see Fig. 2).

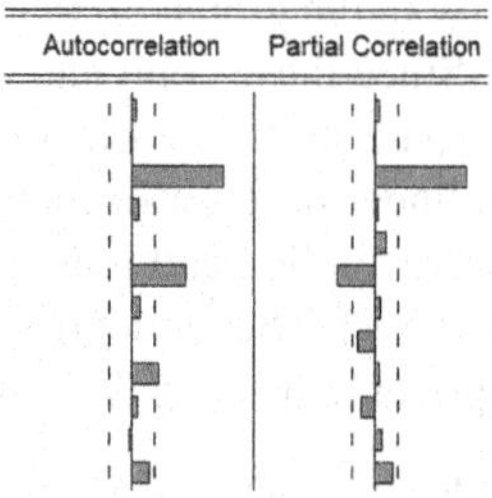

Fig. 2. Correlogram of imported gas prices

After this step, the data set is divided into training and test data set (last 8 months). In Fig. 2, we see significant values of up to 6 delays according to autocorrelation and partial autocorrelation values. Based on this, the ARIMA (6, 1, 6) model was executed and the most suitable model was determined as the following ARIMA (3, 1, 6) according to the Information Criteria and coefficient significance. Coefficients are shown in Table 1. According to the results in Table 1, imported gas prices are affected by their pre-3-period values and shocks up to 6-period.

Table 1. ARIMA (3, 1, 6) model. The correlogram of the residual square obtained from this model was examined and ARCH-LM (nR^2 (6) = 3.43) test was performed. No conditional heteroscedasticity was found as a result of the test.

Sample: 2011M02 2019M04		
Included observations: 99		
DLOG (imported gas price)	Coefficient	Std. Error
Constant	0.0005	0.011
Ar (3)	0.31***	0.10
Ma (3)	0.78***	0.11
Ma (6)	0.59***	0.08

***Significant at 1%.*
***Significant at 5%.*
Significant at 10%.
R^2: 0.69, Akaike: -4.32, Schwarz -4.20, HQ: -4.28
Residuals are white noise.

Training and test sample performance of this model is presented in Table 2.

Table 2. Performance measures of ARIMA (3, 1, 6)

	RMSE	MAE	MAPE
Training	1.23	0.69	1.44
Test	0.99	0.68	1.37

Since gas prices are determined indexed to oil, there is a serious correlation with oil prices. Therefore, especially the increase in oil prices until the end of 2018 is reflected in gas prices. Given the serious factors such as sudden shocks, uncertainties in prices, political risks, and supply capacity in the global oil market, the course of oil prices may remain open to serious changes. Since these contracts will be affected by these fluctuations, imported gas prices will also be seriously affected. For this reason, this effect can be examined by establishing nonlinear time series models. For this purpose, Threshold Autoregressive Models (TAR) were applied and nonlinearity was confirmed by the Bai Perron test (F: 10.44, significant at 5%). The model results are given in Table 3. According to Table 3, if the value of oil prices is below $47.7/Barrel 6 months ago, the increases

Table 3. Results of TAR model

DLOG (imported gas price)		
Included observations: 93 after adjustments		
Selection: Trimming 0.15, Sig. level 0.05		
Threshold variable: OIL PRICE (−6)		
Variable	Coefficient	Std. Error
OIL PRICE (−6) < 47.7 – 14 observations		
C	0.003	0.007
DLOG (imported gas price) (−3)	0.93***	0.16
DLOG (imported gas price) (−6)	−0.83***	0.17
47.7 < = OIL PRICE (−6) – 79 observations		
C	−0.005***	0.00
DLOG (imported gas price) (−3)	0.93***	0.11
DLOG (imported gas price) (−6)	−0.11	0.11

***Significant at 1%.
Significant at 5%.
Significant at 10%.
R^2: 0.74, Akaike: −4.50, Schwarz −4.33, HQ: −4.43
Residuals are white noise.

and decreases in natural gas prices are fast. If the price of oil is realized at $47.7/Barrel and above 6 months ago, natural gas prices tend to increase rapidly[1].

In order to forecast in this model, the forecasting value of Oil Prices must be determined in the model. For this reason, a separate model was estimated by using the Imported Gas Price (−4) as a threshold variable for the forecasting. Training and test sample performance of this model was obtained as in Table 4.

Table 4. Performance measures of TAR model

	RMSE	MAE	MAPE
Training	1.18	0.64	1.29
Test	1.00	0.88	1.81

Although the training sample performance of this model is better than the ARIMA model, out of sample (test) performance is lower.

Analysis Based on Scenario 2: In this scenario, the price was analysed considering Turkey as an international natural gas hub. Therefore, the aforementioned variables Oil Price ($/Barrel), Coal Price ($/Ton), Carbon Emission (€/Ton), Heating Degree Days (HDD), Herfindahl-Hirschman Index (HHI), Industry Index, Natural Gas Storage Amount (Sm3), Hydroelectric Power Generation (GWh), Wind Power Generation (GWh), Solar Power Generation (GWh), Natural Gas Price in Importer Country ($ per Million Metric) are included in the analysis of the estimation of gas prices.

After taking the logarithm for variance stability, we control for seasonality. These are followed by seasonal smoothing of the Heating Degree Days (HDD), Herfindahl-Hirschman Index (HHI), Natural Gas Storage Amount (Sm3), Hydroelectric Energy Production (GWh), Wind Energy Production (GWh) and Solar Energy Production (GWh) variables. Finally, unit root tests are performed for all the variables. The result of Augmented Dickey-Fuller (ADF) and Phillips-Perron (PP) tests show that all variables were I (1) (see Table 5).

After this step, lag length criteria were firstly determined to examine whether these variables affect imported gas prices. According to Schwarz and Hannan Quin criteria, the appropriate lag length is 1, and according to the Akaike information criterion is 7. Since the number of data is not very large, Schwarz and Hannan Quin criteria were preferred and it was decided to continue with 1 lag.

---

[1] After this step, the estimation of ESTAR and LSTAR models was made, but only 1 model had a significant threshold. Achieving the high slope parameters of the threshold in this model indicated that the model converged to the TAR model. Besides, this model's Sum of Squared Residuals and information criteria indicate that the TAR model is better. In this case, it can be said that the regime change in gas prices is sharp rather than smooth. Therefore, only the results of the TAR model are included in this study.

Table 5. Results of unit root tests

Variables	ADF		PP	
	Level (none)	First difference (none)	Level (none)	First difference (none)
Imported gas price ($/Barrel)	−0.70	−2.13**	−0.28	−11.02***
Oil price ($/Barrel)	−0.53	−8.07***	−0.51	−7.87***
Coal price ($/Ton)	−0.24	−7.94***	−0.21	−8.07***
Carbon emission (€/ton)	0.01	−7.42***	0.13	−7.12***
Heating Degree Days (HDD)	0.53	−9.72***	−0.66	−45.22***
Herfindahl-Hirschman Index (HHI)	1.10	−9.09***	0.39	−19.08***
Industry index	2.50	−15.58***	2.00	−15.19***
Natural gas storage amount (Sm3)	0.08	−9.78***	0.17	−10.17***
Hydroelectric energy production (GWh)	0.16	−15.94***	0.37	−19.23***
Wind energy production (GWh)	3.31	−11.64***	2.64	−17.57***
Solar power generation (GWh)	0.03	−5.49***	0.06	−5.49***
Natural gas price in the importer country ($ per million metric)	−0.73	−9.08***	−0.71	−9.20***

***Significant at 1%.
**Significant at 5%.
Significant at 10%.

Afterwards, an appropriate short-term equation was established and variables that affect gas prices were determined by the stepwise method. Natural Gas Price ($ per Million Metric), Industry index and oil prices in Russia affect short-term natural gas prices (R^2: 0.13). Thus, Vector autoregressive analysis (VAR) continued with these variables. The lag length criteria specific to these variables have also been determined. Following this, the appropriate delay number was determined as 4 and 6, respectively, based on the Schwarz and Hannan Quin criteria, and based on the Akaike information criteria. The analysis was continued with the length of 4 lags and the results are presented in Table 6.

Table 6. Results of VAR model. All variables are in logarithmic differences.

Sample (adjusted): 2011M06 2019M04

Included observations: 95

	Imported gas price	Oil price	Natural gas price in the importer Country_ Russia	Industry index
Imported gas price (−1)	−0.11 (0.11)	−0.85** (0.34)	−0.59** (0.27)	0.03 (0.09)
Imported gas price (−2)	−0.09 (0.07)	0.02 (0.21)	−0.07 (0.17)	−0.03 (0.05)
Imported gas price (−3)	0.66*** (0.06)	0.43** (0.20)	0.03 (0.16)	0.11** (0.05)
Imported gas price (−4)	0.09 (0.10)	0.47 (0.30)	0.60** (0.24)	−0.10 (0.08)
Oil price (−1)	0.12*** (0.04)	0.36*** (0.11)	0.29*** (0.08)	0.02 (0.02)
Oil price (−2)	−0.04 (0.04)	−0.01 (0.12)	−0.02 (0.10)	0.02 (0.03)
Oil price (−3)	0.09** (0.04)	−0.22* (0.12)	0.17* (0.09)	−0.04 (0.03)
Oil price (−4)	0.07* (0.04)	0.13 (0.13)	0.15 (0.10)	0.01 (0.03)
Natural gas price in the importer Country_Russia (−1)	−0.01 (0.05)	−0.05 (0.14)	0.27** (0.11)	−0.02 (0.03)
Natural gas price in the importer Country_Russia (−2)	0.09** (0.05)	0.16 (0.14)	−0.11 (0.11)	−0.02 (0.04)
Natural gas price in the importer Country_Russia (−3)	0.05 (0.05)	−0.24 (0.15)	0.15 (0.12)	−0.01 (0.04)
Natural gas price in the importer Country_Russia (−4)	0.04 (0.05)	0.24 (0.15)	−0.04 (0.12)	0.002 (0.04)
Industry index (−1)	−0.13 (0.15)	0.44 (0.45)	0.44 (0.36)	−0.48*** (0.11)
Industry index (−2)	0.06 (0.17)	0.51 (0.50)	0.42 (0.40)	−0.12 (0.13)
Industry index (−3)	−0.16 (0.17)	0.02 (0.50)	0.21 (0.40)	−0.08 (0.13)
Industry index (−4)	−0.29** (0.15)	0.39 (0.45)	−0.22 (0.35)	0.08 (0.11)
Constant	0.002 (0.003)	−0.009 (0.009)	−0.006 (0.008)	0.006*** (0.002)
R-squared	0.75	0.25	0.35	0.32
Adjusted R-squared	0.70	0.10	0.21	0.18
Log likelihood	220.89	115.51	137.64	247.28
Akaike AIC	−4.29	−2.07	−2.54	−4.85
Schwarz SC	−3.84	−1.62	−2.08	−4.39

Standard Errors are in parentheses.
***Significant at 1%.
**Significant at 5%.
*Significant at 10%.

Table 7 presents the predictive performances of gas prices depending on the training and test sample that are based on the VAR model results.

Table 7. Performance measures of VAR model

	RMSE	MAE	MAPE
Training	1.11	0.82	1.66
Test	1.30	1.01	1.97

Assuming that Turkey hosts a natural gas hub, we use machine learning to analyse how the determinants that affect natural gas prices may potentially shape these prices. In this context, more than one machine learning algorithm has been studied and the price estimation has been made by using Stacking Regressor as a result of the evaluations. Stacking (or Stacked Regression) is an ensemble machine learning algorithm. It uses a meta-learning algorithm to learn how to best combine the predictions from two or more base machine learning algorithms. The idea is to use cross-validation data and least squares under non-negativity constraints to determine the coefficients in the combination (Breiman 1996). The 3 independent variables selected as a result of the work done in the previous section constitute the input of the study to be described in this section. Therefore, Brent-oil price with natural gas prices, industry index (IND) reflecting the economic development level of the country, and Russian natural gas price are included in the analysis.

The 88-month values of the 3 independent variables were selected for the analysis between January 2012 and April 2019 were used to complete the training process of the algorithm. Then, the forecast performance of the algorithm was examined by considering the 8 months' test values between May 2019 and December 2019. Forecasting performances of gas prices according to the training and test sample obtained according to this algorithm are given in Table 8.

Table 8. Performance measures of Stacking Regressor

	RMSE	MAE	MAPE
Training	1.94	1.68	4.09
Test	2.17	1.81	3.55

In this context, for the oil prices (till the end of 2021), we take the monthly estimates of the Short-Term Energy Outlook (STEO) presented by EIA (2020c). For the period up to 2025, the 2050 projection data presented in the Energy Outlook 2020 by EIA were used (2020b). For the industry index and Russian gas prices, we use the forecast values obtained in the previous section.

4.1 The Impact of COVID-19 Pandemic

The outbreak of COVID-19, which started in Wuhan, China in the last months of 2019, affected the world dramatically. The World Health Organization declared COVID-19 as a global pandemic on 11th of March, 2020 (WHO 2020). This is followed by a series of restrictions, such as banning international travel, temporary shutdowns, lockdowns and/or home office working, etc., all widely implemented by the governments and businesses. Due to these developments, there were serious fluctuations in foreign exchange and commodity prices, while oil prices also dropped sharply.

Our study has been prepared based on the data realized as of the end of 2019. However, the effects of this pandemic on a global scale have been tried to be examined as a subsection. Our prediction study with machine learning was also rerun with the realizations of the first quarter of 2020. To do so, oil prices from the end of 2021 were compiled from the EIA's May STEO (EIA 2020b), and for the period from 2022 to 2025, oil prices were compiled from Deloitte's (2020) first-quarter report. The estimates made by the aforementioned institutions have added value to our study as they have a pandemic effect in line with the actual data and the latest prices.

For the industry index, both the realized up to March and afterwards the results obtained by the time series method; and for the Russian gas price, the actual results up to April and then the results obtained by the time series method were used. According to the performance of our Stacking Regressor algorithm, a serious decrease in natural gas prices is observed in 2020 with the effect of the pandemic. It is anticipated that the effects of this decline will only begin to disappear after 2021 and will reach the normal level after 2023 (see Fig. 3).

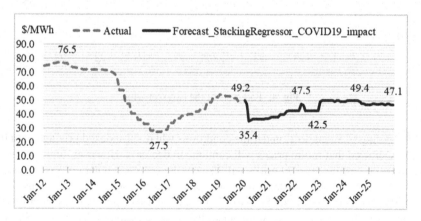

Fig. 3. Forecasts of the Covid effect.

5 Comparison of Scenarios and Discussion

Natural gas prices in Turkey were examined under two scenarios: (i) the current commercial structure (or business as usual), and (ii) assumption of a natural gas hub. In

Scenario 1, ARIMA and TAR have estimated the prices based on time series. In Scenario 2, the relationship between supply and demand factors and their effects on prices are examined. Also, the results of the VAR and machine learning studies are obtained. The natural gas price estimation values calculated under both scenarios are shown in Fig. 4.

Monthly prices realized during the period from January 2011 to December 2019, and the estimated prices using "ARIMA, TAR, VAR, and Stacking Regressor" between January 2020 and December 2025 were obtained as shown in Fig. 4. While the ARIMA forecast under Scenario 1 estimates prices at $44/MWh by the end of 2025, the VAR analysis estimates under Scenario 2 shows a downward trend to $37/MWh at the end of 5 years. On the other hand, with the results of machine learning, which is also within the scope of Scenario 2, it is predicted that it will move to reach the level of $48/MWh at the end of the forecast period. Furthermore, in this analysis in which the effect of COVID-19 is also analysed, although serious decreases of prices in the short term are expected, it is predicted that after 2023 this effect will start to disappear altogether.

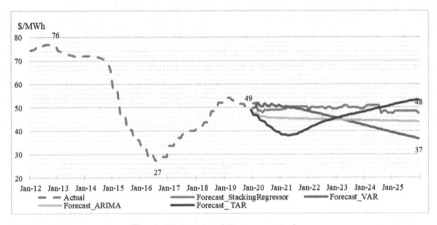

Fig. 4. Forecasts of the two scenarios.

According to Scenario 1, under the conditions where oil-indexed pricing continues, ARIMA showed that future prices will continue to decrease. However, future volatility and potential thresholds in oil prices will likewise be reflected in natural gas prices, and hence, the result of TAR model is more acceptable for this scenario. Also, considering the market prices formed under Scenario 2, although the short-term price increases were seen in the VAR analyse, prices were generally in the direction of decreasing; Stacking Regressor application shows more stable prices. As a result of the statistical analysis, the predictive dynamics of the VAR analysis is provided by using the historical values of the relevant variables. Predicted prices resulted from the Stacking Regressor application considers the impact of future projections of the variables affecting gas prices. Therefore, the prices obtained using machine learning will be taken as the basis for Scenario 2.

6   Conclusion and Recommendations

It is observed in the literature that the medium-term and long-term energy price forecasts are studied mainly using the regressors and the time series analysis. This study is motivated to present the effect of a possible hub construction in the Turkish natural gas market. Hence, two scenarios are constructed to analyse the natural gas prices in the middle term of 2020–2025. The first one is "As Is", hence the time series gives reliable predictions. The second scenario assumes the existence of a hub and the impacts of oil price, coal price, renewable energy usage, competition index, industry index, carbon emissions, gas storage capacities, heating days are considered as well as the time series on prices.

Currently, Turkey imports natural gas mainly from Russia with bilateral contracts indexed to the oil prices. This allows BOTAS, the state company importing natural gas to determine the price without allowing the market balance of the demand and supply. Scenario 1 is structured using these facts and a time series analysis of 8 years is made using ARIMA and TAR methods to forecast prices for the years 2020, 2021, 2022, 2023, 2024, and 2025. Yet, forecasts with ARIMA show a linear trend after a small descent in parallel to the oil prices, whereas TAR shows continuous price drops but after mid-2021, it is expected to increase.

Scenario 2 with the hub does not have market prices since such a market does not exist in Turkey but assumes that the historical import prices are the market prices. The impacting criteria are analysed using the VAR and Stacking Regressor algorithms to achieve monthly price forecasts for the period 2020–2025. This method shows steep drops in prices down to $37/MWh. Although VAR is well known to show the impacts of different criteria on the dependent variable, and therefore it is very strong in short term forecasts, the results demonstrate the weakness of these methods in medium-term forecasts. Both impacts of different criteria and the time series on the natural gas price are considered only by the Stacking Regressor implementation. This is why medium-term price forecasts for scenario 2 are more reliable and realistic to have almost stable results dropping from $49 to $ 47.6 when Stacking Regressor is used.

With the COVID19 shocks the Globe lived in the last three months, we studied the COVID19 effect in the forecasts. Stacking Regressor is used as the most reliable method and showed the decrease of prices in short term dropping down to $35.6, but recovering prices and finding almost the same figures over $47 at the end of 2025.

All the price analysis run for Scenario 2 showed correlation with Russian gas prices, oil prices, and industry index. Correlation with the oil prices is clear due to the input of bilateral contracts. However, the analysis revealed that there is a significant level of correlation not only with oil prices but also with IND and Russian gas prices. All the different levels of correlations with other criteria show that the natural gas price forecasts should not only be based on time series analysis but either direct or indirect impacts of the nine criteria studied should always be taken together in Turkey.

Analysis for constructing the Hub in Turkey shows the most realistic predictions for the future. Even with the impact of COVID19, Turkey seems more secure if the hub is constructed. There is a continuing strategical plan to create a Natural Gas Market similar to the Power Market and the law is announced but the market is not yet established (EPDK

2018). It would be wise to consider the natural gas storage options and international hub construction before the market is structured.

Turkey is a continuously developing country with geopolitical importance. As industrialization grows energy markets will have strategic importance. Turkey does not have natural gas reserves and depends on the importation of the resource. A potential natural gas hub constructed in Turkey will make the country stronger in import strategies and might influence the energy security of the European Natural Gas market. This study is giving a foresight for the natural gas prices in Turkey in case a hub is created. Achievements of this study will support the energy decision-makers and Natural Gas policies in Turkey.

References

Acaravcı, S.K., Reyhanoğlu, A.G.: İ: Enerji fiyatlari ve hisse senedi getirileri: Türkiye ekonomisi için bir uygulama [Energy prices and stock returns: An application for Turkish Economy]. Nevşehir Haci Bektaş Veli Üniversitesi Sosyal Bilimler Enstitüsü Dergisi **3**, 94–110 (2013)

Asche, F., Osmundsen, P., Sandsmark, M.: The UK market for natural gas, oil and electricity: are the prices decoupled? Energy J. **27**(2) (2006)

Bachmeir, L.J., Griffin, J.M.: Testing for market integration: crude oil, coal, and natural gas. Energy J. 55–72 (2006)

Beyazgül, D.: Liberalisation of the Turkish natural gas market. Ph.D. dissertation, Politechnico Di Milano (2016)

Biresselioglu, M.E., Kaplan, M.D., Ozyorulmaz, E.: Towards a liberalized Turkish natural gas market: a SWOT analysis. Energy Sour. Part B **14**(2), 25–33 (2019)

Box, G., Jenkins, G.: Time Series Analysis: Forecasting and Control. Holden-Day, San Francisco (1970)

Breiman, L.: Stacked regressions. Mach. Learn. **24**(1), 49–64 (1996)

Burger, C., Weinmann, J.: Germany's decentralized energy revolution. In: Distributed Generation and its Implications for The Utility Industry, pp. 49–73. Academic Press (2014)

Business Insider (2020). https://markets.businessinsider.com/commodities/historical-prices/co2-european-emission-allowances/euro/1.1.2006_10.4.2020. Accessed 24 Apr 24

Ceperic, E., Zikoviç, S., Ceperic, V.: Short-term forecasting of natural gas prices using machine learning and feature selection algorithms. Energy **140**, 893–900 (2017)

De Vany, A., Walls, D.W.: Pipeline access and market integration in the natural gas industry: evidence from cointegration tests. Energy J. **14**(4), 1–19 (1993)

Dodge, Y.: The Oxford Dictionary of Statistical Terms. Oxford University Press, Oxford (2003)

Deloitte: Price forecast – Oil, gas & chemicals (2020). https://www2.deloitte.com/content/dam/Deloitte/ca/Documents/REA/ca-en-e&r-oil-gas-price-forecast-Q3-report-aoda.pdf. Accessed 24 Apr 2020

EIA (2020a). https://www.eia.gov/dnav/pet/hist/LeafHandler.ashx?n=PET&s=RBRTE&f=M. Accessed 24 Apr 2020

EIA (2020b). https://www.eia.gov/outlooks/aeo/data/browser/#/?id=12-AEO2020&region=0-0&cases=ref2020~highprice~lowprice&start=2018&end=2050&f=A&sourcekey=0. Accessed 24 May 2020

EIA (2020c). https://www.eia.gov/outlooks/steo/data/browser/#/?v=8&f=M&s=0&start=201601&end=202112&linechart=WTIPUUS~BREPUUS&maptype=0&ctype=linechart&map=. Accessed 5 June 2020

Enders, W.: Applied Econometric Time Series, 2nd edn. Wiley, Hoboken (2003)

EPDK: Doğal Gaz Piyasası Sektör Raporu – 2016 [Annual Natural Gas Sector Report-2016] (2017). https://www.epdk.gov.tr/Detay/Icerik/3-0-107/yillik-sektor-raporu

EPDK (2018). https://www.epdk.gov.tr/Detay/Icerik/3-0-78/kanunlar. Accessed 20 July 2020

EPDK: Doğal Gaz Piyasası Yıllık Sektör Raporu – 2018 [Annual Natural Gas Sector Report-2018] (2019). https://www.epdk.gov.tr/Detay/Icerik/3-0-107/yillik-sektor-raporu. Accessed 24 Apr 2020

EPDK (2020). http://www.epdk.org.tr/TR/Dokumanlar/Dogalgaz/YayinlarRaporlar/Aylik. Accessed 24 Apr 2020

EPIAS (2020a). https://seffaflik.epias.com.tr/transparency/uretim/gerceklesen-uretim/gercek-zamanli-uretim.xhtml. Accessed 24 Apr 2020

EPIAS (2020b). https://seffaflik.epias.com.tr/transparency/uretim/yekdem/lisanssiz-uretim-mik tari.xhtml. Accessed 24 Apr 2020

EPIAS (2020c). https://www.epias.com.tr/genel/gun-oncesi-piyasasinda-azami-fiyat-limiti nin-01-nisan-2020-teslim-gunu-ve-sonrasi-icin-yeniden-2000-tl-mwh-olarak-belirlenmesi/. Accessed 20 June 2020

Geidl, M., Koeppel, G., Favre-Perrod, P., Klockl, B., Andersson, G., Frohlich, K.: Energy hubs for the future. IEEE Power Energ. Mag. 5(1), 24–30 (2007)

Gianfreda, A., Grossi, L., Carlotto A.: The European hubs for natural gas: an integration towards a single area? In: 9th International Conference on the European Energy Market, Florence, pp. 1–5 (2012)

Gokırmak, H.: The energy policies for a sustainable economic growth in Turkey. Int. J. Energy Econ. Policy 7(1), 55–61 (2017)

Hemmes, K., Zachariah-Wolff, L., Geidl, M., Andersson, G.: Towards multi-source multi-product energy systems. Int. J. Hydrogen Energy 32, 1332–1338 (2007)

Herbert, J.H., Kreil, E.: US natural gas markets how efficient are they? Energy Policy 24, 1–5 (1996)

Herrera, G., Constantino, M., Tabak, B., Pistori, H., Su, J., Naranpanawa, A.: Long-term forecast of energy commodities price using machine learning. Energy 179, 214–221 (2019)

Kobek, M.L.P., Ugarte, A., Aguilar, G.C.: Shale gas in the United States: transforming energy security in the twenty-first century. Norteamérica 10, 7–38 (2015)

Kocaslan, A.G.D.G.: Avrupa birliği'nin doğalgaz politikasi ve bu eksende türkiye'nin önemi [European union's natural gas policy and the importance of Turkey in this context]. İstanbul Üniversitesi İktisat Fakültesi Mecmuası 61(2), 235–255 (2011)

Manzur, D., Seiflou, S.: Are crude oil, gas and coal prices cointegrated? Iran. Econ. Rev. 15(28), 29–51 (2011)

MGM (2020). https://www.mgm.gov.tr/veridegerlendirme/gun-derece.aspx?g=yillik&m=06-00&y=2012&a=02#sfB. Accessed 24 Apr 2020

Mishra, P:. Forecasting natural gas price – time series and nonparametric approach. In: World Congress on Engineering, London England (2012)

Misund, B., Oglend, A.: Supply and demand determinants of natural gas price volatility in the UK: a vector autoregression approach. Energy 111, 178–189 (2016)

Moeini-Aghtaie, M., Dehghanian, P., Fotuhi-Firuzabad, M., Abbaspour, A.: Multiagent genetic algorithm: an online probabilistic view on economic dispatch of energy hubs constrained by wind availability. IEEE Trans. Sustain. Energy 5(2), 699–708 (2014)

Mulder, M., Hulshof, D., Maat, J.: Market fundamentals, competition and natural-gas prices. Energy Policy 94, 480–491 (2016)

Naderi, M., Khamehchi, E., Karimi, B.: Novel statistical forecasting models for crude oil price, gas price, and interest rate based on meta-heuristic bat algorithm. J. Petrol. Sci. Eng. 172, 13–22 (2019)

Nalbant, H., Kayalica, M.Ö., Kayakutlu, G., Kaya, G.: An analysis of the natural gas pricing in natural gas hubs: an evaluation for Turkey. Energy Syst.1–25.https://doi.org/10.1007/s12667-020-00395-8

Nikoobakht, A., Aghaei, J., Shafie-khah, M.: Catalão, JPS: Co-operation of electricity and natural gas systems including electric vehicles and variable renewable energy sources based on a continuous-time model approach. Energy **200**, 117484 (2020)

Osicka, J., Ocelik, P.: Natural gas infrastructure and supply patterns in Eastern Europe: trends and policies. Energy Sour. Part B Econ. Plann. Policy **12**(4), 358–364 (2017)

Salehnia, N., Falahi, M., Seifi, A., Adeli, M.: Forecasting natural gas spot prices with nonlinear modeling using Gamma test analysis. J. Nat. Gas Sci. Eng. **14**, 238–249 (2013)

Santibanez, G.: A modelling approach that combines pricing policies with a carbon capture and storage supply chain network. J. Clean. Energy Prod. **167**, 1354–1369 (2017)

Serletis, A., Rangel-Ruiz, R.: Testing for common features in North American energy markets. Energy Econ. **26**, 401–414 (2004)

Siliverstovsa, B., L'Hégaretb, G., Neumannc, A., von Hirschhausena, C.: International market integration for natural gas? A cointegration analysis of prices in Europe North America and Japan. Energy Econ. **27**, 603–615 (2005)

Su, M., Zhang, Z., Zhu, Y., Zha, D., Wen, W.: Data driven natural gas spot price prediction models using machine learning methods. Energies **12**, 1680 (2019). https://doi.org/10.3390/en1209 1680

Tanaka, N.: Big Bang in Japan's energy policy. Energy Strat. Rev. **1**(4), 243–246 (2013)

TEIAS (2019a). https://www.teias.gov.tr/tr-TR/kurulu-guc-raporlari. Accessed 26 May 2020

TEIAS (2019b). https://www.teias.gov.tr/tr-TR/aylik-elektrik-uretim-tuketim-raporlari. Accessed 26 May 2020

Turkstat (2020). http://www.tuik.gov.tr/PreTablo.do?alt_id=1024. Accessed 24 Apr 2020

Wang, J., Lei, C., Guo, M.: Daily natural gas price forecasting by a weighted hybrid data-driven model. J. Petrol. Sci. Eng. **192**, 107240 (2020)

WHO (2020). https://www.who.int/news-room/detail/27-04-2020-who-timeline---covid-19. Accessed 5 June 2020

Wiser, R., Bolinger, M.: Can Deployment of Renewable Energy and Energy Efficiency Put Downward Pressure on Natural Gas Prices. Lawrence Berkeley National Laboratory, Berkeley (2007)

Wong-Parodi, G., Dale, L., Lekov, A.: Comparing price forecast accuracy of natural gas models and future markets. Energy Policy **34**(18), 4115–4122 (2006)

Xunpeng, S.: Development of Europe's gas hubs: implications for east Asia. Nat. Gas Ind. B **3**(4), 357–366 (2016)

Predicting Power Deviation in the Turkish Power Market Based on Adaptive Factor Impacts

Denizhan Guven[1](✉) iD, Avni Ozozen[2] iD, Gülgün Kayakutlu[3] iD,
and M. Ozgur Kayalica[3] iD

[1] Eurasia Institute of Earth Sciences, Istanbul Technical University, 34467 Istanbul, Turkey
guvende@itu.edu.tr
[2] Axpo Turkey, 34340 Besiktas, Istanbul, Turkey
[3] Energy Institute, Istanbul Technical University, 34467 Istanbul, Turkey

Abstract. Energy market models are generally focused on energy balancing using the optimum energy mix. In countries where the energy markets are not fully liberalised, the State Regulators reflect any cost of being off-balance on the utility companies and this affects the consumers as well. The right short term prediction of the market trends is beneficial both to optimise the physical energy flow and commercial revenue balance for suppliers and utility companies. This study is aimed to predict the sign trends in the power market by selecting the influencing factors adaptive to the conditions of the day ahead, 10 h, 5 h, 2 h and 1 h before the electricity balance is active. There are numerous factors consisting of weather conditions, resource costs, operation costs, renewable energy conditions, regulations, etc. with a considerable impact on the predictions. The contribution of this paper is to choose the factors with the highest impacts using the Genetic Algorithm (GA) with Akaike Information Criteria (AIC), which are then used as input of a Recursive Neural Network (RNN) model for forecasting the deviation trends. The proposed hybrid method does not only reduce the prediction errors but also avoid dependency on expert knowledge. Hence this paper will allow both the market regulator and the suppliers to take precautions based on a confident prediction.

Keywords: Energy market balancing · Auxiliary power market modeling · Turkish power market · Adaptive prediction · Genetic algorithm and recursive neural networks

1 Introduction

The structure of the monopolistic power industry controlled by the government has been changed by the development of deregulation and the emergence of competitive markets since the beginning of the 1990s. Since then, electricity as an indispensable commodity has been traded based on the market rules with spot and derivative contracts [1]. On the other hand, as electricity storage for long durations is not economically feasible at present, it is very crucial to set a balance between generation and consumption for

© IFIP International Federation for Information Processing 2021
Published by Springer Nature Switzerland AG 2021
E. Mercier-Laurent et al. (Eds.): AI4KM 2021, IFIP AICT 614, pp. 213–234, 2021.
https://doi.org/10.1007/978-3-030-80847-1_14

the sake of the electricity grid. Ensuring a complete balance between them is hardly accomplishable because of the uncertainness in both electricity supply and demand. That is why avoiding perfect grid imbalance is not possible. To inhibit grid unstableness, these imbalances should be neutralized by the Transmission System Operator (TSO) [2].

With the transition through cleaner electricity generation, the structure and requirements for supply security are consistently evolving. Since the share of Renewable Energy Sources (RES) in electricity generation increases gradually, the prediction of electricity generation becomes more difficult. This situation leads to make Ancillary Services (AS), such as voltage and frequency control (system services) more critical to ensure a consistent electricity network [3]. System services also called balancing, assures that the active power insertion and withdrawals are met in real-time to keep the frequency constant [4].

In this respect, Turkey is one of the leading countries determining its direction towards cleaner electricity generation from RES. Although electricity generation is dominated by fossil-based power plants, the share of electricity from RES has increased from 26.4% to 40% in the last decade (author's calculation based on EXIST [5] and TETC [6]). In this period, the RES capacity of Turkey has jumped from 15.5 GW to 49.5 GW [7]. On the other hand, this situation may cause electricity system imbalances due to the instability of electricity generation from RES.

With the balancing and settlement regulation published in November 2004, the Day-Ahead Balancing system was adopted to facilitate real-time balancing and improve system security in Turkey [8]. Since then, Balancing and settlement regulation have undergone various changes as a result of the studies carried out in line with the demands of the market participants to ensure the healthy execution of real-time balancing in the electricity market and to fully respond to the needs of the market participants.

Balancing Power Market (BPM) is operated by the Turkish Electricity Transmission Company (TETC). Although a market with balanced production and consumption amounts is presented to the system operator (National Load Dispatch Centre-NLDC) with the Day-Ahead Market, deviations may occur in real-time. For instance, if a power plant is out of order due to a malfunction or the electricity generation from RES does not meet the foresight or a large consumption facility starts to operate/stop working suddenly, it disrupts the system balance (See Fig. 1). In this case, NLDC tries to achieve the system balance by using the offers submitted to the BPM to ensure the balance.

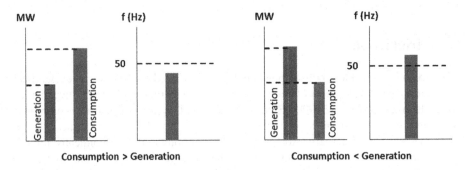

Fig. 1. Frequency imbalances

Therefore, this study aims to present a new methodology combining the Genetic Algorithm (GA) model and the Recurrent Neural Network (RNN) model to predict grid imbalance volumes in Turkey. GA is applied to select the best regressors, and RNN is utilized to predict the grid imbalances for different forecast horizons. Although there are numerous balancing price forecasting studies in the literature, only a few studies are focusing on volume forecasting. In this context, this study contributes to the literature by filling two gaps. Firstly, this study will be the first study that combines these methods to forecast grid imbalances. Secondly, as far as is known, there is not a single study for forecasting imbalance volume specific to the Turkish electricity balancing market. As a country with very high grid imbalance volumes, this study is very crucial for Turkey.

This study is organized as follows. An overview of grid imbalance studies is given in the next section. The third section presents a review of the methodology used in this study. In the fourth section, the proposed model is run with appropriate data specific to the Turkish case. Finally, the last section concludes with the discussion on estimation results.

2   Literature

The number of studies for the electricity market imbalance is progressively increasing in the literature. These studies can be grouped under three different types, namely, fundamental, price forecasting, and volume forecasting. Within the scope of fundamental works, while some studies aim to form a framework for how the balancing market works, some studies analyse the impact of Renewable Energy Sources (RES) on the balancing market structure. In this context, Ortner & Totschnig [9] aimed to evaluate the suitability of electricity balancing markets in Europe based on the different scenarios for 2030. A large-scale market model was established to obtain a perception about market shares and revenues of day-ahead, intra-day and balancing markets. The result of the model exhibited that balancing volume will grow in the mid-term, but the financial magnitude of the balancing market will range in a few percent of day-ahead market volumes. In another example, Lago et al. [2] discussed whether the grid, which is controlled by Transmission System Operator (TSO), is not efficient with respect to grid imbalances. It was stated that market players may help to compensate grid imbalances under the supervision of TSO. As a result of this study, it was proven that the new market structure may contribute between 10–20% of the total balancing energy needed and reduce the balancing costs.

Unlike previous studies, Borggrefe & Neuhoff [10] analysed the ongoing designs of intraday and balancing markets in North America and Europe. They evaluated these market structures whether they are capable of sufficiently dealing with the reliability of wind. To evaluate market structures, they defined six criteria, and it was presented that none of the power markets in Europe can completely meet all these criteria. On the other hand, some electricity markets in North America, such as New York ISO, Texas and California satisfy all criteria. Similar to this study, Goodarzi et al. [11] assessed the impact of both wind and solar energy forecasts errors on electricity market imbalance volumes and spot electricity prices in Germany. Ordinary Least Squares (OLS) regression, quantile regression and Auto-Regressive Moving Averages (ARMA) methods were performed to determine these relationships. This study showed that higher wind and solar forecast errors cause an increase in the absolute values of imbalance volumes, and therefore this situation may lead to higher spot prices. More recently, Sirin & Yilmaz [12] examined the impact of RES on the Turkish balancing market prices utilizing quantile regression and investigated how imbalances are altered based on the renewable energy technology with Ordered Logistic Regression. As a result of this analysis, it was found that an increase in renewable energy production suggests lower prices, but superior positive imbalances for the electricity grid.

In addition to studies explaining the fundamentals of balancing electricity markets, the bulk of the literature focuses on price forecasting on the balancing market. Kölmek & Navruz [13] attempted to model the balancing market price using Artificial Neural Networks (ANN) for Turkey. After establishing the best proper configuration, the results were compared with a model built with an auto-regressive integrated moving average (ARIMA). It was also stated that the ANN model performs better than the ARIMA model with an average error rate of 14.15%. Similar to the previous study, Mordasiewicz [14] utilized three econometric methods, including Moving Weighted Average (MWA), OLS, and Autoregressive Moving Average with Exogenous input (ARMAX) to forecast balancing price in Poland. ARMAX method was found to be the best method for this purpose. As one of the latest studies, Lucas et al. [15] used three machine learning models, namely Gradient Boosting (GB), Random Forest (RF) and XGBoost to forecast balancing market prices for the UK. XGBoost method was detected as the most successful model with a Mean Absolute Error (MAE) of 7.89 £/MWh among others.

Although there are many other fundamental and price forecasting studies in the literature as aforementioned, this paper focuses on volume forecasting in balancing markets. Several studies are focusing on the imbalance volume forecasting which is the main scope of this study. However, the literature on this subject is quite limited. Within this scope, Garcia & Kirschen [16] proposed a methodology combining both classical and data mining techniques to forecast electricity grid imbalance volume for England and Wales. It was stated that the proposed model shows great potential, but the accuracy of forecasts is found to be still low. For the Czech Republic, Kratocvil [17] developed an imbalance volume interval forecasting model which also involves a variety of exogenous variables. Depending on different intervals, accuracies of imbalance forecasts were found to be ranged between 60 and 70%. In a similar study, Contreras [18] built up a random forest model to forecast electricity grid imbalance volume and utilized a genetic algorithm for applying the bidding plan minimizing the imbalance costs in Spain. As a result of this study, the random forest technique was found to be completely applicable for forecasting electricity system imbalance volume. Parallel with the aforementioned studies, Ferreira [19] applied both Boosted Decision Tree regression model and Decision Forest regression machine learning techniques to forecast balancing power volume and balancing power price for Nordic countries. The forecasting model showed high accuracy (87%) at determining the direction of the total imbalance. The model also succeeded to detect the peaks in the magnitude of the total imbalance. More recently, Salem et al. [20] presented a quantile regression forests model to forecast two-hour-ahead imbalances in the form of prediction intervals for Norway. This established model was found to have great potential towards a fully automated decision support tool with a longer prediction horizon.

Despite the number of studies surveyed above, the imbalance volume forecasting in Turkey has not been sufficiently analysed. This study attempts to fill this gap by selecting the best variables with the Genetic Algorithm (GA) method and forecasting imbalance volume with the Recurrent Neural Network (RNN) method. More importantly, to the authors' knowledge, this is the first study combining GA and RNN methods to forecast electricity grid imbalance volume (Table 1).

Table 1. A brief summary of Literature

Reference	Type	Region/Country	Concept
[16]	VF	England & Wales	Proposing a new imbalance volume forecasting model by combining classical and data mining techniques
[14]	PF	Poland	Forecasting balancing market price using MWA, OLS, and ARMAX
[10]	F	Europe & N. America	Evaluating the impact of wind intermittency both on the current intraday and balancing markets
[21]	PF	Europe	Analyzing the impact of the imbalance pricing mechanism on market behavior with Agent-based modelling
[22]	F	Spain	Proposing a new scheme to minimize the use of ancillary services
[1]	PF	Review	Explaining the complexity, strengths, weaknesses, opportunities and of price forecasting tools
[23]	F	Germany	Analyzing the interactions between balancing system and variable renewable energy sources
[24]	PF	–	Benchmarking time series based balancing market price forecasting models
[13]	PF	Turkey	Forecasting balancing market price using ANN
[17]	VF	Czech Republic	Developing an imbalance volume interval forecasting model which also involves a variety of exogenous variables
[18]	VF	Spain	Proposing a random forest model to forecast electricity grid imbalance volume

(*continued*)

Table 1. (*continued*)

[19]	VF	Nordic Countries	Applying Boosted Decision Tree regression and Decision Forest regression models to forecast balancing power volume and balancing power price
[25]	F	Germany	Presenting an empirical examination of the function of intraday trading in the balancing system
[9]	F	Europe	Evaluate the suitability of electricity balancing markets based on the different scenarios for 2030
[11]	F	Germany	Assessing the impact of wind and solar energy forecasts errors on electricity market imbalance volumes and spot electricity prices in Germany using OLS, quantile regression and ARMA
[26]	PF	Hong Kong	Proposing a genetic algorithm based on dynamic pricing
[27]	PF	Germany	Optimizing balancing power bidding strategy with a MILP model considering the price forecasts and spot market prices
[20]	VF	Norway	Presenting a quantile regression forests model to forecast two-hours-ahead imbalances in the form of prediction intervals
[28]	F	China	Examining the impact of imbalance settlement design and utilizing an effective evaluation method
[3]	F	Swiss	Focusing on balancing market design and opportunity cost
[15]	PF	UK	Forecasting balancing market price using GB, RF and XGBoost
[29]	F	NL	Investigating the impact of market design on strategic bidding behavior
[2]	F	NL	Examining the effect of market players on the balancing market
[12]	F	Turkey	Examining the impact of RES on the balancing market prices, and investigating how imbalances are altered based on renewable energy technology

(The abbreviations in the type section: VF-Volume Forecasting, PF-Price Forecasting, and F-Fundamental)

3 Methodology

This study selects the best features to be used in the forecasting model by using the Genetic Algorithm (GA). The Genetic Algorithm concept is derived from biology and its philosophy depends on Darwin's theory of survival of the fittest. Genetic algorithms are a technique based on both natural genetics and computer science. The terms used to describe genetic algorithms are a mixture of terms used in these two sciences. Thus, the terms used in genetics and their responses in GA are shown in Table 2.

Table 2. Terms of GA and their descriptions (Adapted from Vural) [30]

Term	Response in GA	Description
Gene (Bit)	Character feature	It is the element that determines the character of an individual, and therefore its value
Chromosome (String)	Individual	It is the string formed by the combination of genes. Chromosomes are formed by a certain coding system. They show candidate solutions
Genotype	Gene structure of the individual	It is a candidate solution that involves certain groups of genes within the chromosomes
Phenotype	Decoded gen structure	It is an alternative solution set. It is the determination of the original value by decoding the genotype
Allele	Feature value	It is the value set of genes
Locus	Position of character	It is the position (place) of the gene on the chromosome
Population	Candidate solutions community	It is a collection of solutions formed by a combination of chromosomes. It is usually kept constant throughout the algorithm
Fitness Function	Objective function	It is the value that shows the survival status of the individual. Higher values indicate that the individual is more likely to survive
Selection	Selection	It is the selection of living things that can survive from the population

The fundamental characteristic of a GA is the manipulation of a population whose individuals are characterized by having a chromosome [31]. A chromosome can be also formed as strings of binary bits (0 or 1). Every bit has a certain position within the string describing the chromosome to which it belongs. The fitness function (F) provides the connection between the GA and the problem. The F builds a matching from the chromosomes to some group of real numbers. The higher F indicates a better level of adaptation of the individual [32]. This procedure is generative in virtue of three main operators namely, mutation, crossover and reproduction.

The reproduction operator is a mechanism that chooses the best-fit individual strings in accordance with some selection operators and it is responsible for selecting the members which are authorized to reproduce during the ongoing generation. The selection of these members is dependent on the basis of their fitness values and the best-fit individuals are handed down to the next generations.

The crossover mechanism makes the exchange of chromosomes between mated parents possible. Mated parents create a child with a chromosome series that is a mixture of the parent's chromosomes (See Fig. 2). The mutation operator is a background operator which makes random and self-generated changes in different chromosomes. In Fig. 2, four different mutation types are shown. According to Haldenbilen and Ceylan [32], this operator has a very important role in GAs by replacing the genes that are lost from the population during the selection progress so that they can be tried in a new generation or bring the genes that are not present in the initial population.

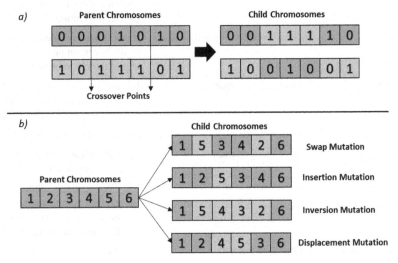

Fig. 2. a) Two-point crossover example b) Mutation examples

The process of GA is shown in Fig. 3. This cycle continues until the stopping criteria are provided. The GA process starts with initial genetic coding. In this very first step of the process, a phenotype is transformed into a genotype. A population is described as a collection of chromosomes and a chromosome as a collection of genes. When a set of solutions are created, it is necessary to determine how good these solutions are. For this, in the second step, the objective function must be defined. One advantage of the GA is that it brings ease of use to problems where it is difficult to formulate the objective function. The third step of the process is to create an initial population. With this step, individuals (parents) to be used in the algorithm are created. The choice to be made here is the number of individuals in the starting population. The starting population number for the best solution is different for each problem type. The population number is generally maintained across generations. The fourth step is the evaluation of fitness which is the function that finds out how good the chromosomes are. This function forms the brain of GA, and it is the only part that works specifically for the problem in GA. The fitness function turns the chromosomes into the parameters of the problem, in a way decoding them.

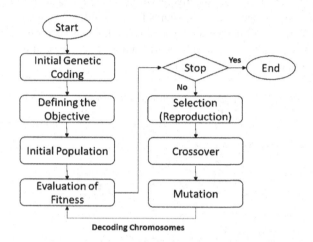

Fig. 3. Steps of the Genetic Algorithm

The next three steps are the generative procedures; selection, crossover, and mutation. After these steps, the last part of the GA process is defining the stopping criteria. The criteria required for the completion of the cycles of the Genetic Algorithm (termination of generations) can be defined differently. Some of the criteria are [33]:

1. After a certain number of generations is finished, the cycles are stopped and it is checked who is most suitable over the generations.
2. As a result of evolution, when the improvement in fitness function falls below a certain value, the cycles are terminated.
3. By giving a certain period for evolution, evolution can be stopped when this time is over.
4. By giving a certain value for the fitness function, the evolution can be completed in the first cycle exceeding this value.

After the best features are selected with GA, the forecasting model was built on the Recurrent Neural Network (RNN) methodology in this study. RNN's are one of the most popular Neural Network (NN) architectures for forecasting problems. The most widely-used RNN architectures are the Elman RNN (ERNN), the Long Short Term Memory (LSTM), and the Gated Recurrent Unit (GRU) [34]. Among the various RNN architectures, only ERNN architecture will be discussed in this study.

ERNN is basic neural networks with a hidden state. However, it does not contain an advanced gating mechanism [35]. ERNN architecture can be mathematically formulated as

$$h_t = f(W_i x_t + W h_{t-1} + b_h) \tag{1}$$

$$z_t = g(W_0 h_t + b_0) \tag{2}$$

where $h_t \in \mathbb{R}^d$, $x_t \in \mathbb{R}^m$, and $z_t \in \mathbb{R}^d$ represent the hidden state of the RNN cell, input and output of the cell at time t, respectively, while d and m indicate the size (dimension) of the cell and input, respectively. W_i stands for the hidden weights of input, W is the recurrent weight matrix of the hidden layer and b_h is the bias vector for the hidden state. $W_0 \in \mathbb{R}^{d \times d}$ and $b_0 \in \mathbb{R}^d$ are the weight matrix and the bias vector of the cell output [34, 35]. The structure of ERNN is shown in Fig. 4.

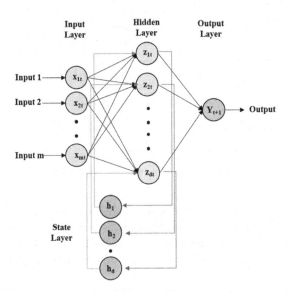

Fig. 4. Structure of ERNN

RNNs have some advantages, such as nonlinear prediction abilities, quicker convergence, and more accurate mapping capability. In RNN architecture, the hidden layer outputs are permitted to feedback onto themselves over a buffer layer, called the recurrent layer. This feedback provides ERNN with some capability, including learning, recognizing, and generating temporal patterns. Every hidden neuron has a connection with only one recurrent layer neuron. Thus, the recurrent layer virtually comprises a duplicate of the state of the hidden layer one trice before. The number of recurrent neurons is equal to the number of hidden neurons [36]. The current hidden state is contingent upon both the hidden state of the prior time step and the current input. The feedback cycle in the RNN architecture linking its current state to the next state supports this dependency. These connections have a crucial role to take into account past information when updating the current cell state [34].

4   Imbalances in State Regulated Power Markets: Case of Turkey

Since renewable energies take a growing share in the energy resource portfolio, short-term forecasts considering the effect of intermittent resources on both the price and imbalances of the power market as in Jiang et al. [37], Qiu et al. [38] and Gligoric et al. [39]. These researches either try to reduce the prediction errors for the day ahead analysis or introducing stochasticity and fuzziness. However, the wind and solar energies are very much dependent on meteorological conditions and that is why they change by the hour and with the impact of several factors at a time. There are certainly grid or turbine outage predictions to realize the power market balances [40]. Market imbalances are more important in partly liberated markets since the cost will be effective on both the suppliers and the consumers. This is shown in the spread differences drawn for Germany and Turkey, shown in Fig. 5.

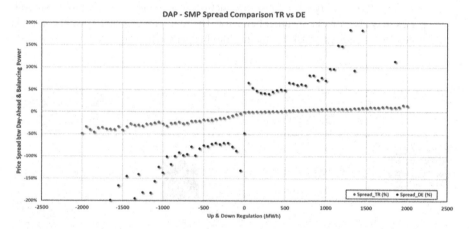

Fig. 5. Comparison of Germany and Turkey

After having reviewed the imbalance studies and observing the power markets we can conclude with the following list of items that cause the imbalances in the power markets:

- **Power markets fluctuate a lot in the short term**. There are unavoidable prediction errors whether the analysis is made for the day ahead conditions or the hour ahead. The prediction errors are very sensitive to the demand because of industrial and commercial demand variations. However, the meteorological conditions vary in even seconds to affect renewable energy resources. Intermittent energy flow due to the operational conditions of the supply unit or transmission infrastructure are also unavoidable. Prediction errors cause the market regulator to apply penalties to the suppliers and utility companies.
- **Supplier behavior in planning the available capacity.** Opportunity costs of upward or downward regulations are important for the suppliers. If the suppliers see some profit in tertiary balancing or a chance to avoid penalties on imbalances, they might

give day ahead commitments accordingly. Unexpected commercial behavior of the suppliers might cause imbalances in supplier unit outages. There are even outage problems based on suppliers running the operations without any plans.

- **Discrepancies between market operations and physical energy flow.** It is a fact that the power markets operate time-dependent which means the actions are taken in minutes, hours or days. That means the market operations are run and regulated with a discrete approach, whereas the resource flow, i.e. the physical energy flow is continuous. The stochasticity in the continuous flow should be considered when any forecast of wind or solar resources or plant outages applied, though the load dispatch schedules are planned by combinatorial optimisation.

- **Unexpected Grid Outages may occur.** Grid operators try to balance the power market in terms of frequencies (50Hz) and the TSO ensures a balance between the production and electricity consumption 24 h a day 7 days a week. Any trend for the negative outage will cause blackouts. Suppliers may put the balance in danger through unplanned plant outages, TSO asks for higher or lower production. The regulator's behavior to smooth the prices may also affect consumer behavior. The regulator can have special contracts with the big consumers or ask for the use of cheaper tariffs (Fig. 6).

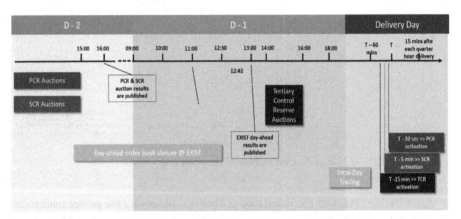

Fig. 6. Timeline of Power Trading in Turkey (Finalized generation/consumption schedules are nominated to corresponding TSO by the BRP on D-1 at 16:00 each day. The nominations can be updated every 30 min after the corresponding intra-day product's gate closure)

All the above-mentioned imbalances can only be balanced through the TSO interventions by purchasing or reducing regulations (Fig. 7). Balancing the imbalances have a considerable cost for the regulator which cannot be reflected onto the end consumer. In some countries, it is socialised and the generation imbalances penalties are given for the suppliers, whereas in emerging countries like Turkey, the penalty is shared among the supplier and the utility company, which has some influence on the end consumers. The ideal market should be the one where commercial regulations are designed to motivate the mitigation of imbalances. As long as the ideal market does not exist we should have more reliable predictions for the benefit of all the role players in the market.

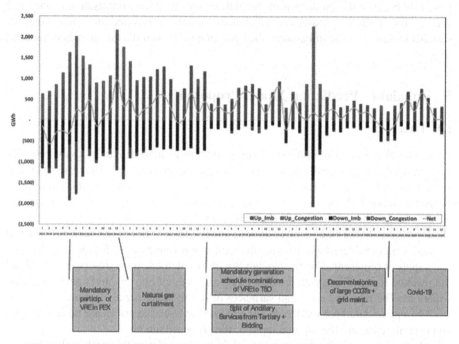

Fig. 7. A Sample of TSO regulations in the past years in Turkey (based on TETC data)

Better predictions will support the trading optimisation, which is not only considered by the suppliers but has beneficial impacts on TSO and the utility companies as well. Though recently there are new technologies like smart meters, load shedding and electricity storage, it is wise to avoid the costs before investing in the new technologies. That

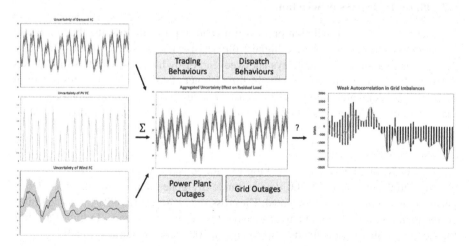

Fig. 8. Is there a transfer function to represent imbalances?

is mainly because the prediction of imbalances will help the optimisation of physical energy flow. If all the resources of imbalances could be transferred into a mathematical formula to represent the imbalances the operation costs would be immediately reduced (Fig. 8).

5 Imbalance Prediction Model Proposed

5.1 Data

Prediction of the trend in imbalances (upwards/downwards) demand, supply, resource data are used considering the financial values and variances as well. The meteorological conditions and the day and time effects are also taken into account in addition to price as seen in Table 3 (Appendix).

Demand, wind strength and solar irradiation history are taken as one day and one week previous to the day of prediction to see the trends. Both the financial Cost and variances are considered while taking the return on revenue values for the same history.

Supply is represented by the availability of dispatchable units, reserve margins and the residual loads. These data are also taken to represent one day and one week ahead situations. The financial costs and variances of supply items are also input.

As to price data both market prices and ancillary service prices are taken as input. Opportunity costs are the original input of the proposed model.

All the above are taken for each hour of 24 h of each day of the week, differentiating the holidays and workdays. When this multiplier is considered for each hour we have $33*2*7*24 = 11,088$ regressors giving the imbalance trend as an output. Each of the data is a time series of at least in time series of a few years.

The time-series data is preprocessed in order to fulfil the missing data and to normalise in binary form to have consistency.

5.2 Phase 1: Regressor Selection

In order to reduce the prediction process time and improve the results, the number of regressors is selected to have the highest impacts for the considered hour of the day. These change a lot by the weekdays and weekend or by holidays. Our GA model uses Akaike Information Criteria (AIC) for the fitness function to be optimised. This is a linear regression model which minimises the least squared error of learning which penalises the high number of factors as it tries to avoid both local optima trap and data overfit.

$$AIC = -2(\text{log-likelihood}) + 2K \tag{3}$$

where K is the number of factors and log-likelihood is the fitness measure.

An initial population of 700 data is randomly generated, of which 15% of best performing chromosomes are selected. The cross-over is applied as 80% for fast learning. A mutation rate of 10% will be used to avoid fast local convergence. In this algorithm, the stopping criteria are defined as no change in 100 consecutive runs (Fig. 9).

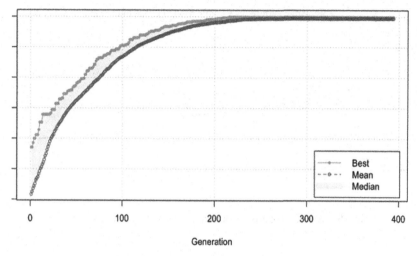

Fig. 9. Regressor Selection using GA

5.3 Phase 2: Imbalance Trend Prediction

The output of Phase 1 is used as input of Phase 2. Hence, regressors with the highest impact are chosen and used as an input for a recursive neural network (RNN) to process classification to predict the next hour (day) imbalance to be upwards or downwards. Elman RNN is modelled to benefit the memory recording.

The transfer function is chosen as *tanh* because it realizes the overfitting and corrects fast in classification application. It is used both between the input and the hidden layers as well as between the hidden layer and the output with a learning rate of 10% to allow fast learning. The number of hidden nodes are tried as similar to the number of input nodes, half of the number of input notes, double the number of input nodes and two times the average of the number of input and output nodes. Best results are achieved by the last one. The prediction errors are calculated using Mean Absolute Percentage Error (MAPE). The formulation of MAPE is given as

$$MAPE = \frac{1}{n} \sum_{t=1}^{n} \left| \frac{A_t - F_t}{A_t} \right| \qquad (4)$$

5.4 Results and Discussions

The model is applied to perform a prediction for the day ahead (12 to 36 h), 10 h ahead, five hours ahead, two hours ahead and one hour ahead. The results are compared with the naive flipping coin, linear regression, GA and long term average which are generally accepted methods applied by the suppliers, which are given in Fig. 10.

Flipping a coin can easily be defeated by long term averages. The linear regression model (OLS) uses the benefits of modelling with certain parameters. The most relevant parameters are chosen by GA and the difference can be recognised. Signals in real-time are only observed in the proposed model.

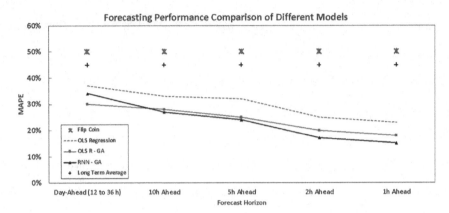

Fig. 10. MAPE comparisons of predictions in different time horizons

These results can be achieved by a dedicated expert to whom it would cause a lot of time. The proposed model processes automatically using the machine learning method and it spends just a few seconds of computer time. In a complex world of energy markets, a number of input factors are non-stop changing which would need the model to be renewed if an adaptive model like the proposed is not used.

Moreover, using the GA with random populations, cross over and mutations avoid the shade of the historical conditions but adapt to the current situation by choosing the regressors at the last hour applied. Using the RNN method helps that by improving what is kept in the memory cell.

The achievements of this study imply that the proposed model will be most beneficial in intraday markets, where prediction up to 1–2 h are more critical. The benefits are equally important for the commercial players and the regulator who will perform the balance faster with the suppliers being well prepared. The cost of active energy, capacity loans and planning costs will be reduced in the long term.

The suppliers can also increase the revenues by avoiding the capacity loans and having more knowledge about the business conditions in the market.

6 Summary and Conclusion

This study aims to forecast grid imbalance volumes by combining the Genetic Algorithm and Recurrent Neural Networks methods. The Genetic Algorithm method is used to select the best regressors, whereas, Recurrent Neural Network is applied to forecast grid imbalances for different forecast horizons using these selected regressors. After running the established model with the appropriate data, the results are compared with that of Ordinary Least Squares Regression in the presence and absence of Genetic Algorithm models.

The proposed model will be a leader in adaptive prediction in the power markets where real-time is difficult to handle due to deterministic and discrete regulations. The adaptive approach gives a new angle by changing the input based on changes in the market as close as one hour.

Achievements of the proposed model will contribute to all the role players in countries with partly liberated power markets. In those countries, the regulator reflects all the costs on the suppliers and the utility companies, that is why even the end consumers will take some share of the cost of imbalances.

In future studies, more variety of the features can be analysed. We suggest that the features are selected using the swarm optimisation so that regressors will be selected not only by impact performance but also being uncorrelated with the other features. stochasticity and continuity in the factors are to be handled by using a stochastic Deep Learning method, which can also add more precision in predictions.

Appendix

Table 3. Potential inputs

Day-Ahead (12 to 36h)	10 h Ahead	5 h Ahead	2 h Ahead	1 h Ahead	Pre-Process	Capturing
D-1 Demand					Normalized btw min-max	Participants' behaviours
D-7 Demand					Normalized btw min-max	Participants' behaviours
D Demand FC	Update	Update	Update	Update	Normalized btw min-max	Forecast error of participants
D Demand FC Variance	Update	Update	Update	Update	Normalized btw min-max	Forecast error of participants
D-1 Wind					Normalized btw min-max	Participants' behaviours
D-7 Wind					Normalized btw min-max	Participants' behaviours
D Wind FC	Update	Update	Update	Update	Normalized btw min-max	Forecast error of participants
D Wind FC Variance	Update	Update	Update	Update	Normalized btw min-max	Forecast error of participants

(*continued*)

Table 3. (*continued*)

Day-Ahead (12 to 36h)	10 h Ahead	5 h Ahead	2 h Ahead	1 h Ahead	Pre-Process	Capturing
D-1 RoR					Normalized btw min-max	Participants' behaviours
D-7 RoR					Normalized btw min-max	Participants' behaviours
D RoR FC	Update	Update	Update	Update	Normalized btw min-max	Forecast error of participants
D RoR FC Variance	Update	Update	Update	Update	Normalized btw min-max	Forecast error of participants
D-1 PV					Normalized btw min-max	Participants' behaviours
D-7 PV					Normalized btw min-max	Participants' behaviours
D PV FC	Update	Update	Update	Update	Normalized btw min-max	Forecast error of participants
D PV FC Variance	Update	Update	Update	Update	Normalized btw min-max	Forecast error of participants
D-1 Residual Load					Normalized btw min-max	Participants' behaviours
D-7 Residual Load					Normalized btw min-max	Participants' behaviours
D Residual Load FC	Update	Update	Update	Update	Normalized btw min-max	Forecast error of participants

(*continued*)

Table 3. (*continued*)

Day-Ahead (12 to 36h)	10 h Ahead	5 h Ahead	2 h Ahead	1 h Ahead	Pre-Process	Capturing
D Residual Load FC Variance	Update	Update	Update	Update	Normalized btw min-max	Forecast error of participants
D-1 Nat. Avg. Temp					Normalized btw min-max	Participants' behaviours
D-7 Nat. Avg. Temp					Normalized btw min-max	Participants' behaviours
D Nat. Avg. Temp. FC	Update	Update	Update	Update	Normalized btw min-max	Forecast error of participants
D Nat. Avg. Temp. FC Variance	Update	Update	Update	Update	Normalized btw min-max	Forecast error of participants
D-1 Availability of Dispatchable Units					Normalized btw min-max	Balancing providing capacity
D-7 Availability of Dispatchable Units	Update	Update	Update	Update	Normalized btw min-max	Balancing providing capacity
D Availability of Dispatchable Units FC	Update	Update	Update	Update	Normalized btw min-max	Balancing providing capacity
D-1 Reserve Margin					Normalized btw min-max	Grid tightness

(*continued*)

Table 3. (*continued*)

Day-Ahead (12 to 36h)	10 h Ahead	5 h Ahead	2 h Ahead	1 h Ahead	Pre-Process	Capturing
D-7 Reserve Margin	Update	Update	Update	Update	Normalized btw min-max	Grid tightness
D Reserve Margin FC	Update	Update	Update	Update	Normalized btw min-max	Grid tightness
Weekday Type					Binary	Pattern recognition
Holiday or Not					Binary	Pattern recognition
Hour of the Day					Binary	Pattern recognition
Ancillary Service Prices					Normalized btw min-max	Generator behaviours
Opportunity Costs of Providing Ancillary Services					Normalized btw min-max	Cost efficiency of system
Day-Ahead Price FC						Participants' behaviours
	Day-Ahead Price	Day-Ahead Price	Day-Ahead Price	Day-Ahead Price		Participants' behaviours
			Past Imb.	Past Imb.		Latest output data

References

1. Weron, R.: Electricity price forecasting: a review of the state-of-the-art with a look into the future. Int. J. Forecast. **30**(4), 10 (2014)
2. Lago, J., Poplavskaya, K., Suryanarayana, G., De Schutter, B.: A market framework for grid balancing support through imbalances trading. Renew. Sustain. Energy Rev. **137**, 110467 (2020)
3. Schillinger, M.: Balancing-market design and opportunity cost: the Swiss case. Util. Policy **64**, 101045 (2020)
4. Nobel, F.A.: On balancing market design. Technische Universiteit Eindhoven: Eindhoven, The Netherlands (2016)
5. [Data] EXIST- Energy Exchange Istanbul: Real Time Generation, 01 January 2020–31 December 2020. https://seffaflik.epias.com.tr/transparency/uretim/gerceklesen-uretim/gercek-zamanli-uretim.xhtml. Accessed 29 Jan 2021

6. [Data] TETC- Turkish Electricity Transmission Company: Electricity Generation and Transmission Statistics. https://www.teias.gov.tr/tr-TR/turkiye-elektrik-uretim-iletim-istatistikleri. Accessed 31 Jan 2021
7. [Data] TETC- Turkish Electricity Transmission Company: Installed Power Plant Capacity Report, December 2020. https://webapi.teias.gov.tr/file/2bd6a902-7b75-4226-9c54-55ae9a fea22f?download. Accessed 11 Feb 2021
8. Cetintas, H., Bicil, I.M.: Elektrik Piyasalarında Yeniden Yapılanma ve Türkiye Elektrik Piyasasında Yapısal Dönüşüm. Optimum Ekonomi ve Yönetim Bilimleri Dergisi 2(2), 1–15 (2015)
9. Ortner, A., Totschnig, G.: The future relevance of electricity balancing markets in Europe-a 2030 case study. Energ. Strat. Rev. 24, 111–120 (2019)
10. Borggrefe, F., Neuhoff, K.: Balancing and intraday market design: options for wind integration. DIW Berlin Discussion Paper No. 1162. SSRN (2011). https://ssrn.com/abstract=194 5724 or https://doi.org/10.2139/ssrn.1945724
11. Goodarzi, S., Perera, H.N., Bunn, D.: The impact of renewable energy forecast errors on imbalance volumes and electricity spot prices. Energy Policy 134, 110827 (2019)
12. Sirin, S.M., Yilmaz, B.N.: The impact of variable renewable energy technologies on electricity markets: an analysis of the Turkish balancing market. Energy Policy 151, 112093 (2021)
13. Kölmek, M.A., Navruz, I.: Forecasting the day-ahead price in electricity balancing and settlement market of Turkey by using artificial neural networks. Turk. J. Electr. Eng. Comput. Sci. 23(3), 841–852 (2015)
14. Mordasiewicz, Ł.: Price forecasting in the balancing mechanism. Rynek Energii (3), 94 (2011)
15. Lucas, A., Pegios, K., Kotsakis, E., Clarke, D.: Price forecasting for the balancing energy market using machine-learning regression. Energies 13(20), 5420 (2020)
16. Garcia, M.P., Kirschen, D.S.: Forecasting system imbalance volumes in competitive electricity markets. IEEE Trans. Power Syst. 21(1), 240–248 (2006)
17. Kratochvíl, Š.: System imbalance forecast. Doctoral dissertation. Czech Technical University, Prague, Czech Republic (2016)
18. Contreras, C.: System imbalance forecasting and short-term bidding strategy to minimize imbalance costs of transacting in the Spanish electricity market. Doctoral dissertation. Universidad Pontificia Comillas, Madrid, Spain (2016)
19. Pires Ferreira, P.: Volume and price in the Nordic balancing power market. Master's thesis. Norwegian University of Science and Technology, Trondheim, Norway (2016)
20. Salem, T.S., Kathuria, K., Ramampiaro, H., Langseth, H.: Forecasting intra-hour imbalances in electric power systems. In: Proceedings of the AAAI Conference on Artificial Intelligence, vol. 33, no. 01, pp. 9595–9600 (2019)
21. van der Veen, R.A., Abbasy, A., Hakvoort, R.A.: Agent-based analysis of the impact of the imbalance pricing mechanism on market behavior in electricity balancing markets. Energy Econ. 34(4), 874–881 (2012)
22. Bueno-Lorenzo, M., Moreno, M.Á., Usaola, J.: Analysis of the imbalance price scheme in the Spanish electricity market: a wind power test case. Energy Policy 62, 1010–1019 (2013)
23. Hirth, L., Ziegenhagen, I.: Balancing power and variable renewables: three links. Renew. Sustain. Energy Rev. 50, 1035–1051 (2015)
24. Klæboe, G., Eriksrud, A.L., Fleten, S.-E.: Benchmarking time series based forecasting models for electricity balancing market prices. Energy Syst. 6(1), 43–61 (2013). https://doi.org/10. 1007/s12667-013-0103-3
25. Koch, C., Hirth, L.: Short-term electricity trading for system balancing: an empirical analysis of the role of intraday trading in balancing Germany's electricity system. Renew. Sustain. Energy Rev. 113, 109275 (2019)
26. Huang, P., Xu, T., Sun, Y.: A genetic algorithm based dynamic pricing for improving bi-directional interactions with reduced power imbalance. Energy Build. 199, 275–286 (2019)

27. Schäfer, P., Westerholt, H.G., Schweidtmann, A.M., Ilieva, S., Mitsos, A.: Model-based bidding strategies on the primary balancing market for energy-intense processes. Comput. Chem. Eng. **120**, 4–14 (2019)
28. Wu, Z., Zhou, M., Zhang, T., Li, G., Zhang, Y., Liu, X.: Imbalance settlement evaluation for China's balancing market design via an agent-based model with a multiple criteria decision analysis method. Energy Policy **139**, 111297 (2020)
29. Poplavskaya, K., Lago, J., De Vries, L.: Effect of market design on strategic bidding behavior: model-based analysis of European electricity balancing markets. Appl. Energy **270**, 115130 (2020)
30. Vural, M.: Genetik algoritma yöntemi ile toplu üretim planlama. Doctoral dissertation. Istanbul Technical University, Istanbul, Turkey (2005)
31. Ozturk, H.K., Canyurt, O.E., Hepbasli, A., Utlu, Z.: Residential-commercial energy input estimation based on genetic algorithm approaches: an application of Turkey. Energy Build. **36**, 175–183 (2004)
32. Haldenbilen, S., Ceylan, H.: Genetic algorithm approach to estimate transport energy demand in Turkey. Energy Policy **33**, 89–98 (2005)
33. Man, K.F., Tang, K.S., Kwong, S.: Genetic Algorithms: Concepts and Designs. Springer, London (2001)
34. Hewamalage, H., Bergmeir, C., Bandara, K.: Recurrent neural networks for time series forecasting: current status and future directions. Int. J. Forecast. **37**(1), 388–427 (2021)
35. Achanta, S., Gangashetty, S.V.: Deep Elman recurrent neural networks for statistical parametric speech synthesis. Speech Commun. **93**, 31–42 (2017)
36. Wang, J., Wang, J., Fang, W., Niu, H.: Financial time series prediction using Elman recurrent random neural networks. Comput. Intell. Neurosci. (2016).https://doi.org/10.1155/2016/4742515
37. Jiang, Y., Chen, M., You, S.: A unified trading model based on robust optimization for day-ahead and real-time markets with wind power integration. Energies **10**(4), 554 (2017)
38. Qiu, J., Zhao, J., Wang, D., Zheng, Y.: Two-stage coordinated operational strategy for distributed energy resources considering wind power curtailment penalty cost. Energies **10**(7), 965 (2017)
39. Gligoric, Z., Savic, S.S., Grujic, A., Negovanovic, M., Music, O.: Short-term electricity price forecasting model using interval-valued autoregressive process. Energies **11**(7), 1911 (2018)
40. Sun, P., Li, J., Chen, J., Lei, X.: A short-term outage model of wind turbines with doubly fed induction generators based on supervisory control and data acquisition. Energies **9**(11), 882 (2016)

Machine Learning Methods in the Inclinometers Readings Anomaly Detection Issue on the Example of Tailings Storage Facility

Wioletta Koperska[1] ⓘ, Maria Stachowiak[1] ⓘ, Bartosz Jachnik[1(✉)] ⓘ,
Paweł Stefaniak[1] ⓘ, Bartłomiej Bursa[2] ⓘ, and Paweł Stefanek[3] ⓘ

[1] KGHM CUPRUM Research and Development Centre Ltd., gen. W. Sikorskiego Street 2-8,
53-659 Wroclaw, Poland
bjachnik@cuprum.wroc.pl
[2] GEOTEKO Serwis Ltd., Wałbrzyska Street14/16, 02-739 Warszawa, Poland
[3] KGHM Polska Miedź S.A., M. Skłodowskiej-Curie 48, 59-301 Lubin, Poland

Abstract. Measurement of structure deformation is one of the two most important elements in assessing the current operating condition of a hydro-technical facility, which is especially important when the object is under constant expansion. This is the case of KGHM's Zelazny Most tailing dam which is the largest tailings storage facility (TSF) in Europe. The considerable size of the facility entails a very complex monitoring system consisting of numerous inclinometers, piezometers, seismic stations, geodetic benchmarks, etc. Interpretation of data from such an extensive system requires a certain degree of automation. It is not possible to perform a real-time complete data analysis through human resources, despite several teams responsible for supervision and maintenance of the TSF. The detection of anomalous events is one of the objectives of the monitoring process. This problem concerns, among others, the readings of the inclinometers responsible for the measurement of surface displacements, necessary in the assessment of tailing dam stability. The article presents methods of finding anomalies on the inclinometer with the use of machine learning techniques, which significantly simplifies the process of identifying attention-requiring areas. The effectiveness of the algorithms was tested on data samples from various measurement points. The best method will be to build learning-based supervised classifiers in the decision-making process of the TSF stability.

Keywords: Inclinometers · Data mining · DBSCAN

1 Introduction

Tailings Storage Facility (TSF) is one of the largest geotechnical facilities made up of earth embankments built to store uneconomical ore and water from the mining process. An example of a large-scale embankment dam is the Syncrude Mildred Lake Tailings Dyke in Alberta (Canada), the length of which is about 18 km and the height varies

© IFIP International Federation for Information Processing 2021
Published by Springer Nature Switzerland AG 2021
E. Mercier-Laurent et al. (Eds.): AI4KM 2021, IFIP AICT 614, pp. 235–249, 2021.
https://doi.org/10.1007/978-3-030-80847-1_15

from 40 to 88 m. It is the largest earth structure in the world by volume of fill. Historic structural damage often resulted in serious catastrophes with large financial losses and a serious threat to the local community and environment. Therefore, facilities of this type are expected to maintain the highest possible safety indicators and the lowest possible environmental impact. For this reason, these facilities develop advanced monitoring systems covering a wide range of sensors in the field of geotechnical, hydrological, geodetic survey, and seismic networks. Additionally, weather conditions are monitored on an ongoing basis, visual inspections in the field are performed, and satellite data are analyzed. Tracking TSF activity parameters is laborious and time-consuming. Existing measurement networks generate huge amounts of data, which are usually analyzed by several teams of employees. Unfortunately, a complete analysis of the collected data is not possible using human resources. To meet the current expectations of the TSF area, an international consortium was formed and the Illumineation project was launched [www. illumineation-h2020.eu]. One of the goals of the Illumineation project is to develop an Internet of Things platform for monitoring the TSF structures and Big Data analytics using machine learning (ML) methods to support engineers in data analysis. The project assumed the development of a sensor network with low-cost sensors and advanced algorithms to improve the efficiency of data processing, track TSF stability parameters, detect and diagnose potential anomalies and identify potential threats, including estimating the impact of TSF on the environment and the local community. Finally, developed technology will be able to "self-learn" and anticipate potential threats and their potential consequences in advance.

One of the critical tasks is the analysis of displacement data for estimating the deformation of the inclinometer pipe. The inclinometers are used for monitoring horizontal displacements using a probe passing along the pipe. The probe contains a gravity sensor that allows measuring inclination with respect to the vertical. The pipe is usually installed in a borehole or fill. The typical applications of the inclinometers include: determining shear zones in the ground, monitoring the extent and rate of horizontal displacement, monitoring of deflection of bulkheads, piles, or retaining walls. Figure 1 shows a typical inclinometer body. After the installation the probe is lowered to the bottom the readings are made as the probe is raised incrementally to the top of the pipe, providing data for the determination of initial pipe alignment. The difference between initial and subsequent readings allows the calculation of absolute horizontal deformation at any point along the inclinometer pipe.

The TSF structures cause a large increase of stress in the ground and it may result in the formation of shear zones. The shear zones are the areas where the shear strength of the ground material is lower than usual. Stability analyses must detect them using the data obtained by the inclinometers.

From an analytical point of view, this problem comes down to the task of anomaly detection. The problem of detecting anomalies in signals is very well recognized in the literature in many areas. It is especially popular in the task of tracking airport security, detecting fraud (e.g. banking) or cyber-attacks, and technical diagnostics of machines and processes. The greatest challenge is to obtain a very high accuracy of anomaly detection (the lowest possible level of false alarms). Depending on the case, the effectiveness of the detection method may depend on the informativeness of the input signals (Sawicki

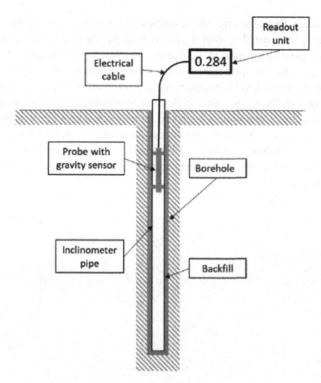

Fig. 1. Inclinometer body.

et al. 2015), the extraction of the robust and effective feature (Ye 2008; Wodecki et al. 2018), the signal-noise separation technique (Ye 2018) or a feature classification method (Ahrens et al. 2019).

The article presents methods of detection of anomalies in the inclinometer readings for the needs of TSF stability monitoring. In the beginning, the characteristics of the investigated object based on the example of Zelazny Most TSF were presented. Then, the measurement network and the description of the basic procedures related to the supervision and maintenance of the facility were described. Next, the input data was presented together with a short statistical description. In the next step, the authors described the methodology of the algorithms proposed for the anomaly detection task. Finally, the article ended with a summary, which presents the further direction of the algorithm development assumed in the Illumineation project.

2   Description of the Research Object and Problem

In the Illumineation project, the main object of research as a test site for developed technology is the Zelazny Most TSF (ZM TSF), the largest reservoir of post-flotation tailings in Europe. Zelazny Most storages waste from mining activities of all KGHM underground copper ore mines located in SW Poland. It is a huge hydrotechnical structure, which covers an area of almost 1,600 ha, and its circumference exceeds 14 km. The height of the dams above the original ground level ranges from 35 m in the southern part to 70 m in the eastern part. The total amount of tailings from the mines in Lubin, Rudna, and Polkowice stored each year at the disposal reaches approximately 30 million tons. The complex monitoring equipment of the reservoir measures all aspects, from geodetic monitoring or water level measurements in piezometers to seismic stations. There are over 40,000 measurement points in Zelazny Most within the developed monitoring network: a geotechnical network, a hydrological network, a geodetic network, and a network of seismic sensors. In total, the network consists of around 2,900 measuring devices and sensors. Field studies, sampling for laboratory tests, and geophysical research are carried out here in cooperation with many national and global research centers (Stefanek et al. 2017) (Fig. 2).

Fig. 2. Zelazny Most Tailings Storage Facility located in SW Poland (Stefanek et al. 2017).

The ZM TSF is located in a complex geological environment. From the ground surface downwards, the foundation soils consist of Pleistocene deposits, including silty lake clays and out-wash sands, rare sandy gravel inclusions, and silty sands. These are underlain by thick layers of freshwater, medium- to high-plasticity Pliocene clays, which incorporate thin, brown coal and sand strata. The Pliocene deposits overlie Triassic strata, which include beds of halite, below which the copper ore body is encountered (Jamiolkowski 2014). The Pliocene deposits contain high-plasticity slikensided clay with very low shear strength. The shear zones occur mostly in those layers. These shear zones are taken into account in stability analyses by modeling the weakened zones with lower shear strength. Hence it is crucial to detect the shear zone in order to obtain an accurate Factor of Safety. Unfortunately, the detection of shear zones is not an easy task. The geotechnical engineer must analyze many factors i.e. inclinometer data, ground conditions, groundwater conditions, etc. Therefore to analyze the inclinometer data more thoroughly there is a need for an algorithm that can learn from the engineers their expertise.

3 Analysis of the Inclinometer Changes

3.1 Data Description

The data includes measurement values for the displacement of the inclinometer from the original state. Measurements were taken up to twice a year from the beginning of the establishment. For each inclinometer, the displacement is measured every 0.5 m of the rod. The displacement is measured in millimeters and its position in the ground is given in meters above sea level. Exemplary data are presented in Fig. 3. The problem of shear zones discussed in the article, visible at 50 m above sea level, is also present-ed. The problem became visible from the measurement on day 26/02/2010.

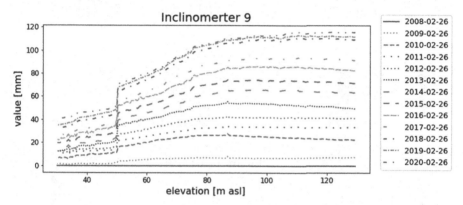

Fig. 3. Value of displacement on the inclinometer over time.

Inclinometers differ in length, location level, and place of implementation as can be seen in Fig. 4. The influence of the substrate on which the inclinometer is located, not considered in this paper. Currently, the surface in which the inclinometer is located is treated as a homogeneous body. It may have a significant impact on the size of the occurred shearing. The factor may be a great addition to the later development of the algorithm.

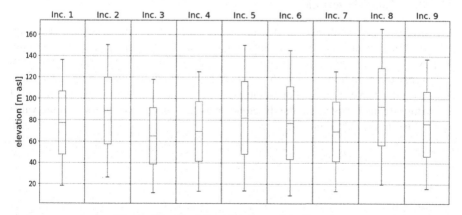

Fig. 4. Elevation's boxplots for each inclinometer.

Shear zones are characterized by a sudden jump to the next level of the inclinometer value. This relationship is clearly visible in the histogram. Figure 5 shows the histograms for the values from the last measurement for 3 inclinometers. It can be seen that they are multi-modal. Local maximums can correspond to the value levels between the shear zones. This shows that it is possible to group values according to the adopted level. Additionally, it indicates that density clustering should be a good choice.

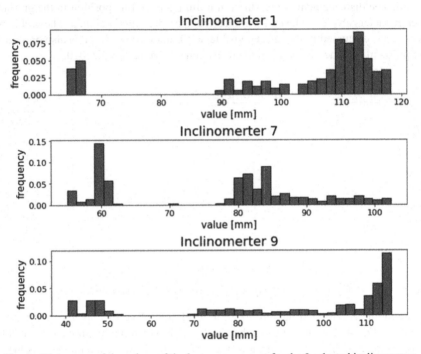

Fig. 5. Histograms of the values of the last measurement for the 3 selected inclinometers.

3.2   Shear Zones Detection

The shear zones are characterized by a quick shift in relation to the previous placement, which deepens over time. The remaining segments of the inclinometer change only slightly.

To find the elevations on which shear zones occurred, tools that emphasize rapid changes in the data were used. For all samples of each inclinometer owned, the values of the sliding standard deviation, the difference between successive values, and the value of the derivative were calculated.

As can be seen in Fig. 6, the shear areas are visible in all statics. They show jumps at the time of the shear. It is easiest to detect on the last measurement.

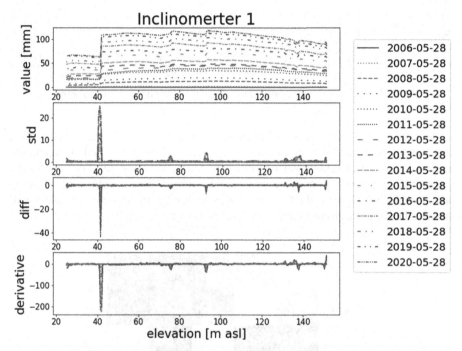

Fig. 6. Statistics values for inclinometer displacement at different elevation levels.

The simplest solution would be to use a threshold or ranges beyond which the data is treated as a shear zone. However, with the current assumptions, the differences between the sizes of the shear zone are so different that it is difficult to determine such ranges. Besides the usual statistical methods, clustering and classification algorithms are commonly used for these problems. The problem can be solved in two ways. With the help of supervised or unsupervised machine learning. The difference between them is that supervised learning needs to input a sample of data (called training data) into the training system. On their basis, the system searches for dependencies corresponding to the given data.

4 Supervised Learning

Supervised learning often produces the best results, which is the algorithm that is best at situational awareness. However, as mentioned before, the most important aspect of this type of learning is having a training sample. In this case, it is information about the presence of a shear, which is shown in Fig. 7.

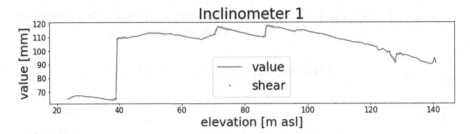

Fig. 7. Inclinometer 1 values with information about the occurrence of shearing.

In order to more precisely describe considered phenomena, additional statistics have been calculated. In addition to the previously presented difference and deviation, the mean value, mean elevation, and kurtosis were added. Values were calculated for the sets containing readings from successive intervals of 5 m. These statistics will constitute predictors set, which we will refer to further as X. The binary response variable Y will indicate the shear occurrence (value equal to one) at a given depth.

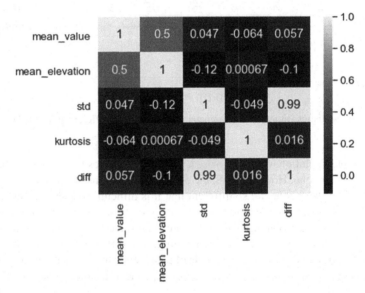

Fig. 8. Correlation matrix.

Figure 8 shows the correlation matrix of selected variables. As previously shown, the deviation and the difference are strongly correlated with each other, so one of the variables can be rejected. Figure 9 also shows that these two statistics split two considered classes most clearly.

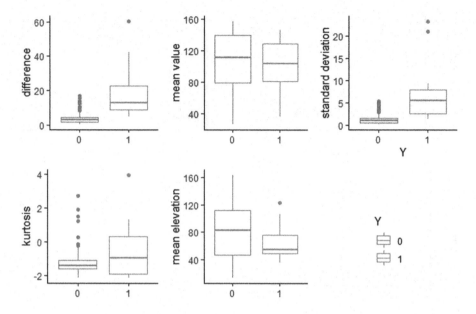

Fig. 9. Selected statistics among two of the considered classes. Y equal to 1 indicates the shear zone occurrence.

As it can be seen, the values of "difference" and "standard deviations" are considerably higher for the samples in which the shear zones have occurred. Yet, it can be seen, that there is a considerable number of samples with high levels of these statistics with Y equal to zero, indicating no shear zone occurrence in that area. The samples with shear occurrence have usually lower elevation values and have a much wider spread of kurtosis statistics (Fig. 10).

In this approach, a set of different classifiers will be tested out:

- Logistic regression (LR): involves directly modeling the conditional probability of shear occurrence given the set of beforementioned statistics. In other words, in logistic regression, the conditional distribution of Y (shear occurrence) is being modeled given the set of predictors X.
- Linear Discriminant Analysis (LDA): in this approach, the distribution of X is modeled for each of the response classes, and is then converted using the Bayes formula. This approach assumes, that observations in each class are drawn from the Gaussian distribution.
- Quadratic Discriminant Analysis (QDA): unlike LDA, assumes that each distribution of the response classes has its own covariance matrix. This means, that QDA is significantly more flexible than LDA, and therefore will have a higher variance.
- K-nearest neighbors algorithm (KNN): being the non-parametric method will provide an even more flexible approach to the problem and should benefit the prediction if the assumptions of LR, LDA, and QDA will be not met.
- Neural Network (NN): which is often best suited for high-dimensionality problems.

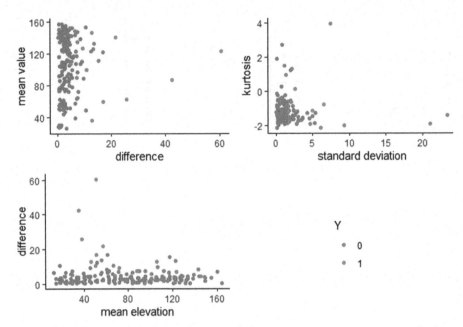

Fig. 10. Summary of individual statistics plotted against each other. The zones with shear occurrence were marked with blue dots.

5 Unsupervised Learning

With unsupervised learning, there is no information about the occurrence of the shearing, therefore the problem must be described in a different way. The shear zones can be treated as anomalies in the data, an unexpected pattern that does not match the general behavior. The main idea behind this is to teach an algorithm to detect normally behaving data and then use that information to pinpoint points that do not meet these assumptions. The advantages are that in addition to detecting points outside certain thresholds (extreme values), it also detects those that do not occur frequently (Çelik et al. 2011). In this case, due to the lack of a final number of clusters, some of the methods like the k-means algorithm cannot be used. DBScan meets all the assumptions. Moreover, in (Thang et al. 2011) it is shown that the application of the DBScan algorithm gives very good results in relation to the previously proposed methods.

The DBScan method allows dividing the samples into groups without prior declaration of the number of clusters. The number of groups is selected by the algorithm. The algorithm groups together points that are close to each other based on a distance measurement (usually Euclidean distance) and have a specified minimum number of points. At the same time, the method indicates points that could not be classified into any of the groups, such values can be understood as outliers - an anomaly occurring in the data, which is exactly what is needed to be highlighted to solve the problem.

The DBScan algorithm takes two initial parameters:

- ε - if the considered point is at ε distance from another point, the algorithm will distinguish these two points as neighbors. Otherwise, the point is considered an outlier.
- minPoints - the minimum number of points in the vicinity of the particular point that allows the area to be considered as dense.

The DBScan checks the surrounding of each point in the sample, and labels them as a:

- Core point if it meets the condition of the minimal number of points in its vicinity. These points form separate clusters.
- Border Point - this is a point that does not meet the density condition, however, there is a core point in its vicinity. It is part of the cluster and constitutes its border.
- Outlier - it is not in the position of the principal point and also does not satisfy the density condition itself.

Points parameterized by DBScan can create three different links between each other. Points are directly density-reachable when at least one of them is a core point and these two are within ε distance from each other. Points are density-reachable when there is a core point that both points are directly density-reachable with. Density-connected points can be located on the opposite sides of the cluster, as long as there is a point density reachable with them.

Given the above definitions, the DBScan algorithm can be described in the following steps of the algorithm (Fig. 11).

The algorithm should divide into groups the places where the distortion levels are within the norm and indicate between them moments of shear, which are anomalies not classified into any of the groups.

The following 3 feature vectors were used for clustering:

- elevation values,
- distortion values for the last (newest) sample,
- vector of distortion derivatives at each point (gradient) – it will mainly point to an anomaly (sudden jumps occur then).

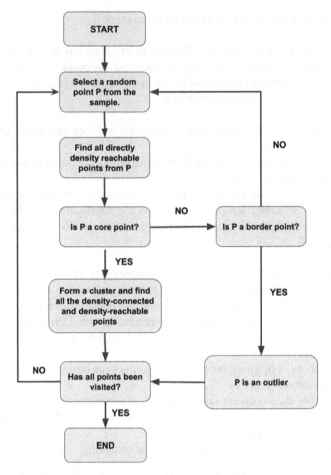

Fig. 11. Scheme of DBScan algorithm.

6 Application to Industrial Data

After selecting the variables and assumptions, each of the selected methods was applied to the available data. It was applied to those inclinometers for which occurrence of shear zones was certain. For example, the results of clustering with DBScan for 3 inclinometers are presented in Fig. 12. The plots with the results (the first plot for each inclinometer) were compared with the plots with the manually marked shears (the second plot for each inclinometer).

As can be seen in the attached picture, the algorithm divided the signal into sections with normal behavior and determined all anomalies. All the shear zones have been detected. However, it is worth noting that the method does not only detect shearings, but also other unusual fragments of the signal.

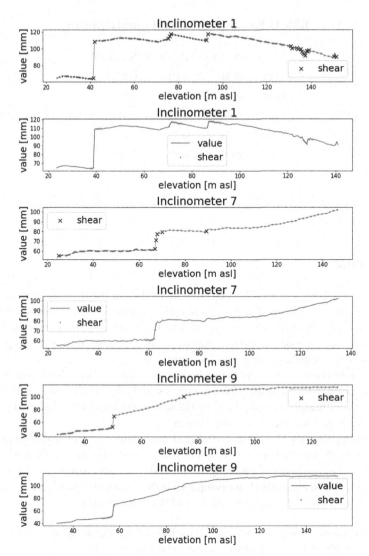

Fig. 12. Clustering result for the presented inclinometers.

Similar analyzes were performed for the remaining methods. The results were compiled in the form of a table (Table 1) with calculated performance measures. One of the goals for problem solving is to choose a method that selects false shearing more often than ignores true ones. It comes down to reduce the false negative error, so sensitivity must be maximized.

From the point of view of assumptions, the best methods were obtained by QDA and NN. The methods are characterized by high accuracy and precision. QDA has the highest sensitivity among all the methods, NN has a slightly lower sensitivity, but it is

Table 1. Performance Measures for used algorithms.

Method	Accuracy	Precision	Sensitivity
LDA	0.94	0.89	0.32
QDA	0.94	0.67	0.71
LR	0.96	0.90	0.47
KNN	0.93	0.57	0.49
NN	0.93	0.88	0.67

clearly more precise. LDA, which was originally intended to be suboptimal, actually has the lowest sensitivity.

7 Summary

The article describes methods for detecting anomalies in the inclinometer time series resulting from shear planes. The tests were carried out in the Zelazny Most TSF plant. In order to obtain the required accuracy of detection, a multi-year monitoring database obtained from all measurement points was used. One of the main goals in designing the algorithm was to reduce the false negative error.

The article presents different methods from two types of machine learning: supervised and unsupervised learning. The methods use only data from inclinometers, which once again significantly extends the potential area of application far beyond the largest facilities with an extensive monitoring system.

The main goal of the algorithm is to support geoengineering responsible for assessing the stability of the tail dam in the area of detecting anomaly readings. In the next step, the algorithm will be used to build a training sample under the supervision of a domain expert. This, in turn, will be used to build tools supporting decision making and forecasting based on the fusion of data from various sources and Big Data analytics.

Acknowledgments. This project has received funding from the European Union's Horizon 2020 research and innovation program under grant agreement No 869379.

References

Green, G.E., Mikkelsen, P.E.: Measurement of ground movement with inclinometers. In: Proceedings of Fourth International Geotechnical Seminar on Field Instrumentation and In-Situ Measurement, Singapore, pp. 235–246 (1986)

Konak, G., Onur, A.H., Karakus, D., Köse, H., Koca, Y., Yenice, H.: cc. Min. Technol. **113**(3), 171–180 (2004)

Cała, M., Jakóbczyk, J., Cyran, K.: Inclinometer monitoring system for stability analysis: the western slope of the Bełchatów field case study. Studia Geotechnica et Mechanica **38**(2), 3–13 (2016)

Sawicki, M., Zimroz, R., Wyłomańska, A., Obuchowski, J., Stefaniak, P., Żak, G.: An automatic procedure for multidimensional temperature signal analysis of a SCADA system with application to belt conveyor components. Procedia Earth Planet. Sci. **15**, 781–790 (2015)

Ye, N.: Secure computer and network systems (2008)

Wodecki, J., Stefaniak, P., Polak, M., Zimroz, R.: Unsupervised anomaly detection for conveyor temperature SCADA data. In: Timofiejczuk, A., Chaari, F., Zimroz, R., Bartelmus, W., Haddar, M. (eds.) CMMNO 2016. ACM, vol. 9, pp. 361–369. Springer, Cham (2018). https://doi.org/10.1007/978-3-319-61927-9_34

Ye, N.: Analytical techniques for anomaly detection through features, signal-noise separation and partial-value association. In: KDD 2017 Workshop on Anomaly Detection in Finance, pp. 20–32. PMLR (2018)

Ahrens, L., Ahrens, J., Schotten, H.D.: A machine-learning phase classification scheme for anomaly detection in signals with periodic characteristics. EURASIP J. Adv. Signal Process. **2019**(1), 1–23 (2019). https://doi.org/10.1186/s13634-019-0619-3

Stefanek, P., Engels, J., Wrzosek, K., Sobiesak, P., Zalewski, M.: Surface tailings disposal at the Żelazny Most TSF, today and into the future. In: Proceedings of the 20th International Seminar on Paste and Thickened Tailings, pp. 213–225. University of Science and Technology, Beijing (2017)

Jamiolkowski, M.: Soil mechanics and the observational method: challenges at the Zelazny Most copper tailings disposal facility. Géotechnique **64**(8), 590–618 (2014)

Çelik, M., Dadaşer-Çelik, F., Dokuz, A.Ş.: Anomaly detection in temperature data using DBSCAN algorithm. In: 2011 International Symposium on Innovations in Intelligent Systems and Applications. IEEE (2011)

Thang, T.M., Kim, J.: The anomaly detection by using DBSCAN clustering with multiple parameters. In: 2011 International Conference on Information Science and Applications. IEEE (2011)

Illumineation Homepage. www.illumineation-h2020.eu. Accessed 24 Feb 2021

Author Index

Printed in the United States
by Baker & Taylor Publisher Services